Performance Drivers

D0994533

Performance Drivers

A Practical Guide to Using the Balanced Scorecard

Nils-Göran Olve, Jan Roy and Magnus Wetter

JOHN WILEY & SONS, LTD
Chichester • New York • Weinheim • Brisbane • Singapore • Toronto

Original Swedish edition published under the title 'Balanced Scorecard i Svensk Praktik
Copyright © 1997 Liber Ekonomi,. All rights reserved.

Copyright © 1999 for English language rights only by
John Wiley & Sons, Ltd, The Atrium, Southern Gate,
Chichester, West Sussex PO19 8SQ, England
Telephone (+44) 1243 779777

Email (for orders and customer service enquiries): cs-books@wiley.co.uk

Reprinted April, September and December 1999, November 2000, June 2001, December 2002,
February 2004, November 2004

Other Wiley Editorial Offices

John Wiley & Sons Inc., 111 River Street, Hoboken, NJ 07030, USA

Jossey-Bass, 989 Market Street, San Francisco, CA 94103-1741, USA

Wiley-VCH Verlag GmbH, Boschstr. 12, D-69469 Weinheim, Germany

John Wiley & Sons Australia Ltd, 33 Park Road, Milton, Queensland 4064, Australia

John Wiley & Sons (Asia) Pte Ltd, 2 Clementi Loop #02-01, Jin Xing Distripark, Singapore 129809

John Wiley & Sons (Canada) Ltd, 22 Worcester Road, Etobicoke, Ontario M9W 1L1

Wiley also publishes its books in a variety of electronic formats. Some content that appears in print
may not be available in electronic books.

Library of Congress Cataloging-in-Publication Data

Olve, Nils-Göran
    [Balanced scorecard i svensk, praktik, English]
    Performance drivers : a practical guide to using the balanced
scorecard / Nils-Göran Olve, Jan Roy and Magnus Wetter.
        p. cm.
    Translation of: Balanced scorecard i svensk praktik.
    Includes bibliographical references and index.
    ISBN 0-47198623-2 (cloth : alk. paper_
    1. Industrial productivity—Measurement.   2. Strategic planning.
3. Organizational effectiveness—Evaluation.   I. Roy, Jan.
II. Wetter, Magnus.   III. Title.
HD56.04713   1999
658.4′012—dc21   98–37151
                                                                       CIP

British Library Cataloguing in Publication Data

A catalogue record for this book is available from the British Library

ISBN 0–471–98623–2 (Hbk)
ISBN 0–471–49542–5 (Pbk)

Typeset in 11/13pt Times by Mayhew Typesetting, Rhayader, Powys.
Printed and bound in Great Britain by Biddles Ltd, King's Lynn, Norfolk
This book is printed on acid-free paper responsibly manufactured from sustainable forestry,
in which at least two trees are planted for each one used for paper production.

Contents

About the Authors

Nils-Göran Olve is Adjunct Professor at Linköping University. He has worked extensively in management development and co-authored one previous Wiley book, Virtual Organizations and Beyond, 1997. His work concentrates on management control issues, in particular the Balanced Scorecard and the management of IT and immaterial assets.

Jan Roy worked as CEO of several Swedish companies, especially in the retail industry. As a consultant, he mainly deals with strategic change processes.

Jan Roy and Nils-Göran Olve are both active in ConcoursCepro, a Stockholm-based consultancy where Jan Roy is the CEO. ConcoursCepro is part of The Concours Group (www.concours-group.com), which has a growing number of consultants in the US and Europe specializing in the strategic and operational uses of human assets and information technology. Scorecards is an important tool in many of its projects.

Magnus Wetter is a management consultant specializing in strategic development and strategic execution. He has an MSc in Business and Administration from Lund University and also studied at McGill University in Montreal.

Address for correspondence:
ConcoursCepro,
Box 440, SE-101 28 Stockholm, Sweden
Telephone: +46 8 4029800
Fax: +46 8 105469
E-mail: company@cepro.se
Homepage: www.cepro.se (see also: www.concoursgroup.com)

Preface

In 1992 the concept of the balanced scorecard made its first appearance. Since then many companies have tested the ideas embodied in the concept. These have been given rather varied content and taken differing forms in different organizations. There is nothing new or original about the basic notion of combining a number of measures in a compact description of an operation. Yet the experience of the last few years has yielded useful new approaches to management control at a company. These are difficult to capture in a concise definition of the balanced scorecard, since they have less to do with the "scorecard" itself than with how it is used. The new approaches relate to:

- Giving management control a strategic dimension
- Communicating to everyone a clear picture of the purpose of his/her work
- Discussing how our efforts to develop competencies, customer relationships, and IT will pay off in the future
- Creating opportunities for learning by more systematically measuring factors which are important for success, and using these data in an ongoing discussion about the business
- Establishing greater respect for the fact that many of the most important things done at a company do not immediately result in higher revenues or lower costs
- Finding ways to explain to outsiders what a company is and can do, as a complement to the financial picture presented in the annual report

These are important ambitions, and they are not easy to realize. They have made the balanced scorecard a popular theme for conferences, management-training projects, and business-school dissertations. But exactly what is the balanced scorecard?

Our book is a concise presentation of the concept, the process, and the experience of a number of companies. In writing it, we drew on our own experience and benefited from the willing co-operation of many people at a variety of companies and other organizations. They have interpreted and applied the balanced-scorecard concept in a number of different ways. It was important, therefore, to include a representative selection of these organizations in the book. We have used them both as subjects of extensive case studies and as illustrations in our discussion of various aspects of using the balanced scorecard in actual practice.

We also relate the balanced scorecard to other current ideas and concepts, in an attempt to provide additional perspectives on its place in modern management control.

An earlier version of the book which was published in Sweden in 1997 received considerable attention. Our impression is that the balanced scorecard has been most widely used in the English-speaking countries and in Scandinavia. We can now add a number of interesting British examples to our case studies of Swedish companies, most of which have substantial operations outside of Sweden.

In our view the ultimate ambition of a balanced scorecard is the creation of a learning organization. The purpose of the descriptions in the scorecard is to show a more thorough and meaningful picture of a business, suitable for the discussions in which a growing number of company employees should participate:

- *A total, comprehensive picture*: How do our operations fit into the overall picture? Can I understand why we do things the way we do, and does it make sense?
- *A long-term view*: More and more of our time at work is spent on preparing for the future. The cultivation of competencies and relationships is an investment with effects that are often hard to see. How can we convince ourselves that what we are doing is right, and that others at the company are doing what they can to prepare for our common future?

- *Experience*: How do we make use of what we learn? Today many company employees deal directly with customers, make discoveries in the process of their work, and cultivate relationships with other companies and official agencies. How can we benefit from the knowledge which we thereby gain?
- *Flexibility*: The long-term focus and the ambition to learn from experience has to be combined with flexible reactions to a fast-changing environment.

In the book we combine our experience from a number of different fields. Together with colleagues at Cepro, a management-consulting firm based in Stockholm, we have been involved in a number of different applications of the balanced scorecard and have learned about other organizations where the concept has been tested. Thus, several of our colleagues have also contributed to the book. Moreover, we have obtained material from other sources through our own work and our contacts at various academic institutions; we have selected what is most relevant. At the end of the book, there is a list of people whom we would like to thank especially for sharing their experience with us. We owe a particular debt of gratitude to Mr Richard Wathen who converted our text into English. As for the hundreds of others with whom we have discussed the balanced-scorecard concept, we hope that we have made good use of your knowledge! Our sincere thanks to all of you!

A recent questionnaire study of Nordic companies indicates a continued strong interest in the balanced scorecard: "27% (63) of the business units have already done so [ie, adopted scorecards], and in two years 61% (145) of the units may be using a scorecard" (Kald and Nilsson, 2000, p.124). Other countries seem to be following, and we are grateful for receiving e-mails from many different parts of the world in the year since the present book was issued. During the year 2000 it has also been translated into Japanese, Spanish and other languages, evidencing strong interest in the concept in these countries. In the future, this may provide material for studies of the interplay between national management styles and how scorecards are used.

Nils-Göran Olve, Jan Roy, Magnus Wetter,
Stockholm, April 2000

Overview of the Book

The basic structure of this book reflects the different uses for scorecards that we have encountered. Figure 0.1 indicates some possible paths through its chapters. We start by introducing the concept and the reasons why it has appeared at this time (Part I: Chapters 1 and 2).

The basic reason for developing the first set of scorecards (Part II) is usually to improve *strategic focusing and control*. The reader who is primarily seeking practical suggestions in this area is advised to begin with Chapter 3; it follows a step-by-step approach, illustrated with the experience of KappAhl, a Swedish retailer. Chapter 4 then presents case studies showing how the details of the approach can differ, and Chapter 5 discusses some of the issues involved in designing the process and the format for scorecards.

In some of these cases the balanced scorecard was introduced primarily as a method of *operational control*, a complement to financial control that provides a fuller description of organizational performance. While of course this kind of control should also reflect the company's strategy, here the balanced-scorecard process usually began at a lower level of the organization. The initial purpose of using measures often seems to be simply to provide a concise overall picture of the business. We discuss this subject in Chapter 6, while also introducing some additional case studies; Chapter 7 develops it further in treating the central topic of measures and the linking of different measures.

Sooner or later, this same phase will also be reached in a scorecard process which began with a definition of the company's

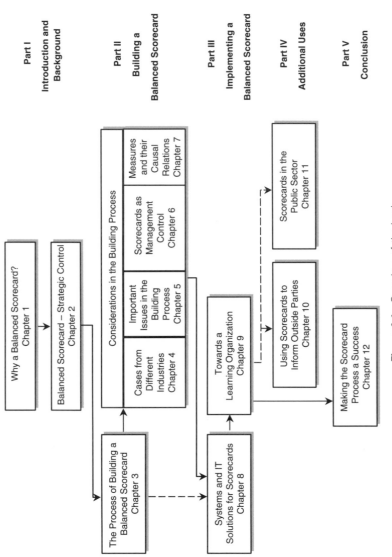

Figure 0.1 Overview of the book

strategy, when it becomes time to find a practical way to measure progress. The reader who is considering the initiation of a strategic scorecard process may move directly from Chapter 3 to Part III (Chapter 8), and later, during the course of implementation, turn to Chapters 5–7. This "shortcut" is indicated in Figure 0.1.

We do feel, however, that in every scorecard project management should carefully consider its position on the issues raised in Chapters 8 and 9. Chapter 8 describes the use of IT as a support for scorecards, and Chapter 9 leads on to the increasingly important field of organizational learning and knowledge management.

The two chapters in Part IV are designated "Additional Uses", and may be regarded as optional for most readers. In Chapter 10 we bring up the subject of adding some kind of scorecard presentation to a company's financial accounting. The balanced scorecard has sometimes been associated with the discussion on valuation of companies and intellectual capital, and there have been proposals that non-financial information in a scorecard format should be required. We find this debate interesting but feel that for now scorecards should mainly be regarded as a tool for internal management processes. For this very reason, however, there is clearly a place for scorecards in the public sector (Chapter 11), since the entire operation of a state or municipality could be viewed as a single organization, comparable to a large industrial corporation or group of companies.

Finally, in Part V (Chapter 12), we summarize our advice by again considering scorecards in the context of management control. One conclusion from our company cases is that a scorecard process may be used for strategic as well as operational purposes, and that the design of a successful process has to reflect this.

Part I

Introduction and Background

1

Why a Balanced Scorecard?

In this chapter we introduce the balanced scorecard – a concept and a method to help us in our discussions on where our business should be heading. The idea of looking at a business in terms of a "scorecard" has aroused considerable interest since 1992 when it was introduced. The reason, we believe, is that more and more managers find that they need something more than the short-term reports so prevalent up to now.

DESCRIBING THE ESSENTIALS OF WHAT WE DO

Responsibility and trust are watchwords at today's companies. But what is a manager responsible for? For decades we have been talking about "decentralized profit responsibility". We usually measure results in monetary terms. The income statements which we prepare for particular business units and departments are modelled on the income statement of the company.

Is this enough? Is the mission of the various parts of a company simply to create profits and return on investment? In many cases probably not. Wise executives know that their company must develop the capabilities which it will need to prosper in the future. But doing so will produce no profits in the current year, only costs.

Here, we believe, lies the fundamental reason why companies require a *balanced scorecard*. The need is even clearer for the many organizations without profit as a goal, including government agencies, internal staff units in industry, and others. We have to do more to describe what we expect of an operation, and how well our expectations are being met.

Perhaps this matter was less urgent before. Both sales and production were primarily focused on the short run. Preparing for the future was something companies did in their development departments and through requirements of centralized authorization for capital expenditures.

Today we no longer consider this approach adequate. Preparing for the future is about investing in competence, cultivating customer relationships, and creating data bases. Much of this work is done elsewhere in the organization than at headquarters. There is a danger that profit targets will clash with long-term decisions.

Later we will consider how profit targets can be reformed so as better to reflect what is really important. But for many employees throughout the company, other ways of describing what they do will say more and be more convincing. These other ways are what we want to use in our scorecards. The balanced scorecard is a method for reaching agreement on where an operation should be heading and for making sure that it stays on course.

Using terms other than monetary ones to explain what you are doing is nothing new. Various kinds of key ratios can be found in abundance in business and the public sector. The difference lies in focusing on a deliberately selected set of measures – few enough to keep track of – and in using them to achieve and communicate a shared view of the organization's strategy for its future development. As the term implies, the scorecard is an aid in creating a "balance" among various factors to be considered. The balance adopted reflects the strategic choices of the business.

We regard the measures selected as a complement to financial controls, and as a means of reducing the danger of a harmful short-term approach while at the same time making the employees of the organization more aware of the meaning of their work and of the underlying assumptions about the future and about the company. Some refer to a change of approach from economic control to strategic control. However, the question is really one of economy in a deeper sense than the monetary one carelessly used in everyday parlance. Good economy means good resource management. Today's companies are so much more than just an investment in monetary capital. For many of us, how we manage talent, market position, and accumulated knowledge is at least as important!

An Example

For a number of years the Product Company had been endeavouring to spread profitability awareness throughout the organization. Capital turnover was satisfactory, and production costs had been squeezed down. Selling efforts were focused on the most profitable products.

But there was a hitch. The factory was extremely reluctant to modernize its technology, and sales gave higher priority than ever to existing customers. The reason was their concern with profitability. Certainly the Product Company was anxious not to spend too much on uncertain projects for the future. But the managing director realized that the company would be in trouble if something happened to the existing plant and equipment or to existing customers. The board of directors had just been discussing visions and strategies for the coming century. But were the employees also thinking along these lines?

The managing director brought up this subject with the financial vice-president, who agreed that financial control at the company tended to be short-sighted. But there was a way to add other considerations beside profitability awareness, and to emphasize a balance between profits today and preparedness for tomorrow. The method, referred to as the balanced scorecard, meant that employees would share the vision of the board of directors.

A SIMPLE BASIC CONCEPT

The initial thinking on the balanced-scorecard concept was presented in an article by Robert S. Kaplan and David P. Norton in the first issue of the 1992 *Harvard Business Review*. In viewing a

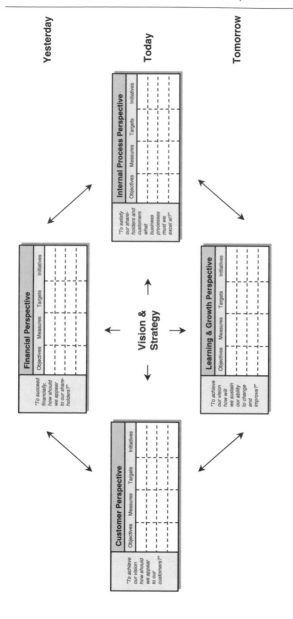

Figure 1.1 The balanced scorecard. Adapted and reprinted by permission of *Harvard Business Review.* Exhibit from "Using the Balanced Scorecard as a Strategic Management System" by Robert S. Kaplan and David P. Norton, January–February 1996, p. 76. Copyright © 1996 by the President and Fellows of Harvard College; all rights reserved

company from four vital perspectives (Figure 1.1), the balanced scorecard is intended to link short-term operational control to the long-term vision and strategy of the business. In this way the company focuses on a few critical key ratios in meaningful target areas. In other words, the company is forced to control and monitor day-to-day operations as they affect development tomorrow. Therefore, the balanced-scorecard concept is based on three dimensions in time: yesterday, today, and tomorrow. What we do today for tomorrow may have no noticeable financial impact until the day after tomorrow. The company's focus is thus broadened, and it becomes relevant to keep a continuous watch on non-financial key ratios.

Key ratios or non-financial measures are nothing new. It has long been known that running a company can hardly be reduced to optimizing monetary profits, and the necessity of using non-financial measures to keep track of the business is not new, either. But the management style of the 1980s at many companies was based on decentralized profit responsibility and an internal division of the business into a number of separate companies. This recipe had been tried not only at large corporations but surprisingly often at smaller ones as well. Now in the 1990s it was time for alternatives.

Since 1992 interest in the balanced scorecard has become widespread. We have noticed that the concept strikes a responsive chord with many executives. Middle managers have been especially receptive; it has been easy for them to see their operations in balanced-scorecard terms, as a balancing act between different significant interests. At upper levels of management, though, the suggestion that key ratios and non-financial measures be used for control has had a hard time competing with seemingly more businesslike profit goals. Therefore, it is important that we consider carefully what we want from a scorecard and what traps we may encounter along the way.

In this book we will devote special attention to how the balanced-scorecard concept has worked in a number of practical cases. The simplicity of the basic concept has led people to mean and to do different things in the name of introducing it. We ourselves have seen some beneficial effects, but also some efforts which have not advanced beyond the discussion stage. For this reason we will place particular emphasis on the various ways of applying the balanced-scorecard concept in practice.

OUTCOME MEASURES OR PERFORMANCE DRIVERS?

In a balanced scorecard, outcome measures are combined with measures that describe resources spent or activities performed. In principle, the former are located higher up in Figure 1.1, and the latter further down. However, we may want to measure the outcomes of a development project as part of the scorecard's "learning and growth" perspective, and this in turn may be seen as an input for marketing or production, i.e. "internal processes". By talking of "performance drivers", we underline that we want to measure those factors that will determine or influence future outcomes.

Traditionally, management control stresses decentralized profit goals which means that it is mostly focused on outcomes. In Figure 1.2 we use a traditional input–output model to illustrate how goals and measures may be placed along a causal chain, from resource input to the effects obtained. By effect we mean the action of one thing on another, or some kind of outcome: a higher reported profit, a better reputation, or a diminished environmental impact, for example. Several of these effects will in turn influence

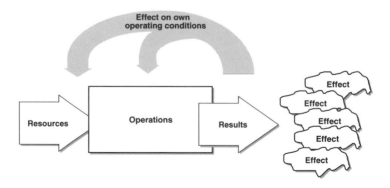

Figure 1.2   Input–output model

the company's future operations, thus becoming a kind of input for the operations of the subsequent period. This relationship is clearest in the case of internal outcomes: new learning, improved processes, a greater volume of registered data on customers.

In general it is better to measure at the right of the figure. Only when we see the effects do we know whether an intelligently planned resource input or a well-managed operation was actually successful. But often the effects which we seek are not immediately or clearly apparent. Moreover, people in charge of an operation may justifiably claim that their performance should be monitored and judged on the basis of how the operation is managed, or even how economically it is managed. The responsibility for whether an operation produces the desired effects lies with the executives who have decided that the operation is to be conducted. Measures should then describe operations or even inputs.

Therefore, in actual practice there are often reasons to exercise management control through measures at the left of the figure. Sometimes these act as "surrogate measures" of conditions closer to the actual effects. We believe that satisfied customers will be loyal, but we do not know for sure. We believe that rapid delivery means satisfied customers, but we do not know the exact nature of the relationship, or at least we would need a certain period of observation to learn how the two are connected. It is because of this that we may refer to the measures at the left of the figure as performance drivers. By understanding them, and taking care to manage them well, we can improve performance in a way which over time will result in better outcomes and effects.

Management control which focuses solely on decentralized short-term profit will fail to present a large part of this fuller picture of an operation. Profit is a good measure, but usually it does not tell us enough about how an operation is managed. At least if the operation is based on some form of identity which is cultivated over time and intended to last over a longer period.

Good scorecards will combine outcome measures, of which profit is only one, with performance drivers. Often it is difficult to draw the line between the two. They are interrelated in a chain of ends and means; for people in charge of logistics, delivery time is an outcome, but for purposes of customer relations it may be considered as one of several performance drivers that can improve customer loyalty. We believe that to an increasing degree score-cards will also illustrate how our business is based on assumptions about *links* among different measures; these assumptions are in turn used to justify the way we do our work.

BEING FORESIGHTED AND YET FLEXIBLE

We are all aware that we live in an era of change. Technology influences our daily lives to a greater extent than we could possibly have imagined only a few years ago. Markets become fragmented when customers realize how they can satisfy their individual demands. This development poses a challenge to the adaptive capacity of business. Communication with customers must be accommodated to suit virtually every individual. This require-ment applies not only to companies that sell to other companies but also to the so-called mass market. Communication fosters growing customer expectations that products will be especially suited to their own needs, perhaps increasingly often even totally individualized.

Such demands can be met. But the conclusion is not that we can avoid planning and content ourselves with reacting defensively. Individually adapted, relationship-based marketing presupposes that we have cultivated the ability to manage customers and products accordingly. For there are no standard recipes, no ready-made solutions which we can purchase as needed. To an increas-ing extent, the decisive factors will be information systems and employee competence. And of course the goodwill capital which we have built up in our customer relationships.

All these requirements call for dynamic organizations with a high degree of employee autonomy. Traditional financial control is ill-adapted to such an environment. Not only is the information which it produces often outdated and too imprecise to provide a basis for decisions on customer relationships or products; in addition, autonomous employees need goals and incentives other than the usual ones based on profit and return on investment and modelled on the income statements used in financial accounting. Other guides are needed to show the way consistent with the comprehensive vision or concept of business. The organization as a whole must be aware of and understand the overall strategies and rules of the game. These in turn should be based on a consensus regarding the necessary priorities.

For these reasons, we believe that the balanced scorecard has its place and an important role to play. The concept is an aid in the essential process of arriving at a shared view of the business environment and of the company. It also provides a new foundation for strategic control.

2

The Balanced Scorecard – Strategic Control

By balanced scorecard we mean not only a particular structure for the "scorecard" itself, but also the processes involved in using it. The balanced-scorecard concept is thus an element of a well-developed system of strategic control and a response to the criticism levelled at traditional management control. We relate Kaplan & Norton's original suggestions about the balanced-scorecard concept to other, similar proposals and to the idea of a company's intellectual capital. With the balanced-scorecard concept, financial responsibility and financial control are replaced by a richer picture of reality. Not that monetary measures have become less important, but in this respect, too, we must strive for a balance.

FROM FINANCIAL CONTROL TO STRATEGIC CONTROL

In the last decade there has been a growing criticism of traditional management control as too narrowly focused on financial measures. The reason is that conditions today are no longer the same as when traditional management control emerged.

For most of the twentieth century, traditional management-control systems have existed in an environment of mature products and stable technologies (Hally, 1994). It has sometimes been said that traditional management control stopped developing in 1925. At that time virtually all of the accounting procedures presently used were already in existence: budgets, standard costs, transfer pricing, the DuPont model, etc. (Johnson & Kaplan, 1987). The role of the management-control system was to see that a company remained efficient; as a result, management concentrated on costs while paying less attention to revenues.

Since World War II industry has undergone massive technological change, and most organizations have become larger and more complex. Sophisticated technologies and production processes have led to new demands on company systems of management control. Financial measures showed the effects of decisions already taken but failed to provide adequate guidance for long-term strategic development. Many began to realize that to be competitive a company needed more complete reporting on the various aspects of its business. For this reason a number of concepts and tools began to emerge during the 1980s; examples are Kaizen, total quality management (TQM), lean production, and business process redesign (BPR). However, the initiative seldom came from the accounting staff or the financial control department. The aims of the new instruments could conflict with traditional management control, or at least their relationship to the latter was unclear, since they emphasized continuous improvement over time by drawing on ideas and suggestions from within the organization. A company strategy based on employee control of processes which satisfy customer needs is not consistent with the short-term thinking that easily results from focusing on financial measures alone.

But the established systems of management control were not only criticized as a means of internal control. A new strategic direction calls for new information for planning, decision-making, monitoring progress, and control. Therefore, management control must also take account of external factors and be broadened to include strategic information which will indicate whether or not the business will continue to be competitive in the future.

THE CRITICISM OF TRADITIONAL MANAGEMENT CONTROL

The financial environment in which today's companies do business puts new and different demands on management control and on the control systems which companies use. During the past 10 years traditional management control has been increasingly criticized, and we will attempt here to summarize some of the views advanced in this debate.

Traditional management control[1]

- *Furnishes misleading information for decision-making* – Information on costs, revenues, and profitability provides the foundation for company decision-making. Traditional financial measures show the results of past activities. Information of this kind can lead to action inconsistent with strategic objectives (Goldenberg & Hoffecker, 1994).
- *Fails to consider the requirements of today's organization and strategy* – The fixation on measurement in monetary terms has led companies to ignore less tangible, non-financial measures such as product quality, customer satisfaction, delivery time, factory flexibility, new-product lead time, and a higher level of employee know-how. The measures used send misleading signals about the efficiency and profitability of the business (Peters, 1987).
- *Encourages short-term thinking and suboptimization* – Financial control also discourages long-term thinking; for example, it can lead to reductions in R&D, cutbacks in training, watered-down incentive and motivation programmes, and postponement of investment plans. The main problem is thus one of "suboptimization over time", and the critical challenge is to achieve a balance between the short and long run.
- *Plays second fiddle to the requirements of financial accounting* – The external-information requirements of financial accounting have determined the design of management-control systems. The stakeholders in the company want continuous information on how the enterprise is doing so that they can compare it with alternative investment opportunities. Financial measures alone do not provide a true and fair view of how a business is developing (Johnson & Kaplan, 1987).
- *Provides misleading information for cost allocation and control of investments* – Traditionally, cost control has not analysed why a cost has been incurred; it has only indicated the amount

and the cost centre. The traditional basis for cost allocation – with indirect costs allocated on the basis of direct costs – is outdated. The relationship between direct and indirect costs has changed as a consequence of increased R&D expenditures, synergies, streamlining production, etc. Cross-subsidies among products make it difficult to measure the actual profitability of any one product. Moreover, it is often impossible to assess the long-term cost of developing a product. Costs must be allocated in some other way than by the traditional method of standard add-ons, such as ABC calculation (Johnson & Kaplan, 1987).

- *Furnishes abstract information to employees* – Another weakness of financial measures is that they are meaningless to a large part of the organization, consisting of the many employees who do not see how their work is related to the numbers shown in the various quarterly and monthly reports. The systems are often much too complicated and are thus an obstacle to flexibility of action on the front line (Shank & Govindarajan, 1993).
- *Pays little attention to the business environment* – Traditional systems of financial measurement ignore the customer and competitor perspective and thus cannot give us early warning signals of changes in our company's industry and business. The financial key ratios found in most management-control systems have an internal rather than an external focus. These measures are used to make comparisons with previous periods on the basis of standards which have been developed internally. It is thus more difficult to compare the company fairly with its competitors, although this information is at least as important as the company's performance in relation to the goals which it has set for itself (Eccles & Pyburn, 1992).
- *May give misleading information* – Today's leaders tend to focus on monthly and quarterly reports, a factor which tends to favour short-term investment decisions. Furthermore, this short-run perspective encourages manipulation of financial measures, so that the financial key ratios may be misleading and lack credibility for purposes of analysis and decision-making (Smith, 1992).

SCORECARD – RECORD OR PROCESS?

"A record of points made (as in a game)" is the Merriam-Webster definition of the noun "score". For the verb there is another definition, "to assign a grade". When we speak of a *balanced* scorecard, we mean that the grading should reflect a balance among several important elements of performance.

We think it is important that the scorecard be seen not only as a record of results achieved. It is equally important that it be used to indicate expected results. The scorecard will then serve as a way to illustrate the business plan and thus the mission of various company units. As a result, the balanced scorecard has sometimes been regarded as a substitute for a budget. In addition, the entire planning process is affected by the format of the scorecard. It helps us to focus on critical issues relating to the balance between short and long run, and to the appropriate strategic direction for everyone's efforts. The scorecard often becomes a catalyst for discussions which actually could have been held without it but which become essential when it is used. Thus, a written record passively prepared after the fact may constitute a scorecard in a formal sense, but not in our view.

Therefore, the perspective throughout this book extends far beyond creating a system of performance measurement. The book also reflects our experience from different companies. While many people are talking about the scorecard (and not just in English), they take it to mean different things. We have found that scorecards have been used in different ways, which we will describe. They all have a common feature: the scorecards have emerged in recent years at companies which have perceived a need for parallel use of different kinds of metrics on their business in all phases of the planning and control process.

THE BALANCED-SCORECARD MODEL OF KAPLAN AND NORTON

The first more widely published description of the balanced scorecard is found in an article by Robert Kaplan and David Norton in the *Harvard Business Review* (1992). The authors, both of them successful researchers and consultants, had worked together with a number of companies to develop methods to measure performance in the "organization of the future". After several more articles, they summarized their findings in a book (1996a). We have already presented the four perspectives which comprise their basic model:

- To succeed financially, how should we look to our share-holders?
- To succeed with our vision, how should we look to our customers?
- To satisfy our shareholders and customers, at what internal business processes must we excel?
- To succeed with our vision, how shall we sustain our capacity to learn and to grow?

Thus, an explicit vision and strategy underlie all four perspectives. And for each perspective, we formulate strategic aims, measures, specific goals, and action plans.

A continuous process centred on the scorecard combines the four perspectives; in it the role of the scorecard is to highlight what should be the focal points of the company's efforts. Kaplan & Norton (1996b) describe the process as a cycle (Figure 2.1). The vision is made explicit and is shared. It is communicated in terms of goals and incentives. These are used to focus the work, allocate resources, and set targets. Follow-up results in learning, which leads us in turn to re-examine our vision. At every step, the scorecard serves as the means of communication.

The learning process places special emphasis on how different measures are interrelated. If we are to be profitable, our customers must be loyal; if they are to be loyal, we must provide good service. To provide good service, we need appropriate and well-functioning processes, and for that purpose we must develop the capabilities of our employees. "Thus, a properly constructed balanced scorecard should tell the story of the business unit's strategy. It should identify and make explicit the sequence of hypotheses about the cause-and-effect relationships between outcome measures and the performance drivers of those outcomes. Every measure selected for a balanced scorecard should be an

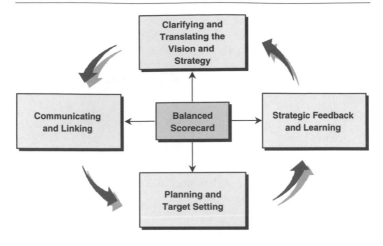

Figure 2.1 Kaplan & Norton's description of the balanced-scorecard process. Adapted and reprinted by permission of *Harvard Business Review*. Exhibit from "Using the Balanced Scorecard as a Strategic Management System" by Robert S. Kaplan and David P. Norton, January–February 1996, p. 77. Copyright © 1996 by the President and Fellows of Harvard College; all rights reserved

element in a chain of cause-and-effect relationships that communicates the meaning of the business unit's strategy to the organization" (Kaplan & Norton, 1996a, p. 31).

It should be noted from the above that measures can describe either what is achieved (*outcomes*) or what affects outcomes (*performance drivers*).

For companies, financial performance is usually the long-run aim, but the other measures provide early signals and are more appropriate for keeping the business on course. Not all measures and key ratios even belong on the scorecard; organizations will still have numerous other metrics. The scorecard is intended to help focus on what is important.

We recommend that the scorecard be used as a tool, adapted to the situation, for discussing and communicating the company's vision and strategy. We will develop this point further in the next chapter. Kaplan & Norton outline a process extending over two years to establish an annual cycle for planning and control with the help of the balanced-scorecard concept. The process starts at the top with a small group of senior executives. After the first quarter, middle management has been brought in, and each business unit develops its own scorecard on the basis of the corporate one. At the same time, corporate management can discontinue projects which in light of the balanced-scorecard process now appear unnecessary, or start up new operations in areas where it has become apparent that the group should be active. At the end of Year 1, various operations have been reviewed in terms of the scorecard in parallel processes at different levels. Now the resulting description of these operations can be communicated throughout the organization. In Year 2, more tangible goals are developed all the way down the line to individual employees, and control and incentive systems consistent with the scorecard are introduced.

In our approach to the balanced-scorecard concept, we have largely accepted the pioneering ideas of Kaplan & Norton. These are actually quite straightforward:

- A compact *structure* for communicating strategy
- The requirement that we discuss the *cause-and-effect relationships* among different factors and that we articulate the strategic hypotheses underlying our course of action
- A *systematic procedure* for conducting these discussions, so that they replace traditional planning and control of an almost purely financial nature.

ALTERNATIVE MODELS

In the literature we have found a number of models similar to that of Kaplan and Norton. All of them are designed to measure the business performance and to link the measures used to the company's overall strategy.

Maisel's Balanced-Scorecard Model

Maisel's balanced scorecard (1992) not only has the same name as the Kaplan & Norton model. Like Kaplan & Norton, Maisel also

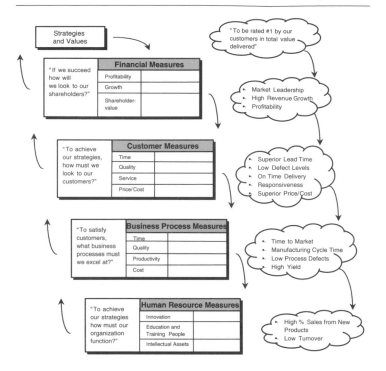

Figure 2.2 Maisel's balanced-scorecard model. Reprinted with permission from Lawrence S. Maisel, "Performance Measurement. The Balanced Scorecard Approach", *Journal of Cost Management* (Summer 1992), p. 50

defines four perspectives from which the business should be measured (Figure 2.2). Instead of a learning and growth perspective, Maisel uses a human-resource perspective in his model. Here he measures innovation as well as factors like education and training, product development, core competencies, and corporate culture. Thus, the difference between the Kaplan & Norton and the Maisel models is not very great. Maisel's reason for using a separate employee perspective is that management should be attentive to, and should measure, the effectiveness of an organization and its people.

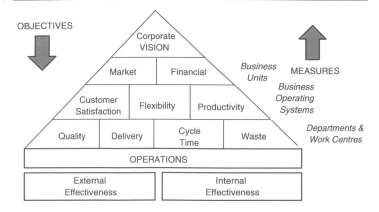

Figure 2.3 The performance pyramid. Reprinted with permission from C.J. McNair, CMA., Richard L. Lynch, and Kelvin F. Cross "Do Financial and Nonfinancial Performance Measures Have to Agree?" *Management Accounting*, November 1990, p. 30

The Performance Pyramid

McNair et al (1990) present a model which they call the performance pyramid (Figure 2.3). As with the other models which we have encountered, the basic principle is that of a customer-oriented model linked to the company's overall strategy, with financial figures supplemented by several other key ratios of a non-financial nature. Traditional management-control information need be provided only at a relatively high level in the company. The performance pyramid is based on the concepts of total quality management, industrial engineering, and activity accounting.

The performance pyramid shows a company at four different levels and provides a structure for a two-way communication system which is needed to institute the company's comprehensive vision at the various levels of the organization. Objectives and measures become links between the company's strategy and its activities. In other words, objectives are translated downward through the organization, while measures are translated upward.

At the top level, corporate management formulates the corporate vision. At the second level, business-unit and divisional goals are expressed in more specific market and financial terms, since from an external standpoint customers and shareholders determine what is important to measure. The third level is not actually an organizational one; rather, it consists of a number of flows within the company. These flows are cross-functional and extend over several departments. Here goals are formulated in terms of customer satisfaction, flexibility, and productivity. This level functions as a link between the upper and lower sections of the pyramid. The three goals at the third level show the performance drivers in relation both to market goals and to financial ones. In addition, this level is the one from which operational goals such as quality, delivery, cycle time, and waste are derived. Of these, quality and delivery are directly related to external effectiveness, whereas cycle time and waste are indicators of the company's internal efficiency.

In the lower section of the pyramid – that is, in the operations part – performance is measured on a daily, weekly, or monthly basis. Higher up in the pyramid, measurements are less frequent and more predominantly financial. In the opinion of McNair et al, a system of measurement should be integrated so that operational measures lower down are linked to financial ones higher up. Thus, corporate management is able to see what underlies the financial measures and what drives them.

EP^{2}M

Adams & Roberts (1993) offer us yet another model, which they call EP^{2}M (effective progress and performance measurement) (Figure 2.4). According to Adams & Roberts, it is important above all to measure what the company does in four areas:

- External measures – serving customers and markets
- Internal measures – improving effectiveness and efficiency
- Top-down measures – breaking the overall strategy down and speeding the process of change
- Bottom-up measures – empowering ownership and enhancing freedom of action

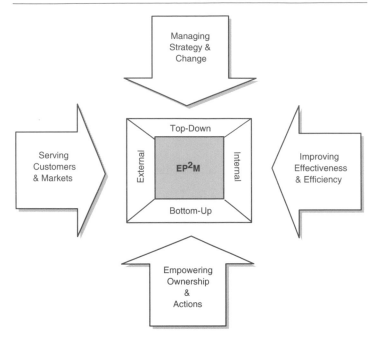

Figure 2.4 The purpose of progress and performance measures. Source: Christopher Adams and Peter Roberts "You are what you measure" *Manufacturing Europe* (1993): 505. Reprinted with permission from the authors

According to Adams & Roberts, the purpose of a measurement system is not only to implement the company's strategy, but also to foster a culture in which constant change is a normal way of life. Effective measures should permit review and provide decision-makers and strategic planners with rapid feedback.

UNDERSTANDING A BUSINESS

The idea of the scorecard is to describe the essential ingredients of business success. Although financial measures are ultimately paramount at a company operating in a market economy, the three other squares below it in Figure 1.1 are needed as "leading indicators", early signals of factors which will not be reflected in financial performance until much later. If there are improvements in these factors, or if they are neglected, we should be informed as soon as possible. And in our planning we should discuss what we want to achieve in regard to them.

Here we are primarily discussing *internal* use of the balanced-scorecard concept. But if we find some way that will impartially communicate how the company has improved its processes or changed its customer base, it may be a good idea to let the shareholders know as well.

Not everyone would agree that the mission and success of a business must be described in terms of several measures, as with the scorecard. To budget a certain profit target and to monitor how well it is being met is simpler and may appear to give greater freedom of action to the managers in charge of the business. It is possible to improve financial metrics so that they more accurately reflect how well the business is managing its customers, developing new products, etc. Internally at a company such improvements can be treated as assets and made visible as "soft" investments. Externally, it may be imagined that a stock market with perfect information would find some way to measure the performance of every company, and that the price of a company's stock would also reflect its long-term prospects. Efforts to broaden disclosure in accounting practices and to find better financial key ratios are intended to improve the correlation between the "correct" course of action by a company and a good growth record for the price of its stock. One example is the discussion on EVA, economic value added, to which we will return later on.

According to this view, modified measures of profit and return on investment are even appropriate for fairly small company units. Decentralized responsibility should promote optimal management of financial capital. When applied well down in the organization, however, control based mainly on financial targets will inevitably involve extensive intracorporate transactions, transfer pricing, etc. Sometimes, of course, senior management will set different ground rules which are less market-like. Other-wise, the business unit might as well be left to function on the market as if it were an independent company. But the basic assumption is that control should centre on goals of profit and return on investment; in effect, small companies are created within the larger one.

The balanced-scorecard approach, on the other hand, emphasizes that the mission of management is about much more than money: in other words, knowledge, the trust of customers and employees, and the question of what future business to be in. If these elements are not present, the profit shown by the company will be worth very little. It is difficult, and not even necessary, to agree on a financial evaluation of everything. Instead, let us openly present a many-sided picture of how well a business is being run!

The approach described above can easily lead to an undesired effect: detailed control and management which thinks that it can tell subordinates what to do all the time. One reason for introducing decentralized profit responsibility in the 1970s and 1980s was to give managers a wider scope of authority to pursue a limited number of clearly stated goals. Actually, such an arrangement is the strength of the market economy, whereas an intelligently designed system of control through multiple measures and multiple goals is often considered characteristic of a planned economy. In fact, neither one of the two is exclusively present at any company. Managers need broad freedom of action and clear goals which may certainly be monetary. To avoid a misguided short-term approach, we should also be interested in another set of numerical goals. We cannot give local management the absolute right to decide which groups of customers it should try to attract, how much the effort should be allowed to cost, what process improvements to invest in, and which competencies to develop. The market will not tell us whether we have made the right choices until it is too late. However, a balanced-scorecard report will help us to decide what to do in all of these areas.

Naturally, our task is not easy. How do we provide concise information on what a division, subsidiary, or department is doing? How do we design a scorecard which avoids tempting us to produce superficially impressive but short-sighted results, one which provides appropriate incentives for all of us to focus our efforts on what really matters? The very description which the scorecard presents in terms of measures must help us to agree on what it *is* that matters! We have already stated that financial measures no longer serve that purpose very well.

The scorecard is termed "balanced" primarily because it expresses a balance between a profit and market approach to control – the uppermost square in the quartet – and control through the use of other measures. The latter should show how the business manages factors which matter in the long run but which are not reflected in short-run profits. Of course these factors vary widely, so that there will also have to be a balance among other areas of focus, among the different measures, between situations at a particular time and changes over a period of time, etc.

A balanced scorecard must not lead back to centralization of matters best managed by local units. On the other hand, we would like it to help us to understand critical long-term factors which probably are often neglected by local units in their determination to be businesslike.

The focus of our interest in this book is internal control. Before we consider whether the description provided by the scorecard is also appropriate for external use in annual reports and other publications, we must have found it relevant and useful within the company. However, we will return in Chapter 10 to external issues, for in some cases scorecards made public outside the company have been an important element in balanced-scorecard projects.

"INTELLECTUAL CAPITAL" AND STRATEGIC DECISIONS

There is ample evidence that the essence of a company, what makes it valuable – whether it is in the private or the public sector – lies in factors which are difficult to describe very precisely. These belong in the lower squares of the scorecard.

We tend to think of long-term and strategic decisions as grand-scale and highly visible, such as investments in new facilities, in new markets, or in major R&D projects launched by corporate or divisional boards.

Today many companies are facing strategic decisions of a very different character. How are we using IT in our customer relationships? Are we encouraging employees to put more work into preparing bids even when the only pay-off is expected to come in the long run? How much information do we gather and make available to each other about our meetings with existing or prospective customers? How many working days should we devote to learning how to use our new Intranet system?

All such efforts cost money, and these areas are easily neglected if there is no incentive to do otherwise or if someone else may reap the benefits. Experience is usually documented for the sake of others; we generally remember our own experience rather well. To cultivate prospective customers or to follow up on previous sales may also benefit someone else more than ourselves – people in other units, perhaps even the people who succeed us in our present positions.

If we really mean that companies should now compete with competence and customer contacts, this point is vital. What companies used to do about the future was probably more visible and budgetable. For investment projects and R&D, there were specific appropriations, decision-making procedures, and people in charge. But the appropriation of funds by a board for particular projects will not ensure that competence and customer contacts are properly managed. These matters are part of everyone's job, all the time. For the right decisions to be made, everyone should be responsible for finding a balance between the short and long run. The balanced-scorecard concept is an aid in bring out the strategic aspects of day-to-day work.

A collective designation for what we are referring to is "intellectual capital". The term has become widespread in recent years. While different writers have interpreted it in somewhat varying ways, the most frequent meaning is "packaged useful knowledge" (Stewart, 1997, p. 67), which is assumed to be the reason why a company is valued at more than the sum of the "hard" assets in its balance sheet, even if these have been written up to their current market value.

Internationally, the Swedish insurance company Skandia is often cited as a pioneer in the area of intellectual capital. In a series of supplements to its annual reports from 1994 onwards, the company presents its intellectual capital as a justification for the premium which it hopes to command on the stock market. Later we will explain how Skandia uses the balanced scorecard to tie its model together as shown in Figure 2.5.

Intellectual capital is cultivated in part by hiring and developing the right kind of employees – in other words, by increasing *human*

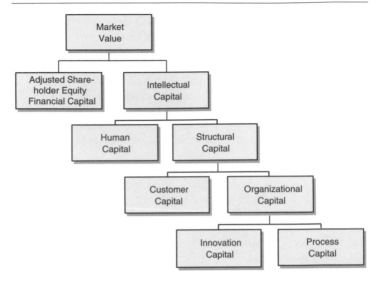

Figure 2.5 Intellectual capital as an element of the company's market value, according to Skandia. Source: Supplement to Skandia's annual report for 1995, "On Processes Which Create Value". By permission from Skandia

capital. But since this resource is volatile, the need for stability must be met by tying accumulated competence and capability to the company in a more lasting way. The development of *structural capital* has *external* aspects: investing in customers' image of the company, e.g. by making the company known to more customers, by presenting them with a more favourable image, or in some other way making them more inclined to patronize the company. The value of these efforts will be enhanced, of course, if we can transform the information obtained from meetings with customers into an asset in the form of well-designed customer data bases, for instance. Then we will "know" something about the customer which otherwise in the best of cases would be known only to individual salesmen – we will have transformed human-resources capital into structural capital!

Structural capital is also closely related to *internal* processes, knowledge, and capabilities. Company investments in IT are generally intended to produce improvements in these areas. The substantial sums expended on software and training are seldom reported as assets in the balance sheet; to the extent that they increase a company's market value, Skandia's model would treat them as additions to structural capital. In this way the model may be used as a basis for discussing the valuation of a company. If a buyer is prepared to pay a premium to acquire a company's stock, one reason would be that the net worth of the reported assets – adjusted shareholder equity in the figure – is understated; the other would be that there are other assets, referred to as "goodwill" in the accounts of the acquirer. When we speak of intellectual capital, we expect that it will become increasingly important. There is some evidence to this effect, but of course it is difficult to be certain. There are several reasons why the market cannot easily determine the value of intellectual capital:

• Cultivation of competence and of market position is difficult to substantiate and to agree on; the expected contribution of these factors to future earnings will depend on our choice of scenario for the company's future environment and its future ability to make such investments pay off.
• Since these factors are competitive weapons, a company may be understandably reluctant to disclose information about them.
• A company's ownership, or at least its effective control, over this "capital" may be limited. Ideas and solutions are easy to imitate, and employees may decide to leave the company. Therefore, when we are considering intellectual capital which is not reported in traditional financial statements, we should also remember that others may claim to own parts of it. In Figure 2.6, we have indicated how ownership rights to human-resource capital, in particular, may be questioned in light of the possible existence not only of intellectual assets but of intellectual liabilities as well. We are thinking primarily of employees who may assert a right to some of these assets. However, sometimes partners with whom we collaborate may be the principal beneficiaries of our company's investments.

The illustration indicates some of the problems of determining what we mean by intellectual capital. Assets in the conventional

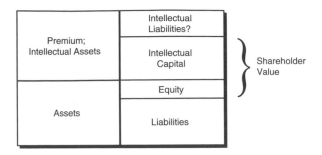

Figure 2.6 Intellectual capital as a market premium

balance sheet are valued as the remainder after accumulated depreciation of our expenditure in acquiring them. We can of course treat competence, market value, and similar items in the same way. But their value to our future business may be quite different – either greater or smaller. This uncertainty may be an element in the valuation of our company by the market.

Other schemes of classification have also been proposed. Sveiby (1997), for example, prefers the term intangible assets, which he divides into external structure, internal structure, and competence of personnel. An important issue – also in the design of a scorecard, as we will later see – is whether employees should be considered as an asset distinct from the company's processes and structures.

There are signs that the market is becoming more inclined to attribute value to intellectual capital. One indication is the growing interest in industries with no "certain tangible assets"; examples would be service industries and IT. Another is found in certain studies of the relationship between stock prices and reported net worth. Such comparisons are always shaky – supposed differences can be explained by a variety of other factors. However, we see significance in the finding by a respected American research company that the share of what we have called intellectual capital has risen markedly during the period 1982–1992 (Figure 2.7).

Further on we will return to the usefulness of the balanced-scorecard concept in financial accounting. In this book, however, we will concentrate on internal control. Of course, if it is becoming

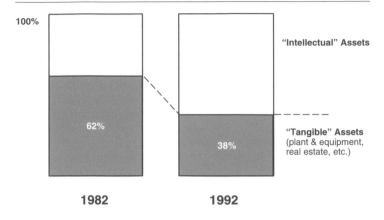

Figure 2.7 The relationship of "tangible assets" to market value for manufacturing and mining companies in the USA. Based on numbers from Blair, Brookings Institution reported in Stewart (1994)

important for more and more companies to cultivate capital which is not reported in the traditional balance sheet, there are major implications for management control. If for management-control purposes a company uses financial-accounting measures of what is being managed and how well it is doing, it will overlook major areas of management responsibility. And in management control, unlike financial accounting, there is no comparable justification for focusing primarily on "hard assets". On the contrary, if we regard management control as strategic control, it will become increasingly important to find ways to communicate how we should be cultivating our intellectual capital, and how well we are succeeding at it.

We believe that this necessity is also the principal reason why the balanced-scorecard concept has emerged at this time. It goes hand in hand with a growing scepticism towards budgeting, regarded by many as the most conservative form of management control, with budgets modelled on profit-centre income statements which in turn are presented in financial-accounting language; we will resume this discussion later in the book. In some instances, people do not even want to talk about the financial aspects of management control. That is what the deputy managing director of ABB Sweden meant when he said, "Now we are moving from financial control to strategic control"; he was referring, among other things, to the use of the balanced scorecard at that corporation (Peter Fallenius, quoted in Wennberg, 1994). This statement raises the issue of what should be included in management control, which is commonly considered a part of managerial *economics*. If we consider competence and customer relationships as resources to be managed, these are certainly to be regarded as having economic relevance. Then measures which can be termed economic – i.e. relevant to resource management – may very well differ from the generally accepted monetary ones.

BUSINESS INVOLVES TAKING CALCULATED RISKS

A fundamental notion implicit in the balanced-scorecard concept is thus that a company must cultivate the capital which it will need for its long-term development. Much of what is meant by the concept was the focus of several "buzz words" used in the 1980s: customer orientation, decentralized responsibility, lean production, and rapid flow. What we learned then has still not been sufficiently implemented, and – moreover – ground already gained must be continually reconquered. The starting point was often an analysis of the customer's situation; it led to conclusions about the so-called characteristics which our company should have. Business purpose, strategies, and goals were specified, and the company adapted to its anticipated market and competitive situation. All that was useful and instructive. But it may not have been enough.

For any number of people can perform such an analysis, and often they will reach the same conclusions. Business success does not primarily require that we determine the nature of demand. The question which we have to answer is whether we are in the running as a supplier. In other words, not just "What is needed?", but also "Why us?" The answer depends on what we can do: our competence and capability. To determine what competencies and capabilities we will need does not mean that we can acquire them overnight. For long-run, sustainable success, we must develop the right capabilities at the right time. To be deft and nimble generally calls for proper preparation.

The articles on strategy in the 1990s developed this idea further. Quinn (1992) referred to *The Intelligent Enterprise* and emphasized the importance of cultivating a "core competency". Even manufacturing companies are becoming more and more dependent somewhere in the value chain on a link consisting of services or intellectual activities. Quinn holds that a business cannot survive without becoming a world leader in some aspect of this nature. That kind of capability is what should be cultivated. Almost everything else can be bought from others. Two other leading American professors in the field of business strategy, Hamel and Prahalad (1994), emphasized how a company must build up its competencies:

> Competition for the future is competition for *opportunity share* rather than market share. . . . Which new competencies would we have to build, and how would our definition of our "served market" have to change, for us to capture a larger share of future opportunities? (p. 31)

When Hamel and Prahalad (1994) speak of competencies, they mean that it takes patient and persistent accumulation of knowledge and understanding to acquire them. We have to ask ourselves, "What can we do that other companies could not easily do as well?" By cultivating the right competence early enough, we open up a lead which we can maintain.

To do so requires that we concentrate on one or a few areas of competence, even when our ambition is limited to becoming the best within sight rather than the best in the world. But fortunately it is now easy to hire others to do the rest – one reason being improved communications. We should not try to do anything ourselves which someone else can do better.

Thus, the concept of core competence brings us back to the thesis that *intellectual capital* is what a company should develop. The following statements summarize the thinking of one of the leading authorities in the area (Rumelt, 1994):

- Core competencies support several businesses and products
- Products and services are only a temporary manifestation of core competence – the latter develops more slowly and is more stable than products

- Competence is knowledge and therefore increases with use
- In the long run, competence, not products, will determine who succeeds in competition

How does someone inspire our enthusiasm to risk investing in intellectual capital? What key ratios can be used to control such ventures? What will the opportunities presented by IT mean for the interplay among independent-minded, creative people? Is the corporation a relevant form of doing business if risk capital is not primarily financial in nature? What American management journals refer to as "the new economy" raises many exciting issues but has so far provided few answers.[2] We will have to make full use of the knowledge and suggestions of the employees concerned. Otherwise we may overlook something which we very much need to know; we will also fail to obtain the commitment which people feel from taking part in our discussions on why we do what we do. One of the main reasons why the balanced scorecard is necessary is that more people – many people – should help determine, and should be aware of, the assumptions on which our actions are based. For the balanced-scorecard concept adds a strategic dimension to management control; by involving many people in the discussion, it enables all of us to understand why we believe in our choice of what we want to become.

NOTES

1. By traditional management control we mean control of decision-making and behaviour in an organization with the aim of improving profits, profitability, and financial position.
2. See, for example, the extensive supplement in *The Economist*, 28 September, 1996.

Part II

Building a Balanced Scorecard

3

The Process of Building a Balanced Scorecard

The purpose of this chapter is to provide a general picture of how a balanced scorecard can be developed. The description should be considered as a framework for the building process rather than as a detailed set of instructions; one reason why the balanced-scorecard concept has been so successful is that the process as well as the scorecard itself are adapted to the company's actual situation – both its market position and its internal organization.

Towards the end, the building process merges into the ongoing use of the scorecard. In this chapter, we have chosen to refer to the latter as a final step in the building of a scorecard: "Implementing the scorecard". This is, however, in itself an extensive subject which we will treat more thoroughly in Part III of this book.

We have argued that scorecards could be used to permeate the company with a sense of the long-term business logic in creating some unique competencies with the expectation of being rewarded in the market-place. This matter is of course relevant both to strategy and to operations. The ideal is to use scorecards for different parts of the business to develop a convincing and communicable logic for the actual cultivation of such competencies. The scorecard is thus used for both strategic and operational control; in this chapter we assume that this combination is desired. But scorecards may also be used when no change in strategy is being considered. Some of our case studies provide examples showing the consequence for the scorecard process: the company may move more directly to formulating scorecards which focus on the features of the business which are critical to its strategy.

However, since it is fairly common that a need to reconsider the company's strategy will be perceived once the scorecard process is under way, we have decided to describe this review in the present chapter. For purposes of illustration we will draw on our experience with KappAhl, a Swedish retail clothing chain.

A COMPREHENSIVE VIEW OF THE PROCESS

The balanced scorecard gives us a valuable tool for enabling employees to understand the company's situation, a must if the company is to achieve the dynamism it needs to be competitive in the long run. The balanced scorecard also provides us with useful documentation for continually developing those measures for control which most quickly will guide the company towards achieving its goals and its vision.

The result will be that daily operations are founded on a shared view of where the company should be headed in the long run. The course to be taken by the company thus becomes a tangible and understandable reality for everyone. In addition, with the scorecard decomposed by area of activity, control of operations will be perceived locally as more relevant than with previous models. Employees will be more understanding and better motivated, and thus more open to change and forceful in implementing company decisions. The organization becomes better at learning and more perceptive and continually develops its competence. The process of formulating and implementing this kind of balanced scorecard touches on a number of different areas. Figure 3.1 illustrates the extent of the process and shows the areas involved.

Strategy Development

Management control starts with the company's vision and strategy, and the scorecard is a method of controlling the business. However, in our experience the descriptive character of the scorecard often leads to new ideas about the company's vision and to a

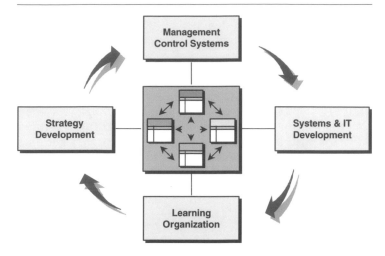

Figure 3.1 The balanced-scorecard process

reconsideration of its strategy. For this reason the first steps in the scorecard process outlined below are about developing a strategy, a phase which may already have occurred in the course of other company processes. In this case preparing the scorecard will merely result in a confirmation of existing strategies, although in the scorecard process these will be expressed in more tangible terms of goals and critical success factors.

Management Control Systems

In Chapter 2 we described the need for a new kind of strategic control and how this need has led to the development of the balanced scorecard and similar models. The process presented in this chapter heavily emphasizes how company strategies are translated into measures and goals for various managers in charge and how the scorecard provides comprehensive, balanced statements of their duties. In principle, the process should be repeated at every level of the company so that all employees are given a sense of participation and can understand their part in the overall strategic scheme. An important part of the process, therefore, is to link together measures in different perspectives and in scorecards for different business units.

In Chapter 2 we laid the foundation for the above in our discussion on cultivation of company competence, in which the company must concentrate its resources on a number of selected areas. This process involves a large number of employees whose contribution is needed in different ways. The scorecards for their various activities should be sufficiently explicit to guide their endeavours in the right direction and to explain how they contribute to the general effort. In Chapters 6 and 7, we will go into this in greater detail.

Systems and IT Development

For the scorecard to be usable in practice throughout the company, the procedure for handling measurements must of course be user-friendly and not overly complicated. Data must be recorded, verified, and made available. Normally the scorecard will draw on a combination of data already in use at the company, and of new measurements, some of which may be quite informal in nature.

In the design of the scorecard for strategic control, it is natural to consider the practical aspects of data collection and existing systems. This statement is especially true of the introductory phase, when the company scorecard has not yet assumed its definite form. But even a provisional system requires practical solutions and answers to a number of questions relating to responsibility for measurement: how often, using what control systems, who is in charge, etc. We will return to these questions in Chapter 8.

The Learning Organization

The primary function of the scorecard is to control company operations. It furnishes a language for describing expectations and performance, thus laying the foundation for discussions on how each individual can contribute to fulfilling the company's vision.

For example, efforts to develop customer data bases or to attract customers in new market segments may not be profitable in the short run, but they may be justifiable in view of the anticipated longer-term benefits. The scorecard provides a basis for determining the appropriate weight to be given to such efforts in the overall balance and for communicating that weight through management control.

By extension, there is also a more cumulative effect. As we gain experience in how the new customer data base is being used, or how sales are developing in the new customer segments, our assumptions about causal relationships will be confirmed or disproved. In this way the use of the balanced scorecard can also facilitate learning. At both individual and company levels, we will develop a better understanding of the relationship between what we do and how well the company succeeds.

Of course it is crucial that we actually use the scorecard. What is needed is an appropriate incentive structure and practical arrangements for handling the information generated, so that it becomes attractive and feasible to develop a set of good scorecard practices. We will go deeper into these issues in Chapter 9.

FROM VISION TO ACTION PLAN

Before we go through the process itself of developing a balanced scorecard, an overview of how the scorecard is developed is provided in Figure 3.2.

- *The vision*: In the uppermost portion of the model there is the company's vision at the highest level. By vision we mean a company's desired future situation. The purpose of the vision is to guide, control, and challenge an entire organization towards realizing a shared conception of the company in the future.
- *Perspectives*: The overall vision is decomposed and described in terms of a number of perspectives. The most frequently used perspectives are the shareholder and financial perspective, the customer perspective, the internal/business-process perspective, and a learning and growth perspective. Certain companies

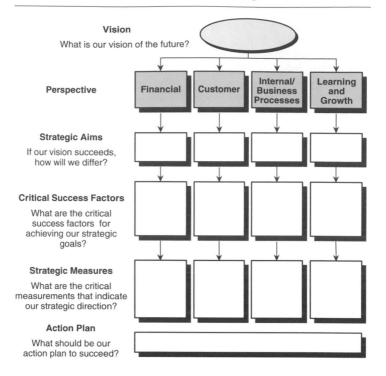

Figure 3.2 Comprehensive view of the process. Adapted and reprinted by permission of *Harvard Business Review*. Exhibit from "Putting the balanced scorecard to Work" by Robert S. Kaplan and David P. Norton, September–October 1993, p. 139. Copyright © 1993 by the President and Fellows of Harvard College; all rights reserved

have added a separate employee or human perspective. A more detailed examination of questions and ideas on this subject is found in Chapter 5.

- *Strategic aims*: The vision is expressed as a number of more specific strategic aims. These serve to guide the company in achieving the vision.

- *Critical success factors*: At this level those factors are described which are most critical for the company's success with its vision.

- *Strategic measures*: This portion of the scorecard describes the measures and goals which have been developed to enable management to follow the company's systematic efforts to exploit the success factors considered most critical for goal achievement. In Chapter 8 the reader will find further discussion on measures and methods of measurement.
- *Action plan*: Finally, to complete the scorecard, there should also be a section describing the specific actions and steps which will be required in the future.

THE CHOICE OF AN APPROPRIATE UNIT

Depending on the size and status of the company, there is good reason at the outset to reflect carefully on the scope of the activities to be covered by the scorecards, on the organizational unit to be covered, and on the pace of introduction. At a smaller company it is probably best to create a scorecard for the entire organization, whereas in a larger company and/or corporate group it may be more suitable to begin with one or two pilot projects. The choice of the appropriate company unit in the latter case should be based on a combination of willingness to participate and suitability for the project, so that the company can make the best possible use of the initial experience in the work to follow. However, it is desirable to gain experience both from staff units and from units with more extensive outside contacts.

We have found that another deciding factor in the choice of a suitable arrangement is the company's situation at the time. If the company is in the midst of turbulent change, the scorecard process in itself may be a useful tool. In such cases teaching company personnel about the balanced scorecard would be suitable and could help to create understanding and consensus on future strategies and on any changes which may follow from the process. In these cases it is thus advantageous to begin by developing a top-level scorecard which in the next phase can be decomposed into appropriate parts. In order to prepare and to gain support for a necessary change in the organization, top management can send out the top-level scorecard for comment. The purpose of distribution for comment is not only to gather support for the overall strategies, but also to initiate a discussion on how the process can be conducted more effectively. The first step, after the top-level scorecard is ready, is to let each department or other suitable group review the scorecard and discuss how it affects their specific situation and how they believe they can contribute to realizing the company's vision and strategic goals. A discussion may also be held on how to work more efficiently and intelligently. Only after this round has been completed should work begin on making any change in the organization. Change usually becomes much easier as an effect of the process just described; a change also gains additional support and is further implemented as scorecards are developed for the respective units of the new organization.

How long the process takes may vary. However, it is imperative not to hurry too much. As we have previously indicated, the process in itself is extremely important; everyone involved must be given enough time to gain the necessary understanding. The time taken is also dependent to some extent on the company's size and situation. At a smaller company the project can be completed in six months at best, whereas if the organization or situation is more complex several years may be required before the entire company has been covered. It should also be noted that the balanced-scorecard process is never really finished. A study at Oxford University's Templeton College (Ruddle & Feeny, 1998) describes transformation processes at a number of large companies and claims that transformational scorecards have been important in the more successful cases. The processes of change concerned here covered a period of four to six years at some companies. Since one of the useful features of the scorecard is that it is a part of strategic control, it must be kept alive and continually adapted to changes in the company's situation and organization.

HOW SHOULD WE BE ORGANIZED AND WHO SHOULD TAKE PART IN THE WORK?

Much of the strength of the model lies in the development process itself, in which a large number of employees participate in jointly analysing and discussing the company's situation and capabilities.

In addition to the discussion and understanding of the vision itself, a central part of the work consists in further analysis to identify strategic perspectives and factors for success. For this reason as many employees as possible should be actively involved in the process, which to the extent possible should be conducted with some form of consensus. It is particularly important that the causal relationships and the priorities which emerge in the discussions be well understood and widely supported. If this understanding is not there, the process will prove very frustrating, with a very high risk that the whole undertaking will come to nothing.

For success in linking the vision with day-to-day operations, it is also important that the development process advances from two directions. At the outset top management must be committed to elaborating the vision and must send that message out to the rest of the organization. Later on in the process, it will be necessary to start a dialogue throughout the organization concerning which activities will be affected and will actively contribute to the success of the vision. The importance of top-management commitment and motivation cannot be sufficiently emphasized. The CEO must be totally committed to the entire process and must take an active part in developing the first basic elements of the scorecard. Subsequently s/he must also ensure that the task is given high priority and is firmly supported by the entire organization.

Who then should be involved in the process? As emphasized above, the process of developing the balanced scorecard is one of the greatest strengths of the whole approach. Therefore, it is especially important to be very particular about who participates and when. In addition to the active participation and interest of top management at the overall level, it is also essential to involve as many opinion leaders as possible in the initial phases, particularly for the purpose of recruiting a number of highly motivated "missionaries" for the work later on. When the process then continues in the other parts of the organization, most employees should be more or less actively taking part. While the degree of participation may vary, in our experience there are major benefits from including as many people as possible in the discussion on how overall goals will affect day-to-day operations and in what ways the individual employee or group can contribute to success.

These discussions often help participants to see matters in a completely new light.

Depending on the size and complexity of the company, it is usually a good idea to put a project-management team in overall charge of the process. The decision on whom to include in project management is critical for success, and management should be careful to ensure that the group will be seen as representative of the entire company. Thus, it would be unwise to staff the project entirely with people from the controller's department, even though they are often the ones who have initiated the project. Let us recall that one of the principal advantages of the scorecard is precisely that it replaces traditional accounting jargon with goals and measures more easily understood and accepted by non-accountants. Project management should continually follow the progress of the work, offer advice, and suggest adjustments which will facilitate an understanding of the process as a whole as well as guarantee the consistency of the scorecard.

A summary description of the various phases of the process follows below. We would emphasize that the model should only be regarded as a very general one, since in reality it must always be adapted to the company in question and to its unique characteristics: its industry, size, ownership, etc.

FUNDAMENTAL PREMISES

A fundamental premise for developing a top-level scorecard for the organization is that all concerned basically agree on the general characteristics of the industry and of the company itself. Therefore, the organization must be given enough time and resources for everyone involved in the project to obtain the information needed to form a well-founded opinion.

In our experience, management often underestimates the benefits to the organization that result when participants possess a comprehensive picture of the actual situation inside and outside the company. This failure is often due to a sort of secrecy surrounding issues and information of this nature. Management does not realize the extent of the problem and that many other employees also require this kind of information in order to make the right

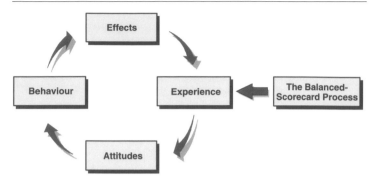

Figure 3.3 An organization undergoing change

decisions, and particularly to respond as rapidly and dynamically as possible to the desires of increasingly discriminating and demanding customers. This point is especially important if employees will have to change their behaviour in some way. It is not enough simply to tell everyone to behave differently from now on. Our behaviour is governed by our values and attitudes, which in turn are based on our previous experience (see Figure 3.3). To bring about necessary changes, we must create an environment conducive to the new experience that will gradually affect attitudes and then behaviour. Often, however, some form of external influence is needed to produce new experience. One purpose of the balanced-scorecard process is to encourage the stimulating discoveries which are so essential. When the organization subsequently sees the effects of its changed behaviour, a form of self-generating process will have been established.

In addition, we are absolutely convinced from our experience that the entire process and the quality of the work will improve markedly if the participants have been provided with relevant background documentation as well as the opportunity both to question it and to develop it further. The improved comprehension of the total situation from giving the organization the necessary information and time will pay off many times over later on in the process as participants return to their day-to-day tasks.

Table 3.1 provides an overview of the process and also indicates the nature of the work and the time required for each step. As

Table 3.1   The steps in the building process

Step	Description	Procedure	Suggested time
1	*Define the industry, describe its development and the role of the company*	Interviews with as many people as possible. Should be done if possible by an outside party to obtain the most objective picture. Research on industry situation and trends	1–2 months
2	*Establish/confirm the company's vision*	Joint seminar attended by top management and opinion leaders	1–2 meetings of 1½ days each
3	*Establish the perspectives*	Seminar attended by top management, the project group, and someone having previous experience with balanced-scorecard projects	1–2 days
4	*Break the vision down according to each perspective and formulate overall strategic goals*	Joint seminar with the same group as in step 2	See below
5	*Identify critical factors for success*	At the seminar above	Total including step 4: 2–3 days
6	*Develop measures, identify causes and effects and establish a balance*	At the seminar above, if possible. However, a certain interval is often beneficial	Included above, otherwise 1–2 days
7	*Establish the top-level scorecard*	Final determination by top management and the project group. Preferably, though, with the participation of someone having previous experience with balanced-scorecard projects	1–2 days
8	*Breakdown of the scorecard and measures by organizational unit*	Suitable for a project divided up into appropriate organizational units under the leadership of the project group. Preferably all personnel involved should take part in the project work of each unit; a suitable form for the work would be a seminar. Progress reports and ongoing co-ordination with top management. Help from an experienced balanced-scorecard architect is especially important in aligning success factors and measures	Total of 2 months and upward. For each local seminar, at least ½–1 day

Table 3.1 *(continued)*

Step	Description	Procedure	Suggested time
9	*Formulate goals*	Proposals by each unit project leader. Final approval of goals by top management	No estimate
10	*Develop an action plan*	Prepared by each project group	No estimate
11	*Implementing the scorecard*	Ensured by ongoing monitoring under the overall responsibility of top management	No estimate

previously noted, the exact arrangement and thus also the time allotted must be adapted to the characteristics and situation of each company.

STEP 1: DEFINE THE INDUSTRY, DESCRIBE ITS DEVELOPMENT AND THE ROLE OF THE COMPANY

The purpose of this step is to develop a foundation for establishing a consensus on the characteristics and requirements of the industry and to arrive at a clear definition of the company's current position and role. Since in addition we are to reach agreement on how the industry will evolve in the future, we will also be building a valuable and necessary platform for proceeding further with the elaboration of our vision and our future strategies. The appropriate form for this work would be individual interviews, primarily with top management and with the most influential opinion leaders at the company.

In the interviews it is important to develop a view of the company and its characteristics from as many angles as possible. For this purpose some of the models presented below may be helpful. The simple teaching approach of these models often makes them excellent catalysts, so that they provide a good basis for discussion in this type of analysis. However, we wish to emphasize that this book is not intended as an in-depth study of the details of strategic environmental analysis or of model-building.

Generally, though, it may be said that practical thinking in strategic management has been heavily influenced by the SWOT

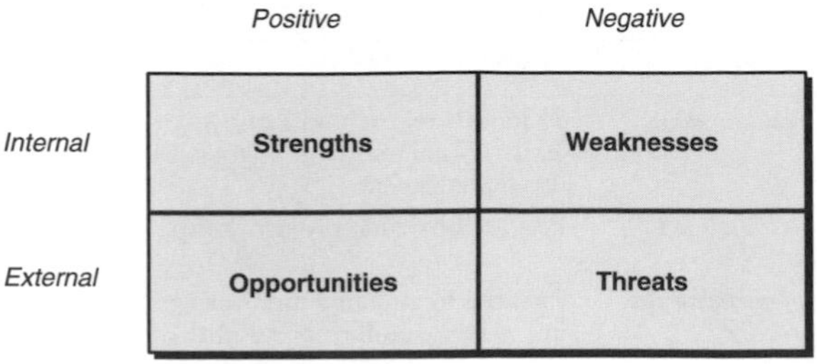

Positive   Negative

Internal   **Strengths**   **Weaknesses**

External   **Opportunities**   **Threats**

Figure 3.4 A SWOT analysis. Reprinted from K.R. Andrews, *The Concept of Corporate Strategy*, 3rd edn, Homewood, IL: Irwin (1987) by permission of McGraw-Hill

(strengths/weaknesses, opportunities/threats) model (Andrews, 1980) developed in the early 1970s (Figure 3.4). With the aid of this model, a company can analyse what it can do today (the organization's strengths and weaknesses) and what it might do in relation to the external environment (external opportunities and threats). At the outset of the 1980s, Porter (1980) introduced his five competitive forces model, in which a company's profitability is affected by the structural forces in its particular industry (Figure 3.5). This approach shifted the focus from the company to the competitive situation in the industry.

In the late 1980s and early 1990s, the pendulum swung back, and with the resource-based approach the focus shifted from the external environment to the resources and capabilities of the individual company (Figure 3.6) (Wernerfelt, 1984; Barney, 1991; Collis & Montgomery, 1995). Some regard this viewpoint as an intermediate one between a SWOT analysis and Porter's five competitive forces model. In dealing with the external environment, a company builds its competitive power on its resources and capabilities. In the 1990s, Hamel & Prahalad (1994) and others developed these themes, using the term "core-competence" (Figure 3.7). In a number of respects, these ideas are derived from the theory of resource-based strategy.

Another major respect in which the theory in this area has evolved is the abandonment of the notion that it is feasible to prepare detailed long-range strategic plans. What people are talking about instead is the importance of creating conditions

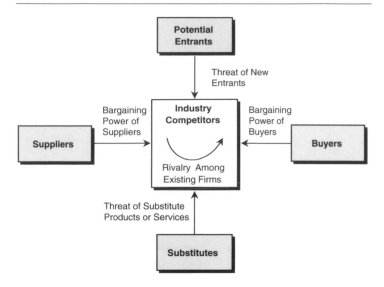

Figure 3.5 The competitive forces that determine industry profitability. Reprinted with the permission of The Free Press, a Division of Simon & Schuster, from *Competitive Advantage: Creating and Sustaining Superior Performance*, by Michael E. Porter. Copyright © 1985 by Michael E. Porter

which favour the development of strategic thinking at a company. This strategic thinking should then guide specific everyday decisions and actions, so that the company acquires the dynamism and decisiveness now required of most companies in most industries.

Since the next step is a seminar for the purpose of creating a kind of consensus on what will matter in the future, it is desirable to document the interviews and to report the opinions which emerge from them, particularly any dissenting views on essential issues. In preparation for the seminar, it is also important to find out what the people concerned believe will happen in the future. This procedure involves a combination of research and interviews with stakeholders and people at different levels in the company. To avoid influencing participants and to learn about their picture of the future, it may even be advisable to start such a discussion by simply asking, "How do you think the industry will develop in the future?"

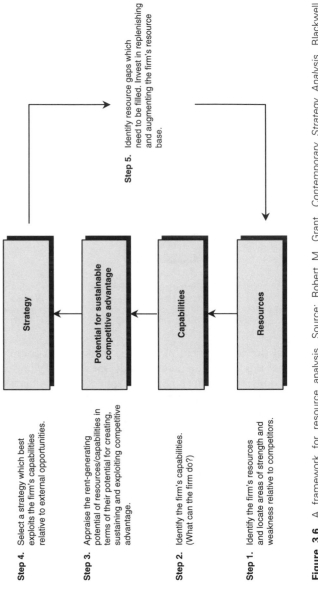

Step 4. Select a strategy which best exploits the firm's capabilities relative to external opportunities.

Step 3. Appraise the rent-generating potential of resources/capabilities in terms of their potential for creating, sustaining and exploiting competitive advantage.

Step 2. Identify the firm's capabilities. (What can the firm do?)

Step 1. Identify the firm's resources and locate areas of strength and weakness relative to competitors.

Figure 3.6 A framework for resource analysis. Source: Robert M. Grant, *Contemporary Strategy Analysis*, Blackwell Publishers (1993): 120. Reprinted by permission

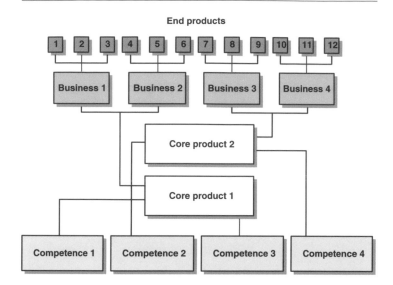

Figure 3.7 Core products are nourished by competencies and engender business units, whose fruits are end products. Reprinted by permission of *Harvard Business Review*. Exhibit from "The Core Competence of the Corporation" by C.K. Prahalad and Gary Hamel, May–June 1990, p. 81. Copyright © 1990 by the President and Fellows of Harvard College; all rights reserved

One purpose of this question is to ascertain the degree of consensus in the group. For this reason it is not advisable to be more specific in defining what is meant by "the industry" or "the future". The benefit of remaining general is that it leaves room for differences in what people mean by the industry and its boundaries to come out. Information about these differences may prove useful later in discussing questions related to the future development of the business, such as in what ways the company might provide value for customers in the future, and – as a consequence – what kind of network collaboration to initiate. At the seminar the comprehensive picture provided by the participants will be presented in summary form. This presentation will usually serve as an excellent basis for discussion by the participants at the seminar and in subsequent steps of the process.

STEP 2: ESTABLISH/CONFIRM THE COMPANY'S VISION

Since the balanced-scorecard model is based on a shared comprehensive vision, it is essential to ascertain at an early stage whether
a jointly held vision in fact exists. Since the scorecard will give the
organization a stronger focus than before, the consequences of
a misguided vision may be extremely serious. To the extent that a
vision is missing, this point presents an excellent opportunity to
begin laying a common foundation for the vision together.

As is evident from the preceding paragraph, there are numerous
models and methods for developing a vision. Since the purpose of
this book is not to describe and evaluate such processes, we will be
very brief in this portion of the discussion.

Examples of Definitions

Vision:
A challenging and imaginative picture of the future role and
objectives of an organization, significantly going beyond its current environment and competitive position.

Mission statement:
Defines the business that the organization is in or should be in
against the values and expectations of the stakeholders.

Strategies:
The principles that show how an organization's major objectives
or goals are to be achieved over a defined time period. Usually
confined only to the general logic for achieving the objectives.

Objectives or goals:
State more precisely than a mission statement what is to be
achieved and when the results are to be accomplished.

As has been indicated previously, there must be a reasonable
shared view of the internal and external situation of the company
before the common vision can be developed. In order to establish
the vision, a number of factors must be considered (Figure 3.8).

For example, a set of issues which cannot be ignored relates to
the ways in which the evolution of IT will affect the company and
the industry. One consequence is that we find numerous examples

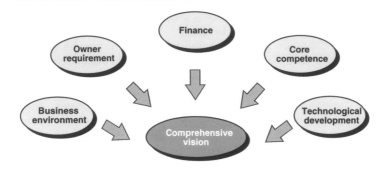

Figure 3.8 Some factors which should be discussed and form the basis for establishing the vision

of how customer needs for products and services are becoming more individualized. The resulting tendency towards fragmentation in a growing number of industries is creating difficulties as well as new opportunities for most companies. With the company's situation as a starting-point, a probable future course of development is outlined. With that outline in view, an assessment is made of what customers will probably appreciate and value. Especially in light of the dramatic changes in the business environment which we are experiencing and expecting, we should remain humble and keep our distance towards established "truths" and previous experience. And particularly in view of the pace of change, it is essential that as much of the organization as possible be actively involved in a continuing discussion on the development of the business. For this reason management should try to find appropriate forms of communication for this kind of discussion and debate. An interesting possibility in this regard is scenario analysis – that will be discussed in more detail in succeeding chapters.

That we consider an established vision important does not mean that the long-range planning should be allowed to lock the company into a preset course of action. What we do believe is that in order to succeed the company must focus on a common course of development, based on a view of the internal and external situation and of the principal success factors which is shared by the entire organization. This focus will give the company the flexibility and dynamism which it needs for continuous adaptation to a changing business environment.

After the vision has been established, but before going on with the development of the scorecard, we should obtain one final confirmation of how each participant perceives the vision. One way would be to have each participant describe how he believes the company will look when the vision has been attained. Thus, everyone would present his or her own picture of the future company from the Financial, Customer, Process, and Development perspectives. An appropriate procedure would be for all the participants in a few keywords to express their interpretation of the vision from the different perspectives. There would then be a concluding discussion on appropriate priorities among the keywords mentioned. Any dramatic differences of opinion here will usually be quite apparent.

The questions below may provide further help before the vision is definitely adopted.

- Does the vision give us the confidence we need?
- Does the vision give us the challenge we need?
- Can the vision help us to formulate our personal goals in a satisfactory manner?
- Do we feel that the vision is meaningful and that it is "ours"?

KappAhl – steps 1–2

As we mentioned at the outset, we will draw on our experience with different companies to illustrate our reasoning. Throughout the present chapter we will be using as an example KappAhl, a Swedish company.

The KappAhl retail-clothing chain was started in 1954 and became one of Sweden's greatest success stories of the 1950s and 1960s. The name tells us a lot about the image of the company. "Kapp" comes from the Swedish word *kappa*, which simply means "coat", or "outwear garment (for ladies)" – a rather basic and unglamorous item in the product assortment. "Ahl" was the name of the founder himself, Per-Olof Ahl. By 1990, when the company had grown quite large and Mr Ahl was well along in years, it was acquired by KF, the Swedish Co-operative Wholesale Society. However, for the time being the days of glory were over, and despite a succession of management changes, it proved difficult to restore profitability.

In the autumn of 1995, a new CEO was appointed. At this point KappAhl had 150 stores and 2000 employees in Sweden, Norway, and Finland. With sales of more than 2 billion SEK and a market share of nearly 5%, the company was one of the largest specialized retail-trade chains in the Nordic countries. But losses grew worse, amounting to almost SEK 150m. in 1995. The new management reorganized the company; at headquarters the staff was cut by 25% and it was renamed "the service office". But more was needed.

In connection with the restructuring, a process to develop scorecards for KappAhl was initiated in the winter of 1995/96; two consultants retained to interview various people at the company conducted a small survey, primarily to find out what was on the minds of employees. Their work led to the first of several seminars; at this one KappAhl's vision would be established. A total of 25 people took part, including a new and enlarged top-management team. Company strengths and weaknesses, and opportunities and threats in the business environment, were considered, and group exercises were held on the subject of the company's future. While the discussion remained on a very general level, a consensus began to emerge that KappAhl had gone too far in imitating the efforts of competitors to focus on a youthful target group. KappAhl's strength and "soul" were to be found in another profile – that of a service company for the general public, but with an up-to-date image.

After summer 1996, the vision, mission statement, and main strategies were revised and confirmed. Management appointed a project group consisting of KappAhl's director of business development, the managing director of the Finnish subsidiary, the KappAhl controller, a controller from one of the buying departments, and a project manager. The latter individual had many years of experience in various positions at the company; in her new capacity she would report directly to the managing director. The project group had as its task to continue the balanced-scorecard process in order to:

- Provide guidance for a relatively decentralized organization towards the comprehensive vision
- Supply tools that would indicate direction and speed
- Signal that the methods to be used for reaching the goals should be determined locally
- Indicate a broader focus than just monetary values
- Provide earlier warnings than conventional accounts.

STEP 3: ESTABLISH THE PERSPECTIVES

After the comprehensive vision and the concept of business have been established, it is time to consider the choice of perspectives on which to build the scorecard. As previously noted, there were four perspectives in the original model of Kaplan & Norton: the financial, customer, internal/business-process, and learning and growth perspectives. However, some companies have preferred to add another perspective, e.g. an employee or human perspective – see Chapter 5 for further discussion. The choice of perspectives should be governed primarily by business logic, with a clear inter-relationship among the different perspectives. The development perspective should thus show the ways in which management intends to develop the organization and the products and services offered for the purpose of streamlining processes and/or adding value for customers. These effects should then be observable from the financial perspective. In our opinion, therefore, any change of perspective should be based on strategic reasons rather than some sort of stakeholder model. It follows that there is seldom need for a separate employee perspective, since the employees are already considered as resources, particularly in the process and development perspectives.

STEP 4: BREAK THE VISION DOWN ACCORDING TO EACH PERSPECTIVE AND FORMULATE OVERALL STRATEGIC AIMS

As we have previously emphasized, the balanced-scorecard model is primarily a tool for formulating and implementing company strategy. The model should be viewed as an instrument for trans-lating an abstract vision and strategy into specific measures and goals. In other words, a well-formulated balanced scorecard is a presentation of a company's strategy. Thus, the purpose of this step is to translate the vision into tangible terms from the estab-lished perspectives and thereby to achieve the overall balance which is the unique feature of the model and the method. This process is one very important part of the actual work of business development. Another is to formulate the overall strategy in more general terms.

The actual concept of strategy is difficult to define specifically. The word has a military origin: each battle must serve the strategic purpose of ultimately winning the war. Strategy may be defined as the relationship between the company's vision and the operational plans to be followed on a day-to-day basis. In other words, a strategy describes the ground rules, events, and decisions required for the company to proceed from the present situation to the one desired in the future, the vision.

The actual process of formulating strategy is usually quite complex and calls for a substantial input of resources. One reason is that usually there are numerous aspects and variables to con-sider. As in many other areas, there is no agreement on the proper procedure for strategy formulation at a company. Nevertheless, there is always the fundamental question of how the company can acquire and sustain a lasting competitive advantage over its rivals. This question lies at the heart of the process of developing and formulating strategy. In our experience, the foremost advantages of the balanced-scorecard model lie precisely in this area. The model makes it easier to decompose the vision into specific, reality-based strategies which people in the organization feel that they can understand and work with.

One way to get this phase of the process under way is to ask participants to describe the general ground rules which would most easily and effectively guide the company to the desired vision. The description should be based on the various per-spectives and to some extent on each of them. An appropriate starting point would be the previous description of how the company is going to look in the future. From there, appropriate ground rules and strategies can be identified in a number of respects: short- and long-term profitability; ways in which the company is to compete, such as pricing and delivery time; company organization and thus the type of competence to be cultivated and available in-house. Other strategies to be set relate to the areas in which the company will develop its products and services, and to who will be responsible for development. On completion of this phase, the group will have a statement for each perspective indicating the principal strategies, in order of priority, for attaining the desired vision.

As an automatic consequence, the strategies will be based on the vision. The organization will be very appreciative, since the vision will be further specified and thus easier to understand in terms of what it will mean in actual practice and how it will affect day-to-day operations. The development of strategies for each perspective is discussed below.

The Financial Perspective

This perspective should show the results of the strategic choices made in the other perspectives, while at the same time establishing several of the long-term goals and thus a large part of the general ground rules and premises for the other perspectives. Here we find a description of what the owners expect of the company in terms of growth and profitability. It is also appropriate to describe which financial risks, such as a negative cash flow, are acceptable. Other issues which may be covered relate to cost and investment strategies, to the maximum permissible amount of accounts receivable, etc. In other words, here one finds many of the traditional instruments of management control in the form of financial measures and key ratios. Kaplan & Norton refer to three strategic themes which primarily relate to the rate of growth and the product mix; cost reduction and improved productivity; and the basic rules for capacity utilization and investment strategy. We have sometimes found it useful to denote this perspective "the shareholder and financial perspective". This serves two purposes. Owners may have such rather more specific expectations, in addition to the more abstract ones of maximum returns. And in certain cases, the owners may have specific demands related to environmental or social effects. When we are considering a company within a corporate group, the parent company may also include in its shareholder and financial perspective other strategic goals, such as expansion of particular markets, etc.

The Customer Perspective

This perspective describes the ways in which value is to be created for customers, how customer demand for this value is to be satisfied, and why the customer will be willing to pay for it. Therefore, the internal processes and the development efforts of the company should be guided by this perspective. One could say that this part of the process is the heart of the scorecard. If the company fails to deliver the right products and services for cost-effectively satisfying customer needs in both the short and long run, revenue will not be generated, and the business will wither and die.

Much of the effort is directed at determining how to increase and ensure customer loyalty. To understand what must be done, we must become thoroughly acquainted with every aspect of the customers' purchasing process. We have to develop an exact picture of what the product/service means to them. If they are an industrial customer, for example, we should ask whether our product is an essential element of their process of creating added value for their own customers, or does not matter very much. How important is price to the customer compared to other values such as quality, functionality, delivery time, image, relationships, etc. Not until we have familiarized ourselves with these details can we decide on our basic strategies in relation to customers and markets and then go on to the other perspectives. It is also important that these analyses rely as much as possible on what the customer in fact appreciates and not, as is so often the case, on the conventional wisdom at our own company.

The strategies chosen should be based on the analyses above and in more or less conventional terms describe the customer segments to be given priority, identify the ways to compete, and specify the policies and rules applicable in these areas. The measures which are a natural consequence of these strategic choices

should provide a comprehensive view from the customer perspective. Preferably, current information should thus be available
on:

- Market shares
- Customer loyalty, measured for instance by frequency of new
  purchases
- Inflow of new customers
- Customer satisfaction with the product/service
- Profitability by customer.

It is also important to learn at an early stage about any changes in
customer preferences and behaviour. One method, among others,
would be by timely interviews to investigate possible changes in
underlying customer values suggested by a customer-satisfaction
index. Further, the company should watch for any changes in
quality, delivery time, delivery capability, frequency of returns, etc.
Preferably it should react before suffering a significant loss of
customer loyalty and thus any major financial damage; in other
words, it should be alert to minor changes and tendencies and
capable of responding promptly. Moreover, the company should
not become overly attached to its existing customers and products.
It may have the potential, including employee competence, to
attract new customers and offer new products. However, these
possibilities should have been explored in Step 2, above.

The Internal/Business-process Perspective

What processes generate the right forms of value for customers
and lead to the fulfilment of shareholder expectations as well? The
answers should emerge from this perspective. We should first
identify the company's processes at the overall level. Porter's so-
called "value-chain" model is useful for this purpose (1985, p. 36)
(Figure 3.9). The model involves describing all company processes
from the analysis of customer needs through delivery of the
product/service. These processes are then analysed in further
detail. The purpose of this exercise is to weed out all processes
which do not directly or indirectly create value for the customer.

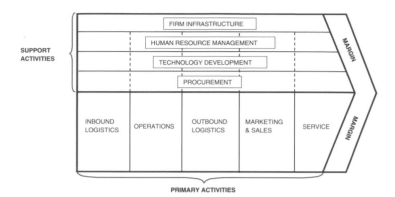

Figure 3.9 The generic value chain. Reprinted with the permission of The Free Press, a Division of Simon & Schuster, from *Competitive Advantage: Creating and Sustaining Superior Performance*, by Michael E. Porter. Copyright © 1985 by Michael E. Porter

The remaining processes should be described in terms of costs, process time, quality assurance, etc. The results will then provide a basis for choosing ways to measure these processes.

Some of the most important processes to describe and analyse are those which tend to enlarge the customer base and those which directly affect customer loyalty. Examples of the latter would be production and delivery processes and service-related processes. Also important are the process of product development and its relationship to customer needs.

The business-process perspective is primarily an analysis of the company's internal processes. The analysis often includes identification of the resources and capabilities which the company needs to upgrade itself (see the previous discussion of the resource-based view on strategy). However, increasingly often the links between the company's internal processes and those of other, collaborating companies are so close as to require consideration here as well. Here we have a choice of what to include in the customer and business-process perspectives:

- Either we may still consider the customer perspective to be completely focused on recipients of the company's goods and services, in which case we must broaden the business-process perspective to include partners with whom we collaborate: suppliers with whom we have long-term relationships and perhaps even share computerized systems, outsourcing partners, as well as others

• Or we may give the customer perspective an "external focus", and in it describe our strategies for all these external relationships, while the business-process perspective retains a purely "internal focus".

In recent years the literature on strategy has identified a trend towards this kind of closer relationship among companies. Normann & Ramirez (1993) refer to "value constellations" and maintain that Porter's process-oriented viewpoint fails to capture how need satisfaction and business success require a number of different circumstances to coincide. A current example may be how educational levels, telecommunications, tax rules, and standards for technical systems must all tie in if selling programmes over the Internet is to be successful. Such a situation is hard to understand in terms of flows. To some extent it may result from planned or long-term collaboration among the actors concerned. But equally often the market is the deciding factor.

The more limited form of collaboration among different participating companies which is necessary for a particular product or service to be made available has been termed the "virtual organization". Suppliers of different constituent elements co-operate in partnership, with or without a binding agreement, so as to give the customer the impression of dealing with a company which does not actually exist in the traditional sense. Hedberg et al. (1997) emphasize that such arrangements put new demands on management; the authors refer to an imaginary organization, based on an "imagination" held by the company taking the initiative.

There are obvious implications for the creation of the top-level scorecard. If we choose to rely on partners, or are similarly dependent on other actors in our business environment, we will clearly need a strategy for more than just our own processes. In collaborating to create value for customers, we must cultivate relationships in several directions. This necessity should be reflected in the scorecard, which should thus include measures and goals for how we manage these relationships. In cases of close collaboration, the scorecard measures may apply to conditions outside our company in the strict sense, but within our imaginary organization. There are also implications for the learning and growth perspective – see below.

The Learning and Growth Perspective

The learning and growth perspective enables the organization to ensure its capacity for long-term renewal, a prerequisite for survival in the long run. In this perspective the company should consider not only what it must do to maintain and develop the know-how required for understanding and satisfying customer needs, but also how it can sustain the necessary efficiency and productivity of the processes which presently create value for the customer. Since know-how to an ever growing degree is a perishable commodity, it will become increasingly important to decide which core competencies (Hamel & Prahalad, 1994) the company should cultivate as a basis for its future development. As a consequence of this strategic choice, the company will also have to determine how to obtain the know-how which it will still need in areas where it has decided not to have its core competence.

A kind of "competence balance sheet" (Figure 3.10) may be used as an aid in making this kind of strategic choice. The reasoning behind the model is as follows: the traditional way of evaluating a company is to analyse its balance sheet. This analysis focuses primarily on the size of shareholder equity, which after miscellaneous adjustments is accepted in principle as the value of the company. Also shown is the ratio of shareholder equity to total assets, a measure of the financial leverage of the company. If the company is too highly leveraged, it is not considered to have a sufficient buffer against the risk of market fluctuations. But leverage should not be too low, either. If the company is overly self-financing, it will have to earn above-normal profits; this requirement may prevent it from expanding as rapidly as its market. Therefore, we seldom find a company that is totally self-financing.

"Assets"	"Liabilities"
Sales	Temporarily employed competence
Service	
Production	Network competence
Product development	
	Partners
Administration	Own competence

Figure 3.10 The competence balance sheet

Drawing an analogy to competence and competence development, we can prepare a competence balance sheet (Figure 3.10). On the asset side we find the capabilities and competencies required for success. The liability side shows how capabilities and competencies are financed – in other words, who provides them. By tradition organizations have "100% self-financed" their own know-how. Since know-how should be increasingly considered a perishable commodity, it is questionable whether such a strategy is appropriate. As with self-financing in the conventional sense, there is reason to fear that a similar policy with regard to competence would hamper the company's growth. In our model, the company performs an analysis on the "asset side" to determine what kinds of knowledge and what capabilities to include in its core competence and then makes a strategic decision on which of these should be "financed" by assistance from external partners, by temporarily retaining outside competence, etc.

In arriving at an appropriate competence strategy, which specifies those areas in which the company will invest to develop its own competence from within and those in which it will resort to collaboration and contacts with outside parties, the following questions may prove helpful:

Figure 3.11 Hamel & Prahalad's competence matrix ("Establishing the Core Competence Agenda"). Adapted and reprinted by permission of Harvard Business School Press. From *Competing for the Future* by Gary Hamel & C.K. Prahalad. Boston, MA 1994, p. 227. Copyright © 1994 by the President and Fellows of Harvard College; all rights reserved

- What does the competence consist of?
- For what should it be used?
- How does it affect value for the customer?
- How specialized is it?
- How does it change over time?
- How frequently is it used?
- How is it affected by IT?

Another model which has proved useful in developing competence strategies is the competence matrix of Hamel & Prahalad (1994) (Figure 3.11).

In addition to developing competence strategies as discussed above, we should also describe the internal infrastructure for transmission of information and the process of decision-making in general terms: in other words, the structure and the conditions which exist for developing the learning organization which is necessary for the unrelenting defence of market position; a structure conducive to developing and sustaining a high degree of motivation and a proper focus on the common mission.

STEP 5: IDENTIFY CRITICAL FACTORS FOR SUCCESS

This next step means moving on from the descriptions and strategies outlined above to discussing and judging what is required for the vision to succeed and which factors will have the greatest effect on the outcome. In other words, the company must now decide what are the most critical factors for success and rank them in order of priority. An appropriate way to begin this part of the process would be to form discussion groups to determine, for example, what five factors matter the most for achieving the strategic goals established previously. In the ensuing joint session which summarizes and continues the discussion, widespread agreement is usually reached on a realistic set of principal factors for success. The list of these factors will then provide a basis for going on to develop key measures.

Align the Success Factors Horizontally and Vertically

Before the work of developing the measures begins, it is important to align the scorecard both vertically and horizontally. In other words, we have to find out whether the scorecard is internally consistent to a reasonable extent in regard to its relevant aspects.

Vertical alignment is more or less automatic as the critical success factors are identified and ranked in order of priority. The easiest way to align the factors horizontally is to prepare a sketch of the scorecard as a flow chart (see Figure 3.12) and examine it to see whether the different perspectives naturally relate to each other. It is equally important to avoid any possibility that a good score on one success factor could be achieved at the expense of another; this warning applies even more emphatically to the measures to be developed subsequently.

KappAhl – steps 3–5

During autumn 1996 the project group worked at the different steps in developing a top-level scorecard. In order to make it possible for the group's members to focus on its task they spent several days in conference away from home. The resulting scorecard was then reviewed and adjusted after being presented to the larger group from the seminar. This phase had a direct impact on the restructuring in progress.

KappAhl's scorecard ultimately included the usual five perspectives, for each of which strategies were formulated. Later on the following strategic goals were identified:

- Finance: high and even earnings
- Customer: increased market share and delighted customers'
- Employees: satisfied employees
- Process: on time; short process times
- Development: innovation force; learning organization.

On closer scrutiny we find that each of the factors involved a number of different issues. KF is a large corporate group normally able and willing to resist financial adversity for some time, but at this point it was being squeezed by profitability problems in several units simultaneously. What would be the implications for the financial perspective, which as we know embodies the expectations of shareholders? How much time did KappAhl have, and what might be its role in the overall corporate scheme of things? Or, turning to the customer focus: would it suffice to satisfy customers in general, or should the company concentrate on particular customer segments? At this point the idea of "going back to our original customers" began to take shape.

For processes the success factors were linked to the relationship between the buyers and the stores. And what form of development was envisioned – in what ways should KappAhl be one step ahead? Hardly in the latest fashions, with the new wave. What were the potential benefits of technical innovation, for example, in terms of better business processes?

By similar reasoning three or four success factors were identified for each focus. For example, the three critical factors for achieving desired levels of profit and cash flow were "fewer seasonal variations", "lower markdowns", and "a more businesslike approach". The success factor for customer satisfaction was determined to be "service perceived as meeting expectations"; in other words, the company should be more attentive to the customer's point of view. The use of the word "service", rather than merely "what the customer buys", should be emphasized.

STEP 6: DEVELOP MEASURES, IDENTIFY CAUSES AND EFFECTS AND ESTABLISH A BALANCE

In this step we develop relevant key measures for subsequent use in our work. As in the other steps, we should start off with some form of "brainstorming", in which no ideas are rejected and all thoughts are made use of in the process. Only in the final phase do we specify and rank in order of priority the measures which seem most relevant, which can be monitored, and which in fact permit measurement. A more detailed illustration of how measures are developed can be found in Chapter 7.

The great challenge is to find clear cause-and-effect relationships and to create a balance among the different measures in the selected perspectives. Therefore, it is important to include a discussion on whether a balance can be reached among the different measures so that short-term improvements do not conflict with long-term goals. The measures in the different perspectives must not lead to suboptimization but must fit and support the comprehensive vision and the overall strategy. Figure 3.12 shows an example of how cause-and-effect relationships among the strategic initiatives and the measures chosen may be analysed and charted.

We have chosen to treat this phase as a single step, even though in practice we have often found it appropriate to divide this step into two parts. First, measures are proposed; then the feasibility of taking measurements is studied, while at the same time the structure is checked for logical consistency (cf. Figure 3.12). Here use is made of what is known in the way of measurable cause-and-effect relationships.

STEP 7: ESTABLISH THE COMPREHENSIVE SCORECARD

When the previous steps have been completed, the top-level scorecard is put together for approval and for presentation to the

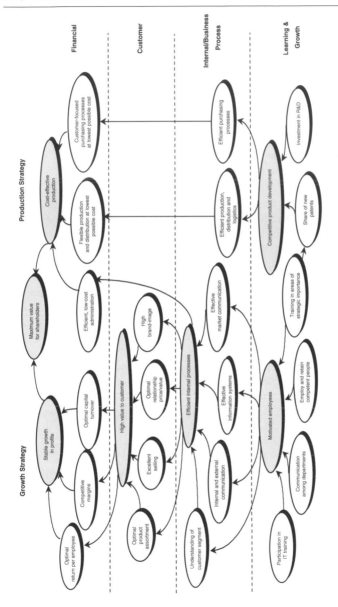

Figure 3.12 Cause-and-effect relationships among strategic initiatives and measures

persons concerned. To facilitate implementation, it is important that everyone in the organization be briefed in some way on the work and the thinking that has gone into developing the scorecard. It is also an advantage if the participants receive supplementary documentation providing explanatory text, possible approaches, and suggestions for group work which can facilitate the continuing process of breaking the scorecard down.

STEP 8: BREAKDOWN OF THE SCORECARD AND MEASURES BY ORGANIZATIONAL UNIT

Depending on the size of the company and the organization, the top-level scorecard and measures are generally decomposed and applied to lower-level organizational units. As an illustration, in Figure 3.13 we show five different levels in a company organization: the company, the business unit, the department/ function, the group, and the individual. Since one of the purposes of the scorecard is to enable employees to see clearly how the company's vision and overall goals affect day-to-day operations, it is necessary to break the scorecard down to a level where it becomes sufficiently tangible and understandable.

If the organization is so flat and small that everyone can see the effect of the top-level scorecard on his own work, no further breakdown is usually necessary. However, in our experience such cases are quite rare; as a rule the scorecard must be decomposed if the company is to benefit from the full potential and power of the balanced-scorecard method. In addition, the process of breaking the scorecard down presupposes that in an earlier phase of the work the company has already determined the most appropriate organizational form for optimal utilization of both internal and external competence, and of past experience as well.

How well the company scores on a particular measure is usually influenced by a number of different activities conducted by various units at various levels of the organization. If as many employees as possible are to see how their work helps the company to attain a good score on its top-level measures, these must be broken down to the most detailed level possible. Therefore, the usefulness of each measure as an aggregate becomes important: how can the

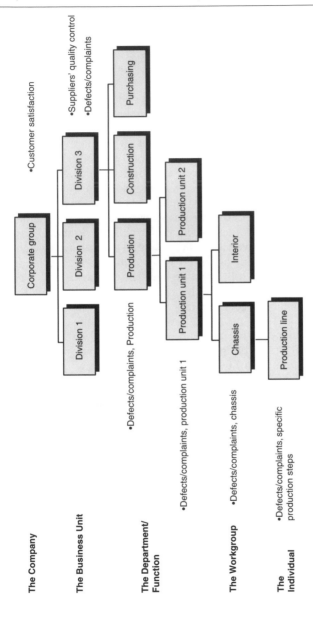

Figure 3.13 Example of a breakdown of a top-level measure, customer satisfaction

various measures be broken down for each department, division, and individual?

We are often asked what level to start from in breaking the scorecard down. Is it possible to start at an intermediate level and develop a vision and a scorecard for, say, a functional unit, or does the scorecard always have to be based on the company's overall strategies and goals? As in so many other instances, the answer varies from case to case. Where the company consists of a number of different business units which are independent of each other from the standpoint of their markets, there is generally little relation between the top-level scorecard and the scorecards for these units at the level below. In such cases it is usually appropriate for each unit/company to develop its own top-level scorecard. In other cases, where the various parts of the company are clearly interrelated, it is usually preferable to have a shared comprehensive vision and common overall strategic goals. Then the groups can be asked to describe on their scorecards how they can and will help the company to score well on the top-level factors for success. If necessary, the groups should also add any unique success factors of their own to the top-level scorecard.

We recommend that guidelines be developed to facilitate the subsequent phases of the work. These guidelines should cover every question from how to interpret the top-level scorecard to what is expected of each individual. To avoid unnecessary misunderstanding, it will also help if there is some kind of simple list of words and concepts.

KappAhl – steps 6–8

The thinking of the project group led to the presentation of a top-level scorecard for KappAhl before the group of 25; the scorecard had been developed to include success factors, measures, and goals. However, action plans were deliberately avoided at this point; these would be prepared by the responsible units once the top-level scorecard had been approved by management. Some elements of the scorecard are shown in Figure 3.14.

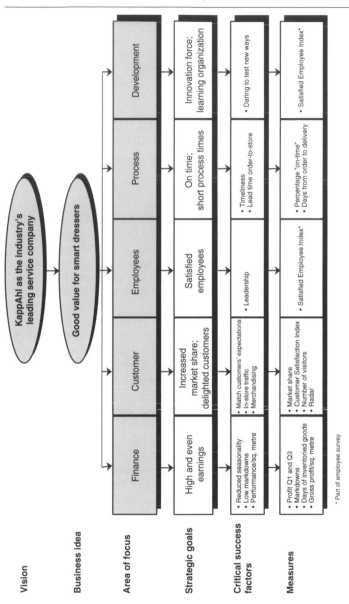

Figure 3.14 An overview of KappAhl's overall balanced scorecard

The measures actually adopted did not really reflect all the fine points of strategies and the success factors, but they had the advantage of being tangible and clear. For example, the measures used in the finance focus were "profit", "markdown percentage", and "gross profit per square metre". For each measure, a method of measurement was specified, so as to assure that the data required would in fact be available. An interesting aspect of KappAhl's company-level scorecard is that it includes certain measures of the performance of units fairly far down in the organization, when these measures are considered to be the principal performance drivers for factors which are critical for the entire company. Thus, the scorecard for the company as a whole does not include a company-wide measure of timeliness, but a measure of how well the unit whose performance is most critical to timeliness is fulfilling its commitments.

This documentation was turned over to 15 different project groups corresponding to units in the formal organization. At this time a new flow-oriented organization had been formulated, with highly decentralized authority. The groups were asked to prepare scorecards for their respective units at KappAhl; each unit was to determine how it could contribute to achieving the vision in the top-level scorecard. However, at this point the process was still limited to the service office (formerly referred to as headquarters) in Gothenburg, where all parts of the company were represented. Each unit adapted its own scorecard to the requirements of its particular business. This stage of the process involved all service-office personnel, who participated in half- or full-day group meetings on two to five occasions. During this phase, which took place during the autumn of 1996, the project group acted as a sounding board for ideas.

As an example, those responsible for the product assortment identified garment fit as a critical success factor in the customer focus. Fit is defined as the degree to which the garment received matches the garment ordered. For the process focus, the same group identified development of new IT support as a critical success factor, with reduction in order-processing time as the measure of success.

In developing measures, KappAhl did not seek identical ones for all levels of the organization. Rather, what was considered important was the logical consistency among measures at different levels. In this critical situation for the company, the process gave employees a powerful impetus to spell out their ideas on how their own departments could further the overall effort. There has never been any lack of suggestions for improvement, or of discontent on the ground that so much could be done in some better way. But it has seldom been possible to see whether a suggestion would actually be good for the business as a whole. Now everyone realizes the complexity of the situation and the need for patience and persistence in bringing about the necessary changes.

The process also led to the realization that everyone did not need to understand every overall strategic aim and success factor but should concentrate on the few which he/she could affect directly. At the same time, however, it is important to see the whole picture, and the scorecard is a valuable method for this purpose.

KappAhl proceeded with the subsequent steps in the various units of the company – that is, of the service office – before extending the process a half year later to the numerous stores of the organization. Since conditions in the different stores are of course fairly similar, the company decided to let one store in each of the three countries first prepare a test scorecard which would be submitted to the project group for evaluation. For this reason most stores were not involved in the process until the autumn of 1997, more than two years after it had begun.

STEP 9: FORMULATE GOALS

Goals must be set for every measure used. A company needs both short-term and long-term goals so that it can check its course continually and take the necessary corrective action in time (see Figure 3.15). As we have previously indicated, it is essential that these goals be consistent with the comprehensive vision and overall strategy, and that they not conflict with each other. For this reason the goals should be aligned both horizontally and vertically. It is also important to create a process of specifying responsibilities for setting goals and for measuring performance. The process should

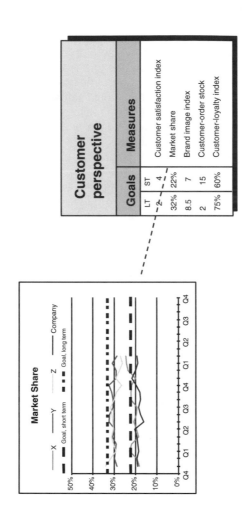

Figure 3.15 Examples of goals and results for the market-share measure

generate answers to the following questions: In what way? For which units? How frequently? And – not least – by whom? See also Chapter 8, which is about measures and measurement.

STEP 10: DEVELOP AN ACTION PLAN

Finally, to complete the scorecard, we must also specify the steps to be taken to achieve the goals and the vision which have been established. This action plan should include both the people responsible and a schedule for interim and final reporting. Since these plans tend to be massive and very ambitious, it is often a good idea for the group to agree on a list of priorities and on a schedule, so as to avoid a lot of unspoken expectations which can later become sources of destructive frustration and irritation. In combination with the measures that have been developed, this list is one of top management's principal documents for control.

KappAhl – steps 9–10

The project group maintained continuous contact with the 15 different units as they were developing their scorecards, both to pass experience along and to see that the process maintained momentum and remained consistent with the purposes indicated in KappAhl's top-level scorecard. The decision was made to give the groups written feedback. It was important to make sure that the measures were well defined and that goals were set at reasonable levels. For example, it is easy to say that lead times from concept to customer should be reduced – but can we agree on when the concept arose, and can we register that determination as a basis for measurement? In this case a simpler measure was chosen: time elapsed from placing the order to availability of the item in the store.

It is also important to observe whether there is potential for conflict between goals. For example, maximizing the percentage of closed sales was found inconsistent with doing the same for average amount of sale. If you succeed in persuading hesitant customers to buy, the amount of their purchases will usually be limited, thus lowering the average. Here it is important to be clear about priorities, or to explain that both measures serve a higher purpose.

Interestingly enough, after a while KappAhl decided to add a fifth, employee perspective to the four usual ones. In the form of a combined value chain (cf. Figure 3.9) and causal analysis (cf. Figure 3.12), the company also attempts to show how measures for different parts of the organization are related to the business of the company as a whole (Figure 3.16).

STEP 11: IMPLEMENTING THE SCORECARD

To maintain interest in the scorecard, it is necessary to follow it up on a continuous basis so that it fulfils its intended function as a dynamic tool of management. For this purpose, relevant IT solutions will be necessary to facilitate reporting and data collection (see Chapter 9).

It is also important that the scorecard be used throughout the organization in the everyday aspects of management. If it thus provides the foundation for the daily agenda of each unit, it will have a natural function in current reporting and control through its impact on day-to-day operations. The implementation plan should therefore include rules and suggested ways to ensure that "balanced scorekeeping" becomes part of the daily work of the company. Finally, the measures selected, particularly for short-term control, should be continually open to question, and in appropriate cases they should be replaced by more current ones.

The above is of course so essential that it cannot be regarded as a simple step in the introductory phase. We raise the point here because only when the scorecard has become a dynamic, functioning part of the everyday life of the company can its introduction be considered complete. Even more – much more – is required for the scorecard to work as an instrument of ongoing management control; we will return to this subject in Chapters 8 and 9.

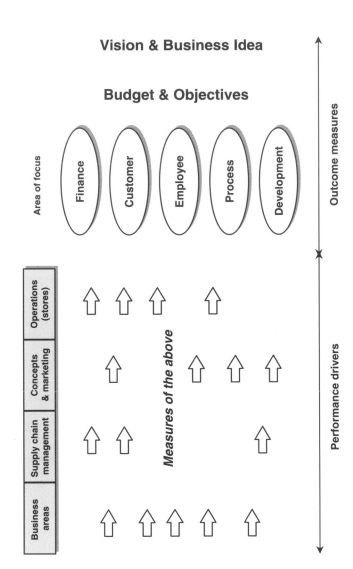

Figure 3.16 How different organizational units enter into the different perspectives at KappAhl

KappAhl – step 11

KappAhl did not begin to introduce more formal reporting procedures until it extended the scorecard process to the stores during the winter of 1997/98. At the service office it had been easy for everyone to adopt the new ideas. True, expectations were not overly high – the concept of a scorecard was unknown, and management tended to be sceptical after having worked with TQM and a number of other recipes for change. However, in the new situation, with new management and the company facing an acute crisis, everyone readily accepted this way of thinking, and even without any formal system of performance monitoring, the scorecards for the different units at KappAhl proved to be a major factor in turning the company around. This undertaking was extremely successful; the company was already showing a profit of over 100 million SEK in 1997.

The managing director deserves much of the credit for the importance given the scorecard process. His own actions and those of the scorecard-project group which represented him made the process highly visible. It was also significant that the project group consisted of people who by virtue of their position and personality demonstrated the priority of the project. It may be noted that accounting staff were present but did not dominate the process; the project manager himself, for example, was not an accountant. While the ultimate goal is of course financial, everyone's thinking focused on how other measures could be used to describe conditions relating to employees and customers.

Moreover, the process fits naturally into the new, more workflow-oriented organization which was introduced at the same time. Business development, planning, and (monthly) follow-up are based on the scorecard of the respective unit. On the other hand, the scorecard has not yet been linked to the system of incentives, although this idea has been discussed.

Two years after initiating the scorecard project, in mid-1998 it is now approaching a stage where it will function as the major control process. Strategic goals have just been revised, and measures have been broken down for the different parts of the flow-based organization. New measurement systems are being introduced, together with new point-of-sales and data warehouse systems. Management has also begun analysing causes and effects in new ways.

SUMMARY

The concept of the balanced scorecard is no guarantee of a successful strategy and vision, but the great strength of the concept lies in the very process of building the scorecard, a process which is an effective way to express the company's strategy and vision in tangible terms and to gather support for it throughout the organization. Viewing the company from different perspectives and in different time dimensions provides a unique understanding of the business as a whole. A common language and basis for discussion are established throughout the organization. In this way the employees can see their part in the total picture, as they must if the company is to achieve its overall goals and comprehensive vision.

4

Cases From Different Industries

In recent years we have encountered a large number of companies which have begun to use the balanced scorecard. Many companies have developed their own design and name for the model, sometimes using only part of it. KappAhl, the company we used to illustrate Chapter 3, may be considered a rather typical case. In its industry, clothes retailing, value resides principally in customer relations and process capability which are not included in conventional, financially based management control. Yet the business is hardly one which we would immediately associate with concepts such as "intellectual capital". So if scorecards are useful to KappAhl, they may be even more so for others. Manufacturing businesses are becoming increasingly dependent on customer relationships, innovative capability, and process know-how, and decreasingly dependent on physical facilities. In the case of service enterprises and government agencies, this trend is even more pronounced.

In this chapter we will present a number of specific examples of organizations that use scorecards or other models resembling scorecards. In our opinion, they all had one feature in common: their operations were difficult to describe in traditional financial terms. Conventional management control threatened values which senior executives realized were important in the long run: making economical use of non-financial resources like market positions, know-how, and IT/information systems (IS); drawing on the experience of many employees; persistently cultivating a distinctive definition of the business adapted to the future scenarios which were deemed conceivable.

ABB 85

We will also use most of these cases to illustrate specific points later in the book. There we will also introduce additional cases.

ABB

ABB is a multinational corporate group in the electrical engineering industry with 1997 revenues of USD 31m. Under the leadership of Percy Barnevik, ABB initiated a "Customer Focus Programme" around 1989/90. It was centred on three principal areas of focus: time-based management (TBM), total quality management (TQM), and supply management. Percy Barnevik's management philosophy has always been based on decentralization: that is, delegating responsibility to lower levels of the organization. This philosophy is clearly reflected in ABB's organizational structure, which includes over 1000 companies.

At ABB Sweden the Customer Focus Programme of the international ABB corporation was introduced under the designation T50; T stood for time and 50 for reducing time by 50%, with the aim of increasing value for ABB's customers. To cut throughput time in half was a specific objective which required improving total quality, as well as collaboration with suppliers. Without high-quality processes and truly well-functioning collaboration with suppliers, this objective would be unattainable.

The T50 project was very well received at ABB Sweden, but in the view of Executive Vice-President Peter Fallenius, it lacked a management-control system that was based on strategic control and that took account of all factors affecting company performance, not just revenues and costs. An urgent need was felt for a management-control system which focused both on the company's processes and on customer requirements. With T50, ABB had identified a large number of measures, but there was a lack of systematization, structure, and focus. For these reasons a project group was appointed in the spring of 1994.

The project group consisted of a project manager and five other members, each of whom represented an ABB company. The objective of the project was to develop principles and an information structure for structured strategic and operational information, to be used for financial and strategic control at all levels. One day a week was set aside for joint conferences to develop a concept for strategic control at ABB which would be based essentially on the ideas underlying T50.

In June 1994, the project group presented its proposal for a concept in which the structure was inspired to a considerable degree by the balanced scorecard of Kaplan & Norton. The project was dubbed EVITA, an acronym derived from the Swedish equivalent of financial and strategic control in the spirit of T50. EVITA was developed by ABB Sweden primarily for use in Sweden.

The principal aims of the EVITA project were the following:

- To make it possible to view the company from a number of different perspectives or areas of focus
- To provide a system of support and control for the activities of a manager's own unit
- To provide a system based on the company's vision and overall strategy
- To create a system of presentation modelled on a cockpit
- To create a presentation-support system based on IT.

According to ABB, EVITA is intended primarily as a means for control of the horizontal processes in groups with defined objectives, but it is also designed to function as an instrument of management.

The principal purpose of EVITA was to create a system of financial and management control which would help the company to accomplish the underlying purpose of T50. Customers and employees are two cornerstones of this philosophy. With these as a basis, ABB has chosen five perspectives: customer, process/supplier, employee, innovation/development, and financial. The possibility of adding a sixth perspective for the environment has been considered, but it is felt that the environment should fit naturally into the other perspectives.

One basic idea underlying EVITA is that each of the various units with defined objectives should conduct its own process to develop the control measures which would appropriately describe its operations in the different perspectives. To facilitate

ABB   87

this process, the project group has modified and further developed a model used by Kaplan & Norton (Figure 4.1). The company's overall vision and strategy provide the foundation for the vision and strategy of the various units. A number of questions are asked concerning the vision, critical success factors, and actions necessary to satisfy the success factors; then the critical measures for exercising control are formulated. ABB recommends that a maximum of five and a minimum of one measure be used for each perspective, with each unit ideally focusing on a total of about 10 measures for all perspectives combined. Further, at ABB it is felt that most measures should be followed up once a month. However, performance on certain customer, profit, and human-resource measures is reviewed only once or twice a year; given their character, it is very difficult to take the relevant measurements more often.

A number of conferences were held to introduce EVITA. The first, in October 1994, was attended by all controllers of ABB's Swedish units. Working in groups, the participants learned about and accepted the ideas underlying the EVITA concept. Two subsidiaries expressed an interest in acting as pilot companies: AB Control and ABB Coiltech. The two companies are similar in some ways, different in others. ABB Control, with approximately 500 employees and sales of about SEK 500m., manufactures electric components. ABB Coiltech is half the size of ABB Control. The production processes at the two companies also differ; most of ABB Coiltech's production involves welding and metal-working.

Hopefully the result will be that most ABB companies will prefer to operate by the EVITA concept in the future. A concept related to EVITA has been recently introduced by ABB's corporate management in Sweden: the idea of "world-class". At the outset of 1997, units began reporting world-class targets in the EVITA perspectives to Swedish corporate management. Each unit determines for itself, preferably by using the EVITA model, which is the critical measurement for that specific unit, as well as the world-class target for that measurement. Reports are to be submitted quarterly. All measures should be reviewed annually to determine whether they are still relevant in terms of the company's vision and strategy. ABB believes that EVITA will

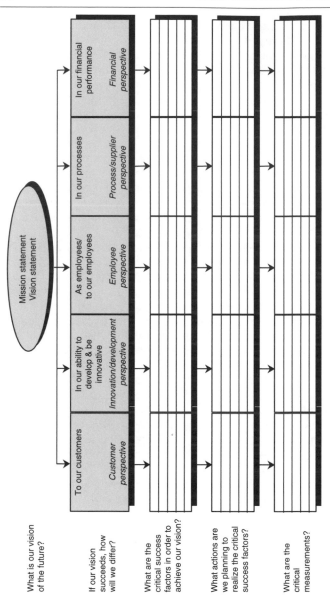

Figure 4.1 Developing a new measurement structure at ABB

serve as a means of clearly showing the role of the units and where they are headed.

Most of the ABB companies in Sweden have accepted the EVITA concept but have in many cases implemented their own version and given their model its own name.

EVITA both calls for and leads to a more open management style and to decentralization of decision-making. It has also been ABB's experience that particularly younger people and non-accountants have found it easier to accept the new way of thinking with EVITA.

ABB emphasizes that the most important aspect of EVITA is the ideas on which the concept is based. The build-up process, in which the vision is broken down by perspective and goals are formulated for each perspective, is particularly critical. Each unit must determine for itself how to proceed from words to action; a detailed action plan is vital to success. It is important that the EVITA concept be used at all levels in a company, but particularly at the operational, target-oriented team level. This means that EVITA is an excellent tool for connecting corporate vision and strategic targets with action for change at the operational level.

HALIFAX

Halifax is a UK-based company with its core business in five sectors: retail operations, customer credit, personal lines insurance, long-term savings and protection, and treasury. Retail operations include the mortgage, liquid savings and retail banking business. In August 1995, Halifax merged with the Leeds Permanent Building Society, with the specific intention of acquiring PLC status, which it did in June 1997. That same year Halifax had a total income of £2957m. and approximately 27,300 employees. With its network of 1000 branches, Halifax is able to serve 18 million customers.

In 1993 one manager at Halifax returned from Harvard as an enthusiastic proponent of the balanced scorecard. His enthusiasm was matched by other members of the Halifax hierarchy, including the CEO. The performance-measurement systems at that time focused mainly on sales targets and financial objectives, with a bias towards process and procedures. The systems ranked the different branches in performance tables, instead of being used constructively to manage and improve performance. And they reinforced the existing culture.

Early in 1994, Halifax decided to develop a new "performance-management system" based on the balanced-scorecard approach. The main goals of the new performance management system were to:

- Keep existing customers and do more business with them
- Win new customers
- Promote a positive culture
- Improve management and branch performance
- Emphasize customer and service objectives
- Encourage employee development
- Reduce paperwork

The first unit to develop a balanced scorecard was Field Operations which represented the mainstream branch activity. This unit was chosen not only because retail distribution was a core business, but also because it had considerable influence on the other units. The first step taken by the sponsor of the project – the head of Field Operations – was to appoint a project manager.

For two years the project manager worked full-time with the project, from the initial idea all the way through the implementation phase. During the process the project manager was assisted by a project group. The core group consisted of 13 people from different parts of Field Operations. The majority of the participants in the core group were from the operational part of the organization. At that time the project group had a number of working parties which made their contributions in different phases of the project, i.e. when a special competence was needed in a particular area.

Unlike many other companies, Halifax did not want to use the balanced scorecard as a strategic tool but as an operational management system. The primary goal was to develop an operational tool for the regional, area, and branch managers – a support system that could help them to manage their day-to-day activities. In other words, Halifax tried to apply a bottom-up rather than a top-down approach. The organization was not ready for a comprehensive process of strategic review; the existing vision and mission statement had only just been modified by the Board of Directors. Since the employees at the operating level also had a great need for a better operational system, the impact of the balanced scorecard would be greater than with a top-down approach. Today, in 1998, four years after Halifax started their balanced-scorecard process at the operational level, the organization is starting to adapt its business-planning process to the balanced-scorecard concept in order to adapt this operational tool for strategic purposes as well.

At the initiative of the new CEO, the Board of Directors – as indicated above – modified the vision and mission statement. As the foundation of the balanced scorecard, these were communicated to the project group. Once the vision and mission had been stated, the project group started to formulate critical success factors and measures for four perspectives: financial and business, customer, internal process, and staff development and improvement (see Figure 4.2). In contrast to Kaplan & Norton, Halifax did not find the learning and development perspective relevant to the scorecard as an operational management tool rather than for strategic planning. The project group found it more appropriate to have a staff development and improvement perspective instead. One key performance indicator for Field Operations was not only to deliver to customers but also to be able to deliver through the staff.

The development phase of the overall scorecard took approximately six to nine months. According to Halifax, this phase was the most important part of the whole process, since the results would greatly affect the subsequent work of implementation. Therefore, the project group continuously reported their thoughts and findings back to the head of Field Operations – the sponsor of the project – and to the board of directors.

When the development phase was complete, Halifax had an overall scorecard with critical success factors and a set of measures for all four perspectives (see Figure 4.2). Initially, approximately 75% of the measures were found from existing

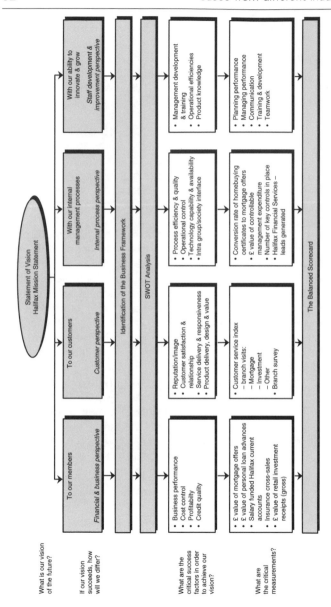

Figure 4.2 Stages in the development of the overall balanced scorecard at Halifax

management information sources. Today, in 1998, all of the originally defined measures are still used. During the phase of developing measures, a number of requirements generally applied: relevance of measures to roles and responsibilities, consistent use of a "cascade" approach, development of targets, secondary measures or management information to provide supporting analysis, and applicability of historical/trend information. At Halifax the following criteria were found for successful measures:

- Availability and accuracy of data
- Relevance to the critical success factors
- Priority/importance of the measure
- Positive impact on behaviour
- Ability of users to influence/control what was measured

Today Halifax has 2–5 measures in each perspective, with a total of 16 measures for the whole scorecard. Of these the Board of Directors follow 10–12. Many of the measures are supposed to be checked every day (e.g. product sales), although some of them are not updated very frequently; certain measures, i.e. those relating to customers, are only updated twice a year.

Some of the measures are revised in the annual "Business-Planning Process"; these measures are mainly non-financial. The other measures – mainly financial – are revised in the budgeting process. The objectives for each measure are set once a year but are reviewed quarterly. Every measure has an "owner", who is responsible for planning, managing, recording, and improving the measure. At Halifax the balanced scorecard has not replaced the budgeting process, which plays a fundamental part in managing the business. With the balanced scorecard, Halifax obtained a system that put the previous performance-measurement system in a broader context of performance management.

SKANDIA

Skandia, a Swedish insurance company, has become well known for what it has done with the balanced scorecard, and its work with the concept of intellectual capital has received considerable publicity even outside Sweden (described e.g. by Kaplan & Norton, 1996a and Edvinsson & Malone, 1997). Two reasons explain this fact: first, the company started fairly early and could integrate its work with the scorecard into a more extensive process relating to "Skandia's intellectual capital"; second, management deliberately chose to give this effort a high profile through publications and conferences. The scorecard is called Navigator to highlight the focus on the control process rather than on the scorecard, as management considers the word scorecard to be too backward-looking (cf. our discussion in Chapter 2).

Skandia has approximately 9000 employees. Its interest in its intellectual capital, however, is linked to its character of a virtual or "imaginary" organization, heavily dependent in its international expansion during recent years on an active network of partners, enabled through information technology (see Hedberg et al., 1997, pp. 2ff).

After several years of experimental work, the company published a supplement to its annual report for 1994, "Visualizing Intellectual Capital in Skandia". Supplements to subsequent annual and semiannual reports have followed every six months; there have also been two CD-ROMs. In these publications, which are also available in English, statistics for various Skandia units are presented in the form of scorecards. These are referred to collectively as the Skandia Navigator; a fifth focus, for human resources, has been added to the original four of Kaplan & Norton (Figure 4.3).

When Skandia decided on a separate human-resources focus, their reason was a desire to stress the interaction between this perspective and the others. For example, the relationship between the human-resources focus and the process focus is described as multiplicative. Results are produced by personnel with the competence as well as customer focus required to exploit the potential of the process.

Skandia thus views the balanced-scorecard concept both as an instrument of internal management control and as a complement to its financial reporting to external stakeholders. A company's balance sheet cannot fully "explain" its value, particularly if the latter consists largely of intangible assets.

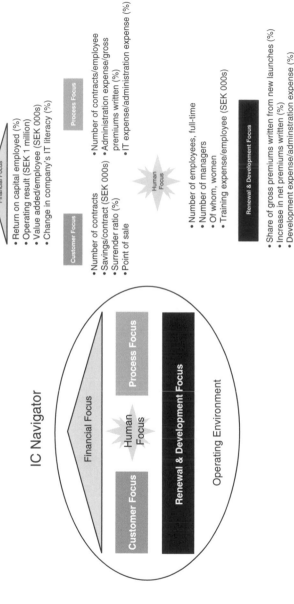

Figure 4.3 American Skandia as an illustration of Skandia's Navigator. Source: ''Customer Value'', supplement to Skandia's 1996 annual report. Reprinted by permission

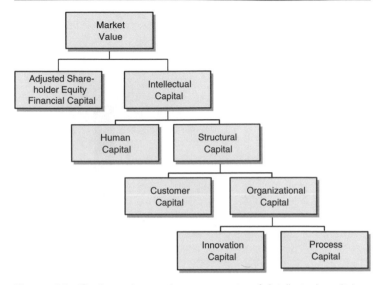

Figure 4.4 IC-value scheme, the components of Intellectual capital as an element of the company's market value, according to Skandia. Source: "Value Creating Processes", supplement to the 1995 annual report. Reprinted by permission

Market value is considered to consist of five different kinds of capital; these correspond to the five perspectives in Skandia's scorecard, the Navigator (Figure 4.4). Here the purpose appears to be to facilitate understanding of the basis for determining the value of Skandia's stock in monetary terms, or calculating its "goodwill" value. Reference is made to the fact that the acquisition value of service companies may greatly exceed the net worth shown in the balance sheet, even after adjusting asset values. The various supplements published by Skandia over the years contain separate sets of measures for the different business units within Skandia, using the five areas of focus; for the most part, different measures are used for each business, although some of them recur. The valuation itself is then left to the reader.

From what we can see, the primary use of the Skandia Navigator is for internal management control, which Skandia likes to call "navigation". Starting in the autumn of 1995, when several units had begun to test this new tool, it has been used in the company's internal business planning. With the Navigator, each unit indicates planned estimates for the principal measures used for control. In this way it is hoped that the traditional focus on monetary values in budgeting can be downplayed. On the basis of its critical success factors, each unit determines its own relevant measures. The process is expected to continue; at this point not all units have begun to use the Navigator. From autumn 1998 it is the company's aspiration to have the Navigator as a global holistic budgeting approach.

Skandia refers to six steps leading to intellectual capital management (Edvinsson and Malone, 1997, p. 54); the progress made by different parts of the company has varied. The six steps are the following:

1. Missionary.
2. Measurement.
3. Leadership.
4. IT.
5. Capitalizing.
6. Futurizing.

Although some initial attempts have been made with the last steps, not all units are yet involved. The reason is that management prefers a voluntary approach. Role models and coaches have presented different variants of the Navigator, and budgets and reports have begun to be remodelled in this form. At American Skandia, management has also introduced a bonus system, in which each of the five areas of focus counts for 20%.

As part of a larger project involving a number of Skandia Future Centres, the company has begun to report Navigator values for selected Skandia units in supplements to the annual report; these also provide easily understood explanations of the model for intellectual capital.

Lars-Eric Petersson, managing director and CEO at Skandia, emphasizes that the Navigator is intended primarily for internal use. Thus, he views the external effects more as a bonus than as a deliberate tactic to make the company's stock go up. While one effect has been to inform the market of Skandia's internal efforts to develop its intellectual capital, the internal effects in themselves have been the main objective and also most satisfying in terms of results. One purpose of the process now under way is to make Skandia "bilingual", in the sense that all managers must be conversant in the operational as well as the strategic language of the company; this aim is given excellent support by the Navigator process. According to Petersson, the intended effect has been clearly achieved, since it is quite apparent that the Skandia units which have introduced the Navigator have also made the greatest progress in developing their strategic language and awareness. This result is manifested in ways which include the growing realization that a higher level of competence is now required and that an enlarged customer base as well as innovation are important factors.

Skandia has continued to develop the Navigator by introducing Navigator terminology in the budgeting for 1997 and 1998. Top-management groups will use the Navigator to monitor progress on a quarterly basis. Up to this time, developing a corporate-wide scorecard has not been given priority. This is a project that will start in during the autumn of 1998. The Navigator is a tool for individuals as well as business units in the Skandia corporate group.

As we have stated, Skandia has made certain attempts to evaluate elements of intellectual capital in monetary terms. Among other things, the company has tried to assess the usefulness of a specific system of task management (Dahlgren et al., 1997). However, the range of possible values turned out to be extremely wide. In spite of experience of this kind, Skandia's ambition is still to find an appropriate way of relating the company's market value to the measures used in the Navigator.

As noted above, the view of different Skandia units provided by the Navigator ties in with the various elements of intellectual capital shown in Figure 4.3. According to the model, the interaction of these elements is supposed to justify the valuation of the company by the market. Skandia's latest publications indicate that different measures can be combined in an overall index (see also Roos et al., 1997). A graph in their latest report shows the trend at American Skandia for the past few years in regard to each of the five areas of focus in Navigator, as well as the overall intellectual capital index. (We will comment later on this index.)

ELECTROLUX

Electrolux is one of the world's leading manufacturers of household appliances. Today it has approximately 106 000 employees in more than 60 countries around the world. Like many other companies, Electrolux operates in an increasingly changing world in which being attuned to customers and their needs is becoming more and more important. For these reasons a wide-ranging project, covering vision, strategy, and quality, was launched at Electrolux in 1993. From the project it became clear that the organization needed more information of a strategic nature rather than data on historical facts. At this time the company had no specific measures of quality and customer satisfaction. Nor were there any measures relating to product development or employee motivation. The only measures of how the company's business was doing were financial.

In 1994 another project was initiated; it would subsequently be named the GIMS Project, with GIMS standing for global integrated measurement system. GIMS was a pilot project conceived as part of a major review of strategy for the white-goods business sector. To search for new ideas, a small group was sent out by corporate management to visit a number of American companies such as Johnson & Johnson, Federal Express, and Xerox. In March, 1995, these observations were included in "The White Book", a document that describes the overall strategy for white goods. At Electrolux the principal benefit of GIMS was that it clearly shows the interrelationship between the company's vision, strategy, and short-term planning.

The GIMS concept, while standing for many things, is based on the following fundamental ideas:

- Moving ahead with the company's strategy
- Supporting the development of business processes

Area	Measure	Follow-up
Customer	• Strategic Accounts Index • Retail Attitude Index • Customer Satisfaction Index • 2 out of 4 Preferred Brands • Green Product % Total Range	• Yearly • Quarterly • Yearly • Yearly • Quarterly
Operational	• Sales • Market Share • Productivity per Head • Order Fill Rate • Service Call Rate	• Monthly • Quarterly • Quarterly • Monthly • Quarterly
Cultural	• Employee Attitude Survey • Self-assessment Profile	• 3 times a year • Yearly
Financial	• Cumulative Operating Profit III (%) • Operating Profit II (%) • Mergers & Acquisitions Expenses (%) • Gross Profit (%)	• Quarterly • Monthly • Monthly • Monthly

Figure 4.5 Electrolux dynamic business measurement (DBM)

- Integrating the organization
- Linking strategy to business plans

Recently GIMS has been modified and renamed DBM (dynamic business measurement) (Figure 4.5). From the beginning GIMS concentrated on the white-goods business sector, but today a number of DBM projects have also been started in other sectors. In contrast to many other companies, the business sectors of Electrolux are heterogeneous; they have quite different distribution channels and final customers. Thus, it is difficult to apply the same measures generally throughout the company.

Electrolux management would like to emphasize that DBM is a dynamic system which must constantly keep pace with changing times. Thus, the corporate strategy and vision are always open to discussion. While the measures used in DBM may be fixed, their focus varies with the competitive situation and changes in the business environment.

At present, DBM concentrates on 16 different key ratios, 12 of which are non-financial. Priorities among these will vary for the six different sectors. No more than a handful of measures can be optimized. Electrolux management explains that DBM should be viewed as a menu of key ratios from which relevant ones may be selected for specific entity and time frames. Because of the complexity of the corporate organization, however, it will not be possible to monitor all these key ratios for all sectors.

Electrolux manufactures and sells approximately 55 million product units per year. Since most of the products are sold through distributors, the final consumers are not registered. Having no direct contact with final consumers, the company must distinguish between their needs and those of its direct retailers; for this purpose it has developed two separate indices, one for consumer satisfaction and one for retail attitude. At this stage management has no intention of developing a corporate-wide measure of customer satisfaction, but hopes instead to determine an aggregate measure for each business sector.

Two years ago Electrolux abandoned its traditional 12-month budgeting process. Today's planning process consists of three steps:

1. Strategic planning – permits greater focus on strategic aims and action plans.
2. Annual planning – follows up on the strategic planning and also uses traditional financial key ratios.
3. Quarterly rolling-budget planning – enables the organization to spot trends early. As reliable and relevant ways are found to take measurements on various non-financial metrics, these are introduced into the quarterly planning process.

The choice of "budget" or "plan" as a term is a matter of semantics, according to Electrolux. However, it is important to distinguish between relevant planning and matters on which there can only be conjecture.

Experience with the GIMS and DBM has shown that it is impossible to give employees too much training. Employees must be informed over and over again. People are accustomed to working with traditional financial key ratios and to using them for control. Therefore, it is very important to inform employees on what the new system means.

Smaller groups of 20 people have been more receptive to the information provided. If the entire organization is to be sold on the concept, it is essential to proceed very systematically downward through the organization. The major challenge is to enable all employees of the organization to see how they and their work as individuals can make a contribution towards achieving overall corporate goals. Employees must realize that DBM is not a "concept of the month", but the product of considerable previous thought.

In the opinion of Electrolux management, it is better to let implementation of the concept take a little time so that people truly understand it, and perhaps even to revise the concept, before informing the entire company about it. Measures are to be viewed as dynamic, since employee and customer attitudes are constantly changing. An organization is a living organism, not a static product.

Electrolux hopes to use television to communicate information to employees in the future. Television will permit the company to provide different parts of the organization with more specific information on their business. It is important to communicate with everyone in the organization; empowerment and delegation are largely about giving each employee a sense of responsibility for manufacturing a product or for performing a service, for example. The bottom line is customer satisfaction. If the customer is not satisfied, there is no tomorrow.

BRITISH AIRWAYS

British Airways is the world's largest international passenger airline with approximately 24 million people carried on international scheduled services in 1994. It was also the seventh largest international cargo airline in the world in 1994.

In February 1997, British Airways celebrated 10 years of privatization. To set the course for the future, British Airways introduced a new mission: "To be the undisputed leader in world travel", a statement that the airline intends to remain clearly ahead, to set the standards for others to follow and to remain alert to challenges for the leadership of the industry.

In order to achieve the mission, the corporate goals and values were also changed. The new goals are to be the "customers' choice," to have "inspired people," "strong profitability" and to be "truly global". The new values are to be "safe and secure", "honest and responsible", "innovative and team spirited", "global and caring" and a "good neighbour".

British Airways is organized basically along three dimensions: strategy, commercial and operations. The idea of this type of organization is that strategy is long-term, commercial is medium-term and the operations is short-term. British Airways do not use scorecards at the corporate level. Elsewhere in the organization, four units on their own initiative are running their business in terms of the balanced-scorecard concept. In recent years the reporting format for monthly reporting was heavily criticized for being too focused on financial figures alone. The Finance Department has also seen that out in the organization the balanced scorecard has been a successful and popular way of running the business.

One example where the balanced-scorecard concept is used is British Airways operations at Heathrow Airport in London, the largest international airport in the world. Here British Airways operates an increasing number of services with a market share of 41% of the total available capacity in 1996, but 46% of the traffic. For 1998 the total cost budget is about £250 million and the staff is approximately 7000 people. The operations at Heathrow are a part of the Customer Service and Operations Department within the operations dimension. This part of British Airways can be characterized as very operational, the rough end of the business. Here people do not want to ponder too much; they just want things fixed, and then go on to the next problem.

During the first part of 1997, operations at Heathrow were going through a difficult time. They were essentially out of control and had a lot of performance problems. In this situation a new director was appointed. His first priority was to build a new performance measurement system. Efforts were concentrated on getting a focus on what really mattered – as soon as possible.

Before assuming the job at Heathrow the new director had been responsible for developing a balanced scorecard for the Cargo Department. Here the concept was well received, since the business had a tendency to focus on only one area at a time (i.e. one year on costs and the next year on customers and personnel, since the cost programme had neglected these areas and so on).

At Heathrow the managers were not that hard to convince about the balanced-scorecard concept. As mentioned, this department was performing very badly at that point of time. It was far from meeting the targets, and management knew that the existence of the unit was on the line. This factor, in combination with the director's positive experience of scorecards, made them accept the proposal of building a balanced scorecard.

The process of building the balanced business scorecard for Heathrow was started in early autumn, 1997. The basis of this scorecard was the corporate goals which by coincidence corresponded to the performance categories chosen at Cargo. Since the Director had done a thorough job, at the Cargo Division, of breaking the mission down to strategic goals in the chosen categories, the process at Heathrow started off with a given mission, given categories, and given strategic goals. There was one exception, though; since it is hard for the operations at Heathrow to be "truly global", this goal was reformulated as getting the "internal processes right".

The overall goal for the project was formulated in the so-called "strategic staircase". The first year the goal was to get the basics right, the next year to get competitive performance, and the third year, to be the market leader.

At Heathrow the organization is divided into Operational Performance, Passenger Services, Aircraft Services, Operational Processes, Programme Office and Business Management

Group. As a first step in the building process, all the line managers were taken away to a workshop (a total of 5 days over a period of 2.5 months) every week until the balanced business scorecard was set. For the whole organization it took approximately four months to build the "business balanced scorecard" for Heathrow.

For the first year the operations at Heathrow will focus only on one objective in each perspective. They want the objectives as simple as possible so that everyone in the organization can understand. In the customer category the objective was; "we want the customers to notice an improvement in punctuality and baggage". In the internal process category, "a performance driven working environment". In the people category, "to recognize that this is a people business". Financial category, "deliver effective and natural management". In the change category, "one team and one game for Heathrow".

For each of these sets of objectives, there is personal accountability at the individual level. The purpose was for people to break down objectives into measures on their scorecards at their department. Every manager was to look for output measures that would indicate progress towards objectives, At the end of this process, every department had its own scorecard.

The scorecard for the group is a mixture of measures that are aggregated from the different departments and measures that are worth highlighting at this particular time. (The measures followed by the group are: punctuality, check-in satisfaction, cost/passenger, cost/bag, total costs, number of failures to deliver a bag, the time for the bag from arriving in the hall until it arrives at the aircraft, number of safety incidents not cleared up, number of accidents, aircraft damage, sickness – a total of 11 measures.) In every scorecard there should only be 10 critical measures. If any measure is above target and is not one of the vital four or five measures, it should be removed from the scorecard.

Once a month the director holds a business review for an hour with every manager. At these reviews the manager goes through the written summary of what happened during the last period, and the progress of each measure is discussed. The scorecards, the summaries, and the comments are then put together in a report called "The Balanced Business Scorecard Report" (Figure 4.6). Once a month the group's scorecard is reported to the director of Customer Service and Operations for BA worldwide (even though the manager does not use the balanced scorecard in every part of the division).

COCA-COLA BEVERAGES SWEDEN

Coca-Cola was formerly represented in Sweden through a licensing agreement with Pripps, the dominant Swedish brewery. Since this agreement was terminated in the spring of 1996, Coca-Cola has been building up new production and distribution capacity in the Swedish market. In the spring of 1997, the new organization assumed responsibility for selling and distribution; since the beginning of 1998, it has also been in charge of production.

In establishing a new business, Coca-Cola seeks to draw on its world-wide experience. As part of the build-up process, Coca-Cola Beverages Sweden (CCBS) is implementing the balanced-scorecard concept in its growing organization. For a number of years, other units of the Coca-Cola Corporation have been doing the same. However, there are no corporate directives requiring all companies to use this model for reporting and control.

CCBS intends to use the balanced scorecard not only to show a comprehensive strategic focus and to control and monitor operations but also to create trust and a sense of responsibility so that the entire company will be working to achieve the same goals. In other words, the aim is to create a model which decentralizes responsibility and clarifies everyone's role at the company. CCBS management would like the company's balanced scorecard to be a specific statement of its strategy. The strategy is "owned" by top management and is communicated to the rest of the organization through a "top-down" process. Thus, the balanced scorecard of CCBS cannot primarily be characterized as a tool in the process of strategy formulation itself.

Figure 4.6   The balanced business scorecard at Heathrow

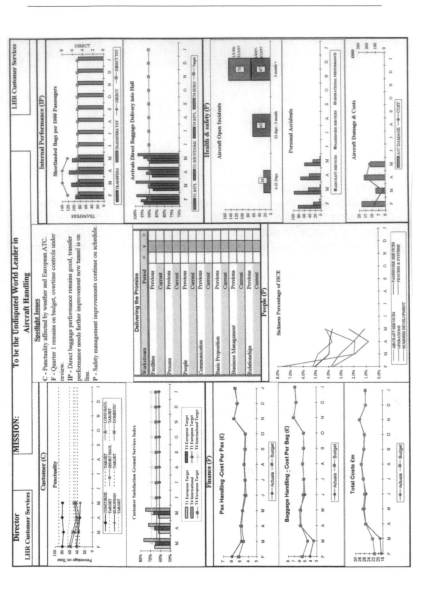

When the balanced-scorecard project at CCBS was started, the company had only 40 employees. At that time only a project manager was appointed; there was no specific project group. In the small organization at the outset of the project, the balanced-scorecard concept was quickly accepted as a tool of management. Since then the organization has grown, and the company's balanced scorecard has come to be viewed as a natural instrument of control. One of the main purposes of the project was thus achieved; the number of employees would grow from 40 to approximately 900 in only one year, and CCBS believes that a strategic framework is necessary for decentralizing responsibility and developing a learning organization.

CCBS had followed the suggestions of Kaplan & Norton in choosing to measure its strategic actions in a financial perspective, a customer and consumer perspective, an internal processes perspective, and an organizational learning perspective.

As a first step in implementing the balanced-scorecard concept, top management at CCBS met for three days. The company's comprehensive business plan was used as the basis for discussion. During this time each executive would perform the following steps:

- Define the vision
- Set long-range goals (approximate time frame: three years)
- Describe the current situation
- Describe the strategic initiatives to be taken
- Define the parameters for the different metrics and measurement procedures

As a consequence of these discussions, there was a need at CCBS for a large number of measures, since the CCBS organization had just been set up. With the organization in a phase of growth, management decided to develop a culture and a system of follow-up in which all the principal parameters would be measured. At different levels the focus would then be on the most crucial measures in relation to the strategic initiatives.

In building the company's balanced scorecard, top management has sought to emphasize the importance of obtaining a balance among the different perspectives. For this purpose

CCBS used a step-by-step process. The first step was to formulate financial measures that would relate to the strategic initiatives. With these measures as a basis, financial goals were then set, and appropriate activities to attain these goals were determined. The procedure was repeated for the customer and consumer perspective; here the initial question was, "How must our customers see us if we are to attain our financial goals?" As a third step, CCBS clarified the internal processes necessary for delivering value to customers and consumers. Then CCBS management asked itself whether they were sufficiently innovative and willing to change for the company to develop in an appropriate way. Through this process CCBS was able to ensure that the perspectives were in balance and that all parameters and activities were leading in the same direction. However, CCBS believes that it may be necessary to repeat the different steps several times before the right balance can be obtained (Figure 4.7).

CCBS has begun to break the balanced-scorecard concept down to the individual level. At CCBS it is considered very important to evaluate individuals solely by measures which they can influence. The aim is for each person to be measured by how well he/she achieves a limited number of weighted targets relevant to his/her particular duties. By basing the bonus system on the employee's rating on the weighted measures, the company can control and focus on the various strategic initiatives.

Strategic aims are set and agreed on both for the corporation as a whole and on the district level. Top management presently intends to follow up the top-level balanced scorecard on a monthly basis. All employees will then be informed of the results through newsletters and regional meetings.

CCBS intends to hold semi-annual career-development interviews with all employees, while monitoring their performance month by month. If a particular target is not being met, the person responsible for it will be required to explain why and to present a remedial action plan.

At CCBS it is emphasized that neither the business plan, nor the budget, nor the balanced scorecard is regarded as fixed for all time; rather, all are considered highly dynamic and are continually reviewed and modified during the year. However, the

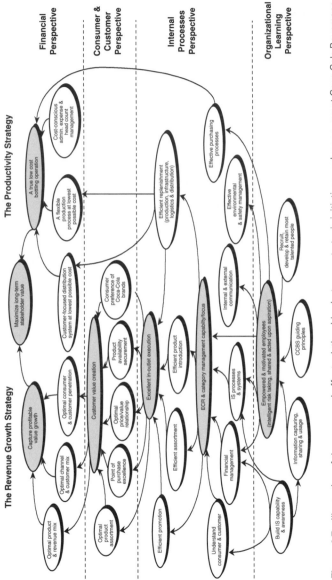

Figure 4.7 Illustration of the cause-and-effect relationships between strategic initiatives and measures at Coca-Cola Beverages Sweden

greatest challenge in implementing the balanced-scorecard concept, according to CCBS, is to find the proper balance among the different measures in the various perspectives, and also to ensure that all information systems required for follow-up are available. In addition, it is vital to success that an individual be responsible for seeing that all information is submitted on time. His/her performance in regard to this aspect of the process should also be measured.

SKF

SKF is the world's largest manufacturer of rolling bearings and currently employs 44 000 people around the globe. The corporation is divided into three business areas comprising a total of nine divisions and their subsidiaries. Early in 1995 management concluded that there was a need to change the system of management control at SKF.

There were two principal reasons why a change was needed. First, there was dissatisfaction at SKF over the calendar-based budget, which in practice was an instrument with too limited a time frame. The budget was ineffective as a planning tool; it was time-consuming and costly, and it encouraged political manœvring within the corporation. For these reasons management was searching for an instrument of measurement and control which could replace control by the budget and help the corporation to adapt more rapidly to the changes in today's business environment.

Second, after a new CEO had taken office in the spring of 1995, SKF's strategy was reviewed and the corporation was reorganized. Management conducted a detailed analysis of the corporation and its market situation; the analysis resulted in a new corporate vision and strategy. In brief, SKF would become less production-focused and more customer-focused. Also, employee competence would be developed so as to ensure stable growth. Corporate management saw a need for management control that would be linked to the new vision and strategy.

In September 1995, SKF launched its balanced-scorecard project after a number of senior executives had read articles on the concept. The finance function together with a number of staff units and divisions were assigned to conduct the process. Specifically, the project groups consisted of six controllers from different staff units and divisions. The aim of the project group in the initial phase was to develop the corporation's own specific balanced-scorecard concept and then to implement it in the organization. The new concept was intended to replace the budget, which was perceived as having largely negative effects, while still retaining the positive features of a budget, e.g. setting targets and discipline in meeting commitments.

For a number of years ideas like TQM had been gaining acceptance. Integrating these into the newly formulated strategy, SKF decided to build its balanced scorecard on the basis of the following four perspectives: shareholder, employee, process, and customer (Figure 4.8).

The balanced-scorecard process itself has also been heavily influenced by the ideas of Kaplan & Norton. However, at SKF another step has been added: both strategic and operational measures were developed. After the metrics had been established, SKF prepared an activity plan for attaining each goal. To set targets and prepare an activity list for each one is much easier when working with the scorecard, as it focuses the company on a limited number of issues. "Stretch targets", aiming at substantial improvement, are frequently set. The process of selecting parameters, setting targets, and specifying activities on the scorecard is an iterative one, with a lot of give and take. This phase is critical for successful strategy implementation.

SKF would like to emphasize above all that it takes a long time to implement a concept like the balanced scorecard. Substantial resources and effort are required to succeed in changing both the organization and human behaviour at a company.

The major problem is not to introduce something new into the organization but to enable it to break the habit of using its old systems and procedures. Some divisions remarked on the absence of an IT-based presentation-support system in the implementation phase, and it was difficult to apply the new philosophy using the old system. Consequently, it is essential that top management always ask for information and reports that are consistent with the new concept.

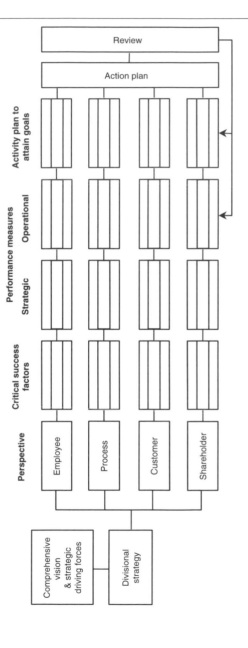

Figure 4.8 Comprehensive model of the balanced-scorecard process at SKF

To succeed with a balanced-scorecard project, it is also important not to have too many other projects involving major change going on at the same time. "Timing is of the essence" for success.

CONCLUSIONS

In this chapter we have presented some examples of how scorecard processes have been introduced in various industries. The corporations concerned are all large, but in several cases the process has started at some or a few local units (ABB, Coca-Cola, British Airways). In some cases a start has been made in one division with the ambition gradually to reach the entire corporation (Skandia, Electrolux, Halifax). In one case (SKF), the ambition clearly was to create a new overall management control for the entire group. We will encounter a few more cases of this in later chapters.

A common experience seems to be that the scorecard process takes quite a long time. Some of the people we interviewed made the point that this is necessary, as the scorecard introduces a new way of thinking. Dictates would be wrong, but active selling and coaching are needed.

Most of these cases took Kaplan & Norton's model as their starting-point. Several added a fifth (human or personnel) perspective to the original four. Electrolux made extensive use of experiences from other measurement-related projects, also in other firms, notably linked to the quality movement. We will meet more such cases later.

5

Important Issues in the Building Process

We have already described the process of developing the first comprehensive scorecard. In practice, however, a number of variations on the process are possible. In the present chapter we address several issues on which choices will have to be made. These issues have proven relevant in a number of case studies which are described in more detail in succeeding chapters. Not all of the companies involved refer to their method as the balanced scorecard, but in our opinion their experience illustrates the fundamental nature of the choices to be made.

Depending on these choices, the process of building the scorecard will vary. The following are some of the issues which we will address in this chapter:

- How should we organize the work, particularly the process of breaking the scorecard down?
- Some companies speak of *perspective*, others of *focus* – does it make any difference? Should we retain the four perspectives of Kaplan & Norton, or are we free to choose our own?
- What are measures, actually? How many should we have? Who decides?
- How far down in the organization should we have a scorecard – all the way to the individual level? Are all measures to be used for setting goals?

HOW SHOULD WE ORGANIZE THE WORK?

We have previously mentioned the importance of a project group with the time and energy to keep the balanced-scorecard process moving. It should carry weight in the organization but at the same time be impartial and open to ideas from all quarters. These requirements may be difficult to reconcile. Most members of the executive team have busy schedules. They may also find it hard to speak freely to everyone who should be involved in the process.

The answer is often to give a controller or consultant an influential role in the process. Such a solution may be an excellent one, even though someone with an accounting background may be looking for the kind of measures with which he/she feels most comfortable – or people in the organization may say what they believe he/she wants to hear.

It is important in any case not to let this one person establish the measures alone; rather, his/her role should be that of process leader. In addition, the project group, including representatives of top management for the business unit concerned, should meet fairly often.

The way in which the work is organized is thus crucial to a successful outcome. Management and other people who command respect in the organization must act as missionaries and demonstrate their interest. At the same time, it must be possible for employees to contribute their ideas and knowledge – a major feature of the new method, of course. Therefore, process leaders must be attuned to what people are thinking. When introducing new ideas, such as measures, their approach should be one of proposing a new method on a trial basis rather than imposing a ready-made solution.

Halifax

According to management at Halifax, the implementation process began when the project was initiated. The entire staff of the organization received continuous information about the project, the balanced scorecard, and how the new system would affect them. There was a continuous learning loop during the process, in which the project group reported what they had accomplished back to the different branches.

In the opinion of Halifax, management support is essential to the success of a balanced-scorecard project; if the CEO and the personnel director had not been supporting the project, nothing would have come of it. While admitting that some things get done without management support, Halifax executives emphasize that implementing a balanced scorecard is not one of them.

BOTH PERSPECTIVE AND FOCUS

In their first article, Kaplan & Norton discussed *perspectives*: How do customers see us? How does our business look in a process perspective?

Later a number of companies began to speak of *focus*. The two terms do not always have the same meaning. The customer perspective is about our company as the customer sees us: a minimum of delays, a pleasant feeling about nice products or a good product line. A customer focus, on the other hand, may be about customers *as we see them*. What is the market penetration of our products in different age groups or industries? Is the number of our customers increasing? Are we vulnerable from selling to a limited number of major customers?

In spite of this possible difference, we will continue to use "perspective" and "focus" as interchangeable concepts. In practice – that is, at the companies which we have visited – both terms are used.

Naturally, we need to consider both "how customers see us" and "how we see our customers". Lead times and quality must measure up to the competition while also meeting our own standards. What is good enough? The test, of course, is the judgement of customers and how we compare to competitors. However, no such test may be available when we invest in a new product or concept. We may decide to build up a business in order to be present when the demand arises, or to reform our business processes in a way that no one has ever thought of before. For example, we hear all the time about how companies should be on the Internet.

In our opinion, a good scorecard should be balanced in several respects. One, of course, is among the four perspectives; in other words, the company should give the lower, more long-term areas of measurement sufficient consideration, and not be satisfied by good short-term financial performance alone. But there are several other ways in which we may speak of a balance. One of these is the balance between "how others see us" (different perspectives) and "how we see ourselves" (different kinds of focus).

A third form of balance which the scorecard should help us to find is between static and dynamic, between a situation at a point in time and a change over time. Measures should tell us about both stocks and flows, just as our customary financial accounting includes both a balance sheet and an income statement. For example, we may need measures to show us both how many customers we have and how rapidly we are gaining or losing customers, or both what we have in our data base and how much it has grown over a period of time. Earlier we discussed intellectual capital. The quantity of this capital is a measure of a situation at a point in time, but surely we will also want a related measure to show how it is changing over time. Thus, in striking a balance between static and dynamic, the scorecard can also help us to avoid the danger of a short-sighted approach. Without a scorecard many investments in the future will only be shown as expenditures until the time – which may be much later – when they bear fruit. If we make these investments fully visible, we help to draw attention to them, to make them more respectable and better managed, and possibly to encourage more of them.

ABB

At ABB it is considered very important to follow the development of each business in all of the five perspectives which have been selected for use. It is necessary to understand the relationships among the perspectives. The process, employee, and innovation perspectives create and provide the basis for customer value which in the long run will affect profits. This reasoning is illustrated in Figure 5.1.

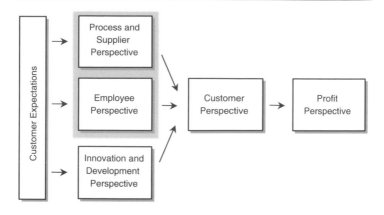

Figure 5.1 The relationships among the EVITA perspectives

Volvo Car Corporation[1]

At Volvo the principal challenge is considered to be that of giving non-financial measures as much weight as the more established financial ones. The latter can be readily used in management control, but not always the former. While it is necessary to see how the different measures are interrelated, Volvo has found it virtually impossible to strike a balance among all measures and to optimize each. This task is particularly difficult in an organization as large and complex as Volvo Car Corporation. One major purpose of the monthly VCC Performance Report is to let each unit know that it is being measured according to a number of specific metrics which show how it is making an important contribution to the company's development and overall performance. The various company units should always be asking: how well have we been progressing, and where are we headed?

In today's turbulent environment the short-run perspective has become more and more compelling, and it is very important to focus on a few critical measures. In the VCC Performance Report the company has found an operational instrument of management control which it previously lacked. However, the whole document is based entirely on the company's long-term strategic planning. At Volvo Car Corporation it is considered difficult for an organization to focus at one moment on the short-term operational aspects of the business and then immediately to switch to the strategic implications at some distant point in the future.

ALWAYS THE SAME PERSPECTIVES?

The Kaplan & Norton scorecard comprises four perspectives. Skandia, ABB, and more recently KappAhl have preferred to add a fifth, a "human resource focus". Volvo does not actually refer to its "scorecards" as "balanced", but has chosen its own design. And at some companies each perspective is devoted primarily to one of several different functions.

Further on we will discuss the use of special measures for employees and IT. Should these be included in our four areas of focus, or should they sometimes be given perspectives of their own?

To us the purpose of the scorecard is to influence the strategic direction of the business. If we want to focus on employees or IT, special metrics would of course be desirable in these areas. If we are referring more generally to the entire business of a department, a subsidiary, or a whole corporate group, the employee or IT metrics should of course be included at this level. We would then need to describe both employees and IT in terms of their role in processes and in innovation/development, as well as customer relationships.

If as we have indicated the scorecard should help us to guide the development of the business, it is natural to consider changing the number of perspectives or areas of focus. Skandia follows a clear logic in relating its five areas of focus to its categories of intellectual capital (cf. Figure 2.5). At Skandia human-resources capital is also considered to have a multiplier effect on process and development capital; without the former, the latter have little value. Nevertheless, we see advantages in retaining the original four areas. There are other possible ways of supplementing them if necessary.

The original model of Kaplan & Norton has the advantage of compactness; one of its main purposes is precisely to focus on a limited number of strategic issues. With the link between the upper perspective and "yesterday", between the perspectives in the middle and "today", and between the lower perspective and "tomorrow", it is easy to scan the entire scorecard and to emphasize its principal message: the balance between short-run and long-run. The financial measures of our past performance show a concise picture on which it is generally easy to agree when presented in terms of a few generally accepted measures used in traditional financial accounting. The customer and process perspectives reflect the balance between the external and the internal aspects of today's business, and also the fact that our present position and direction – as seen both by us and by others – reflect both aspects. For example, we can improve by acting both within the company and outside it. Finally, the perspective on the future, at the bottom, might also be separated into external and internal aspects. But for the most part it relates to internal actions which only we ourselves can plan and implement.

People may properly be considered important in all four perspectives. At companies with a special "human-resource perspective", it has sometimes proven difficult to fill out the "renewal and development" perspective at the bottom in an appropriate way. Particularly at the lower levels of an organization, enhancing employee competence is the most obvious area of concentration for development efforts. Perhaps one of the principal kinds of balance relates to how people apportion their time between preparing for tomorrow, taking care of customers, and managing processes. This allocation of time is not apparent if there is a separate human-resources focus.

Other areas of focus have also been suggested. One example is a special environmental focus. Enterprises which regard themselves as virtual companies may want to have a partner focus, which puts the cultivation of networks on a par with customer relationships. However, we do not believe in transforming the scorecard into a stakeholder model. If the environment or partners are critical to the company's success, we would prefer that the original areas of focus be given a broader interpretation. Otherwise we fear that the scorecard may lose some of its value as a comprehensive survey.

It is primarily the customer perspective which we might like to fill out. Where are the other actors in the company's network:

suppliers, companies with which we collaborate, and representatives of the public interest who make decisions in certain areas critical to our business, and with whom we have an ongoing relationship?

Someone might perhaps want to place these elements in the process perspective, and perhaps suggest that our ability to handle such relations is a critical success factor for our internal processes. Undeniably they have a major impact on how well we run our business. In some cases the relevant measurements for factors like delivery time may encompass several links in a supply chain. While some links may not be part of our company in a formal sense, they do make a difference for the time of delivery to the customer.

What we believe is that there may be a need to focus more clearly on both external effectiveness and internal efficiency; the two perspectives in the middle of the scorecard should remind us of this need. A company's management of its environment is not just a matter of marketing and treating customers properly. It also includes cultivation of the network which we have sometimes called the "imaginary organization" (Hedberg et al., 1997). Compare, for example, our earlier discussion on the competence balance sheet, in which we illustrated how a company may rely on others to supply competence in certain areas. In a modern approach to business strategy, this form of managing relationships may sometimes constitute a clear alternative to improving the efficiency of internal processes. A company which is contemplating outsourcing should see that its scorecard properly reflects its ability to cultivate the necessary relationships.

MEASURES ARE DESCRIPTIONS

The balanced scorecard includes measures of various aspects and conditions which are important to a business. We have emphasized that measures in themselves are not what matters. Just putting a number of measures down on paper will not give us a balanced scorecard. The essence of the scorecard is the process and the discussion relating to the measures – beforehand, during, and afterwards.

And yet measures do have a central role. Before continuing our discussions surrounding the scorecard, it is important that we first develop the most specific indicators possible on a number of important factors which traditional management accounting fails to show with sufficient clarity. Here we immediately encounter a dilemma. Since the measures available are not perfect, may not completely capture the phenomena which interest us, or can be manipulated, their value will surely be questioned. But we do not regard that likelihood as a problem. Good solutions are so often rejected in the search for perfection. Of course we should be looking for the best possible measures, but we should not refrain from choosing measures just because the ones available are less than perfect.

By *measures* we mean compact descriptions of observations, summarized in numbers or in words. These observations may concern a particular subject, such as the health of an individual or the profitability of a company. But just as often measures convey summarized observations on a number of rather similar subjects, such as companies in a particular industry. The measures summarize certain *attributes* of the subjects concerned. Usually the description is numerical, as with blood pressure or profit. Sometimes, however, the measure may be verbal, as when a student receives the grade of "excellent".

When we define measures, we create a language to be used when we describe things to each other. As users we must more or less agree on the meaning of what is expressed in the language. For example, measures often have connotations in addition to what they actually denote; we expect that people who see a measure will agree on its connotation. To illustrate, let us consider how a company is described in its income statement and balance sheet, or how a computer or a house is described in a newspaper advertisement. A good language will enable users of information to interpret the description and to feel fairly certain that they have been presented with a "true and fair view"[2] of the object to be described.

Thus, the intentions and needs of users determine whether a language, e.g. a set of measures, can be considered adequate. The broader the field of intended use, the more difficult it becomes to select and define measures equal to the purpose. A misunderstanding may sometimes result when users have not learned the language sufficiently; for example, they may not know the meaning of various measures of a computer's capacity, or how lead time has been defined. But it may also arise because the measure fails to describe what the user needs to know. For example, the debate on intellectual capital (Chapter 2) implies a questioning whether today's annual reports can provide a "true and fair view" of a company whose future will be determined by its customer data base or computer experience.

Measures emphasize certain attributes of what is measured and lead us to perceive them as important. The language of measures often appears objective. Measurements are data, of course, and are frequently equated with actual observations. But there is always a purpose behind the choice and formulation of measures; sometimes they are motivated by consideration for the needs of users, but there may also be a desire to turn their attention in a certain direction. Companies have long been using financial measures for the purposes of management control. Care has been taken to see that internal measures of profit provide incentives for desired action. If bonuses or other rewards are tied to the measures, the effect is reinforced.

However, how measures are defined is not only important when we want to explain something to each other. Individuals who are summarizing their impressions in terms of the observations measured will also be influenced, perhaps unconsciously, by existing practices. Doctors check the health of their patients by performing various established tests. What they find is affected from the outset by the choice of tests. Similarly, an individual teacher, or an entire faculty, may have certain customs about what questions to ask and what answers are correct. And joggers may have the habit of clocking themselves over certain stretches of their course.

At this point it may be wise to borrow the distinctions in systems theory among data, information, and knowledge. Measurements are *data*, but less structured observations may be as well. When teachers summarize their impressions of a student's performance during the year by giving him/her a grade, the purpose is to describe that performance to someone else. However, the numerical grade will only constitute *information* if the person to whom it is communicated understands something because of it.

Without knowledge of the standards of the teacher or the school, grades mean little. For example, the reader may not even know whether a "1" is the highest or lowest grade on the scale; he may know nothing about the relative frequency of different grades, either. New *knowledge* is added only when data constitute *new* information for the person receiving it. However, a confirmation of what was previously believed but not definitely known may be new information, since it reduces uncertainty. Sometimes people speak of the *value* of information or data to the user; that value is determined in part by the user's psychological reaction to the information, and in part by the resulting effect on his/her continued actions.

Consider, for example, a job application. The applicant has a grade-point average of 3.5. The number itself is indisputable, but what information does it provide? Of course, the nature of the job is quite relevant, but so are the standards of the applicant's school. If the grade is to constitute knowledge and to be of any value, it must in some way affect people's actions. If we know the applicant well from a previous trial period of employment, his/her grades may naturally be of interest, but they will leave less room for interpretation, and provide less new knowledge, than in the case of a person whom we do not know.

This point is important when we are designing measures of performance, such as those to be used in a scorecard. Our task should be easier if the scorecard is to be read by people with the same background as our own, than if it is to be distributed to a larger group, or perhaps published in an annual report. However, we have found that one particular benefit from the scorecard is precisely that it triggers internal discussions on what the measures mean. Both sender and receiver may easily forget that many kinds of information have been eliminated, and that frames of reference are very important for understanding the information provided.

Therefore, there is reason to consider the intended use and purpose of each measure. We believe that Figure 5.2 may be helpful. It shows how some measures are only designed to provide the most neutral description possible; that is, no value judgement is made. In other instances the purpose is specifically to permit comparison or even to set goals and monitor progress. The latter is particularly common in the case of measures for an

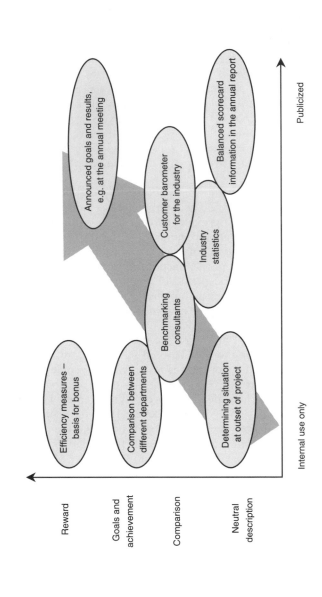

Figure 5.2 Some examples of different purposes and uses for measurements. Source: Modified after Olve & Westin (1996)

organization's internal use. Since the circle of users is fairly limited, it is possible to utilize even measures that call for considerable familiarity with the context. On the other hand, if we intend to publish the measurements generally, e.g. by including a balanced scorecard in the annual report, greater care must be taken to avoid the danger of misinterpretation – particularly in view of the grading function of the upper measures in Figure 5.2.

In Figure 5.2 we provide examples of different purposes of measures. Some of these may also be situations in which a scorecard may be used. We have intended the figure to show that what is required of measures will vary. In between information for internal use and publicized information, we have measures used by a wider but well-informed circle of persons, such as when a trade association explains an industry's situation to its members, or an institute of study does so for its clients. These users can naturally understand measures which might be misleading if more generally publicized. Measurements solely for internal company use require the least care in design, since users – perhaps without even being aware of it – also draw on their previous familiarity with what is described.

In the upper part of Figure 5.2, the criteria for measures become stricter for another reason. "You get what you ask for" – if an inappropriate measure is used as a goal and it is taken seriously, the unfortunate result may be suboptimization. If measures are to be used as a basis for promises to external parties, either at an annual meeting or as a contract clause, it becomes even more imperative that they present a "true and fair view". Because of these factors, as we move up towards the right in Figure 5.2, the design of measures becomes progressively more demanding and potentially sensitive.

The measures which may be considered also differ in other ways, and here a number of fundamental questions arise: How often are measurements to be made? What method will we use? Can we measure directly what we want to know, or must we use surrogate measures – e.g. counting the number of persons with a particular educational background instead of determining their actual skills? Near the origin in Figure 5.2, we may be able to get by with rather limited measures: less frequent measurements, fewer persons interviewed, and surrogate measures instead of measures of actual effects. This approach will be less costly and may suffice for our purposes.

We want to use the measures in the scorecard to enhance our access to the information possessed by the different actors in an organization, knowledge which to some extent is unspoken and perhaps unconscious. We would like "to put people's intuitions in touch with each other". If sender and receiver share the same perception, as we have previously described, this objective may to some extent be possible.

SKF

SKF has come to realize how important it is to establish common definitions for the different measures used. For this reason a reference group on the SKF corporate staff has collected the various definitions and prepared a list of all of them. About 70 measures are found on the list, which includes definitions and persons to contact for each one.

Another problem at SKF has been the inability to measure everything which is relevant. Therefore, it is important to choose the right metrics and to link the various activities to them. Activities must be specified in time, and a person must be put in charge of each one. It will then be possible to see whether there is any relationship between the activities and the metrics.

Electrolux

The Electrolux measurement system, DBM (dynamic business measurement) is intended to be dynamic so that it always keeps pace with changing times. By comparison with GIMS, approximately 50% of the measures in the DBM are either modified or new. Today DBM focuses on 16 different key measures, 12 of which are non-financial. Optimizing all of these is unfeasible, since Electrolux carries 20 product lines. No more than a handful of measures can be optimized. DBM should be viewed as a menu of key measures, from which relevant ones may be selected for specific sectors and time frames. It will not be possible to monitor all these key measures for all sectors.

WHO CHOOSES THE MEASURES?

The measures are of course selected by the process whose main features we described earlier. There we discussed how visions and scorecards for the entire company are decomposed into scorecards for its parts. We were careful to note that this process includes alignments upwards as well as downwards, so that it should not be interpreted as a kind of overcentralized management.

Opinions vary as to whether the same measures are desirable at different levels of the organization. It is important that the scorecard be considered relevant and specific. While this consideration would be a reason for leaving the choice of measures totally up to the local unit, comparisons would then be difficult. For example, Skandia started out with an extremely decentralized procedure for developing scorecards for different units, but later on, when managers wanted to make comparisons, they began to adapt the measures for this purpose on their own initiative. Often, however, it is top management that wants certain measures to be uniform throughout the organization.

What is most important, we believe, is that the same measures, when used by a number of different organizational units, be uniformly defined and applied. Therefore, a scorecard project should probably provide for an interchange of experience on measuring, and establish some kind of library of defined measures among which company units can pick and choose. Subsequently, top management may require that certain measures be used, just as traditional accounting permits some degree of freedom while retaining certain mandatory elements such as a standard format for the income statement.

THE NUMBER OF MEASURES FOR EACH SCORECARD AND PERSPECTIVE

A frequently asked question is how many measures should be used for each scorecard and perspective. The answer depends largely on the level at which the measures are to be used. In other words, the number of measures may vary according to level of the particular scorecard or perspective.

We have found that 15–25 measures per scorecard are customarily used at the corporate and business-unit levels, whereas at the divisional/functional level only 10–15 measures are usually considered critical. At the group and individual levels still fewer measures tend to be needed – generally 5–10.

Why does the number of critical measures decrease as we move down the organization? The explanation has largely to do with the relevance of measures in the sense of the degree to which they can be influenced by the unit or the individual. It is important to avoid measuring departments and individuals on variables which they have no way of affecting.

In addition, we often encounter attempts to combine the measures in each focus into a single overall grade, or index, on the unit's performance – in other words, to reduce the number of measures to a single one. We will subsequently return to this kind of index (Chapter 7). Let us first see how many measures are used at a number of companies which we have studied.

ABB

ABB recommends that a maximum of five and a minimum of one measure be used for each perspective, with each unit ideally focusing on a total of about 10 measures for all perspectives combined. Further, at ABB it is felt that most measures should be followed up once a month. However, performance on certain customer, profit, and human-resource measures is reviewed only once or twice a year; given their character, it is very difficult to take the relevant measurements more often.

Xerox

In 1990 Xerox conducted a comprehensive review of its efforts to meet high standards of quality. This work resulted in a management model drawing on the ideas of Baldrige, Deming,

Xerox Green book, ISO, and EFQM. The model, which was named the business excellence certification, helped top management to focus on a total of 42 specific measures. Today the model has been further developed and has been renamed the Xerox management model (XMM). XMM focuses on 31 specific measures in 6 different categories (Figure 5.3). Since the model has the same format all over the world, it is possible to benchmark the different units, thus simplifying learning and development. The model also provides a framework when the unit is certified once a year. In addition, the measures and categories are reviewed and published every quarter in a self-assessment portfolio.

Every measure has its own "desired state". Once a year goals are set for each measure in three dimensions (results, approach, and pervasiveness). The weight of the dimensions varies for each measure. The goals are set through a process of self-assessment and calibration in comparison with the performance of other companies. For this purpose a rating scale of 7 is used, with 7 standing for "world-class", a measure obtained by benchmarking. Since the rating scale is constant throughout the company, the various units can share their experience in achieving improvement.

Every category and measure has an owner and a sponsor (a person who is always a member of the board of directors). The owner is responsible for preparing a quarterly analysis of the trend in the measure, specifying the reasons for the trend (causal analysis), what is functioning satisfactorily (strengths), and areas for improvement, as well as what action should be taken, by whom (responsibility), by when, and current status (Figure 5.4).

SKF

Metrics within each perspective were established through open discussion, both at the top-management level and further down in the organization. This process led to the selection of five measures to be used by all nine divisions. These measures were return on capital employed, cash flow, one process measure,

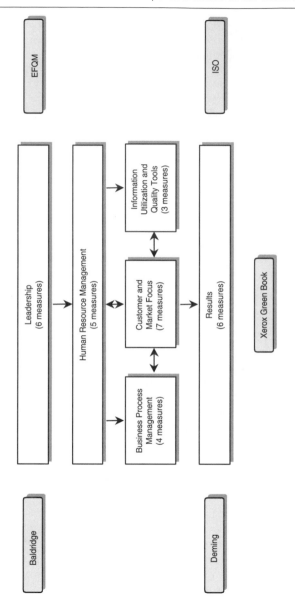

Figure 5.3 Xerox management model

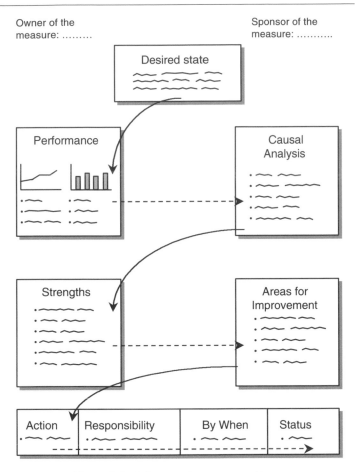

Figure 5.4 Follow-up of measures at Xerox

one personnel measure, and one measure of customer satisfaction. Divisions are to be managed with this model and are
not required to submit a budget to corporate headquarters. The
time perspectives for the various goals differ from division to
division depending on conditions in the respective industries.
To facilitate adaptation of the balanced scorecard to each division

management permits a division to increase its number of mandatory measures to a maximum of 10–15.

Clearly there is a variety of views among companies on what management needs to know and is capable of interpreting. There is probably a difference if many of the measures are only checked to see whether the values recorded lie within an acceptable range – then you should be able to handle a larger number. However, it is questionable whether such measures need to be included in each report. We believe that the total number of measures can be kept at a limited level if a company focuses on a few critical success factors for a certain period and perhaps gradually changes its measures over time. Kaplan & Norton emphasize that a company will normally have many key ratios which do not belong on the scorecard.

Also significant is whether top management must review the scorecards of a large number of units. The need to understand, to follow developments, and to remember the meaning of many different sets of goals increases the danger of misinterpretation, or loss of interest. In either case the benefit of the balanced scorecard is diminished. For these reasons we believe that a reasonably small set of standardized measures is desirable, perhaps three to five at most for each focus.

BREAKING MEASURES DOWN

We have previously discussed breaking measures down for use at lower levels in the organization. Some companies, however, may have begun their scorecard process at lower echelons of the company; here the corresponding step will be to align the measures upwards. But since we emphasize the importance of starting with a comprehensive vision, we assume that this vision will be the basis for the measures adopted at lower levels. (By levels we mean e.g. the company, the business unit, the department/function, the workgroup, and the individual.)

Understanding will of course be enhanced if the same measures are used at different levels. This feature is the principal advantage of traditional financial measures, which use the same terminology to describe the contribution of each unit to the whole. As a practical matter, such uniformity is not so easy to obtain with non-financial measures, not even when the same units of measurement are used.

For example, lead time can be an interesting measure at many companies or departments, but it must be carefully defined if any comparison is to be meaningful. And how are measures at lower and upper levels related? If the company as a whole wants to reduce lead times, how is this goal translated into targets and metrics for the various units? Hardly by setting the same target for all units. Rather, what we need is a comparison with a starting-point or, better still, with external points of reference. The share of sales accounted for by new products is another measure which is appropriate for many company units but which still may be difficult to break down to the unit level. Computing a mathematical average for the company is no problem in itself, but an ambition to increase the proportion of sales derived from new products will probably concern new product areas for the most part.

It may sometimes be appropriate to formulate a top-level measure such as "proportion of salesmen closing deals with at least three new customers during the period", and for the salesmen concerned to adopt the number of new customers as a measure. The important point is to link measures at various levels and to find measures which are perceived as uncomplicated, meaningful, and tangible by the persons concerned. These measures may also be used in setting objectives. The objective need not always be the best possible outcome; sometimes a value within a reasonable interval will do.

Often measures at a more operational level are specific (number of defects at installation), whereas the corresponding measures at higher levels are more general (number of installation contracts completed, with final payment received). If the cause-and-effect relationships of the measure can then be identified, it will of course be even easier to motivate employees to feel committed to the measures. For example, a measure of how quickly defects have been repaired in the past may be linked to one showing the extent of repeat purchases by the same customer. The measure may also concern the financial benefits of minimizing production down time for the customer. Showing these relationships will increase understanding of why the success factors described by the measures are important.

When we discuss relationships among measures, the question of timing often arises – when will the measure react to what should interest us? Kaplan & Norton distinguish between "leads and lags", performance drivers and outcome measures, i.e. between measures which provide an early warning and those which register the effect after the fact. The difference is important, and of course we prefer the "leading indicators". All of the lower squares on the scorecard of a profitable company may be regarded as leading indicators of future profitability. However, measures which provide an early indication will inevitably present an unclear message about future effects, so that we will always have to weigh the benefits of an early warning against the uncertainty which accompanies it.

ABB

In the EVITA system at ABB it is by definition unworkable to combine the readings on the management-control measures of the different units, since each company determines which measures are most relevant. Thus, ABB parts company with Kaplan & Norton in deciding not to use corporate-wide measures.

Volvo Car Corporation

On certain markets and in certain units at Volvo, management has gone quite far in breaking down specific measures to different levels. However, headquarters will not require a breakdown of measures to the individual level, reasoning that this choice should be open to units which find that it would improve employee understanding of the business. Headquarters cannot make this decision for them but can only tell them which parameters to use for the sake of visibility. As an example, the marketing company in England has come quite far with its model that breaks down performance indicators.

SKF

Since the autumn of 1995, the implementation of the balanced scorecard at SKF has moved into a so-called development phase. The purpose of this work has been to proceed from the overall vision and strategy and implement the scorecard throughout the organization. By December 1997, scorecards had been introduced in both operating and administrative units and had virtually replaced the budget. One example is a unit called Spherical Rolling Bearings (SRB). SRB manufactures rolling bearings; its sales were SEK 750m. in 1996. SRB's products are used in machinery and equipment such as rolling-mills, pressing rollers for paper mills, stone crushers, and railroad trains.

SRB's work with the balanced scorecard was initially called PFU (which in Swedish stands for planning, deploy, and follow-up). The term "balanced scorecard" was considered to refer to the instrument itself, whereas PFU put more emphasis on the process of using the balanced scorecard (Figure 5.5). Planning at SRB involves linking the critical success factors both to the unprecedented goals embodied in SKF's vision and strategy, and to the specific goals for the coming year. Acceptance refers to managers' seeing that goals are broken down, communicated, and discussed until accepted at all levels of the organization. Finally, follow-up, as the expression implies, means that specific goals which have been set in the process are followed up and that corrective action is taken as needed so that they will be achieved. Starting in 1998, however, the term "balanced scorecard" will be used as part of a process of standardization at SKF.

INDIVIDUAL SCORECARDS

Some companies seek to break their scorecards down all the way to the individual level. Whether this policy is appropriate depends on the nature of the business. For salesmen and consultants, who are sometimes their own profit centres, it may seem more natural to do

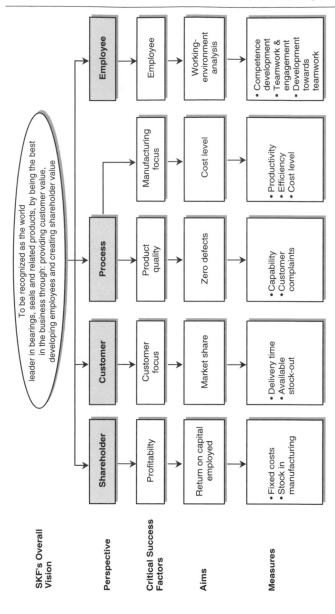

Figure 5.5 A comprehensive view of the balanced scorecard of Spherical Rolling Bearings

so than in businesses where employees are more interchangeable or work in teams. In career-development discussions, however, portions of the scorecard may be useful as a format for presenting expectations and achievement. For example, the scorecard may show how much working time has been devoted to building relationships with new customers, documenting experience, attending courses, etc.

Some of the companies which we have studied are talking about introducing the scorecard at the individual level, and we have also experimented with it ourselves. This step is most natural, of course, when employees are fairly autonomous and are supposed to cultivate customer contacts or special competencies, for example. Scorecards can then provide a suitable format for talks with employees on their career development, but can also be used as a basis for a kind of self-discipline like that of the amateur track athlete who voluntarily keeps a record of his times and performance. However, some companies deliberately avoid linking individual performance measurement to their overall system of measurement.

Electrolux

At Electrolux management believes that the design of the corporate organization limits the extent to which goals can be decomposed. The limit has been set at the division, an intermediate level with four principal business areas. In one business area, though – white goods – management wants to go further and requires that goals be broken down to the level of the sales and/or production subsidiaries. With 25 plants in Europe for white goods and three for vacuum cleaners, Electrolux is engaged in mass production, so that it is difficult to break goals down and to monitor performance on a unit-by-unit basis.

When there are scorecards on the individual level, we quickly reach the question whether bonuses should be based on the measurements reported in the scorecard. Actually, two issues are involved: whether individual bonuses are appropriate at all, and if so whether they should be tied to measures other than financial ones. For example, should a salesman be rewarded for having developed a promising customer contact, or should no reward be given until the deal has been closed, or delivery has been approved and the customer has paid? In some export sectors and at construction companies, for instance, the difference in time may be substantial.

We would like to introduce the scorecard as a means of giving visibility to long-term endeavours as well; thus, for the sake of consistency we should actually reward promising sales efforts from the start. But if we pay out in advance some of the money we expect to earn, the bonus for completing the transaction should be correspondingly reduced. For employees who leave the company in the meantime, this arrangement might be attractive and logical. We wonder, though, how many companies would dare to state that the transaction had created value at such an early stage.

Often management would like to provide incentives for team efforts; here it is natural to link the bonus to performance at a higher organizational level. But perhaps the non-financial measures in the scorecard can reflect the individual's contribution to the team so that he/she can be awarded an appropriate individual bonus.

Clearly, with a bonus system it is particularly important that the measures chosen be well considered. For example, it may sometimes be possible to achieve established goals while neglecting some other area which has not been measured since the need there has appeared obvious. If we like, we may consider such a case as a test of a good scorecard. However, we believe that simply using scorecards to call attention to a variety of conditions in the business will often be sufficient to produce an improvement; therefore, we are not quite prepared to hold that bonus models should be an important element in a balanced-scorecard project.

NatWest Life

According to NatWest Life (NWL), measurements are the key to the success of their improvement initiatives. To back up the cross-functional leadership networking and mentoring schemes, a leadership scorecard is used for self-assessment and objective measurement of management skills. NWL has a scoring system based on a list of approximately 10 things which a good leader is expected to be able to do at NWL. The person scores him/ herself on each criterion. The employee's team may also be asked to score him/her on these criteria. Since the scorecard exercise is repeated every month, it is possible to see how a person's score is progressing over time.

MEASURES AS GOALS

Earlier we stressed the importance of both short- and long-term goals for each measure used. The action plans resulting from the scorecard process should specify the people in charge and the achievement time frame for each measure and its corresponding goal.

A scorecard will generally contain measures with readings that change at different rates; it may not be meaningful to provide new data for some of them as often as for others. For example, studying employee or customer attitudes is often both expensive and difficult, except when the number of persons is large enough to permit subsequent measurements with new random samples. It is also questionable whether rapid changes of opinion are noteworthy, unless they relate to a particular event. Compare voter surveys!

Of course there is the risk that people in charge of an operation will resort to tactical manipulation as the time of measurement approaches. But the same risk is present with financial measures at the end of each accounting year. Actually, we believe that the risk is reduced with the balanced scorecard. Hopefully everyone will be interested in obtaining a realistic picture of the business as a basis for discussing and determining the future course to be followed. The more comprehensive view provided by the scorecard will make it harder for anyone to deceive him/herself or others by manipulating measures.

The use of measures as goals will be illustrated by some of our examples. Later we will return to the question of whether this practice can be a substitute for budgeting, as has recently been suggested.

Xerox

Policy deployment is the name of a process in which Xerox' comprehensive vision and overall strategic aims are broken down to the individual level (Figure 5.6). The process begins some time in October. In mid-December all employees present a list of "Vital Few Actions". The objective is for all to have their own "Bluebook", signed by their supervisor, before the end of January. The goals in the "Bluebook" are the basis for bonuses and other future rewards.

Since everyone is required to go through this annual process of review and analysis, it is natural to use it as a starting-point in setting short- and long-range goals for the coming year. At Xerox a goal, once established, is never changed. In other words, there is no ongoing revision of goals during the year. This process may be compared to budgeting, but it includes consideration of "soft" variables as well.

Everyone is to indicate up to five "Vital Few Actions" to be taken; one of these must have a short-term impact, whereas the others are to show annual progress towards established

Process (forming strategic intentions into an annual business plan)		**Areas** of Priority
1. Setting Guidelines:	Vision, mission and areas of priority 3–5 goals and strategy Annual target & "Vital Few Actions" (maximum of 5)	1. Customer Satisfaction 2. Employee Satisfaction 3. Market Share
2. Development:	Cascade goals and "Vital Few Actions" agreed on	4. ROA
3. Management Process:	Regular review (monthly, quarterly) Annual review/diagnosis	

Figure 5.6 Xerox policy deployment

goals. For each "Vital Action", the employee must also specify the expected outcome, the methods to be used for measurement and setting targets, the person who "owns" the target, and the time when it is to be reached.

SKF

Top management and divisional heads hold quarterly meetings to discuss the performance of each division in relation to the goals on the division's scorecard. While it is difficult to monitor certain non-financial measures more frequently than once a year each division still checks most measures each month. If established goals are not being met, the action plan is reviewed. In this way management attempts as soon as possible to find the causes of any unfavourable development. SKF believes that its operational goals are valid for an average of 6–18 months and should be reviewed and modified at some point within this time interval.

NatWest Life

At NatWest Life (NWL) the vision is integrated into all induction, training, and personal- and team-development activities. All new staff attend a full-day familiarization session called "The NWL Vision and You". On joining the company, each employee is given a booklet describing the guiding principles, management's expectations, and the employee's responsibilities.

At NWL every employee has a role profile, a kind of job description. The profile includes a purpose and a set of key accountabilities for the job. In addition, every employee has a set of objectives for the year; these are set in the annual planning process. The objectives for the employee are to reflect the overall goals in the company's comprehensive Balanced Business Scorecard. Every quarter the individual has a performance review with his/her manager. For each job there is also a set of competencies, normally about 15. (Examples of competencies would be communication, team-working, analytical thinking, etc.) Included are five core competencies which it is vital for the individual to perform satisfactorily. These competencies are assessed every year, training needs are identified and training programmes are then agreed for the individual. (In this way planning-process and company targets in the balanced business scorecard are translated into individual objectives.)

SUMMARY

In this chapter we have discussed in somewhat greater detail a number of the issues which we touched on previously when we reviewed the steps in the balanced-scorecard process.

Even just deciding whether to use *focus* or *perspective* as the term for the parts of the scorecard can influence the selection of measures. This point should be considered in the choice of perspectives, particularly in light of the nature of the discussion which management would like to encourage. The scorecard can emphasize different kinds of balance, such as one between different time frames. In addition, we returned to the question of the *number of areas of focus* needed, and we maintained that the original four of Kaplan & Norton will usually suffice.

We then discussed what we mean by *measures*; they are compact descriptions of observations. We design and select measures for the balanced scorecard for the express purpose of influencing communication within the company. We noted that the values and the previous knowledge of those who will use the measures are important to consider from the outset. The *number of measures per focus* is also relevant. In our experience there should not be more than 5–10; otherwise, there is a danger that the company will fail to focus on the truly critical success factors.

We also touched on the process issues which we will shortly discuss in greater detail. Measures should be *selected* so that persons immediately concerned will recognize that the measures are addressed to them. However, the desirability of vertical and horizontal comparisons within the organization may be a reason to cut back on the number of measures used. It is important that *the individuals in charge be clearly designated* and that *measures can be broken down* or at least related to higher levels in the organization. At this point we noted that it should be possible to use measures in *setting goals*. Later we will further discuss the relationship between the balanced scorecard and control and planning.

NOTES

1. Our main account of Volvo's experiences of scorecards will be found in Chapter 6.
2. "True and fair view" is the official English term used in the legislation on annual reports in the European Union. It is specifically required that balance sheets and income statements which fail to provide a true and fair view be supplemented by explanatory notes.

6
Scorecards as Management Control

The balanced scorecard has been preceded by a number of ideas which resemble it in various respects. In this chapter we will relate our experience with the scorecard to some of these ideas, and in particular to methods for quality management, the workflow approach, and business planning. If anything, however, the fact that numerous companies are already using TQM and similar methods should make it easier to go further and establish a more highly co-ordinated form of management control in which we believe the balanced scorecard should be used. Some regard this form of control as a substitute for budgeting, whereas we prefer to see it as a way of making budgeting more relevant. Figure 6.1 is repeated from the beginning of Chapter 3, and shows how a scorecard process should lead on from the strategy development which we have stressed so far. In this chapter and the next, the emphasis is on scorecards as management control systems. We will come back later to the remaining parts of the figure.

WHAT IS NEW?

It could surely be held that the interest of accountants in non-monetary measures is only a belated awakening to what others have been doing for a long time. Has not the quality consciousness of the past 20 years focused precisely on measures like throughput time and rate of defects? Of course marketing people have always kept an eye on customer attitudes and market shares, particularly

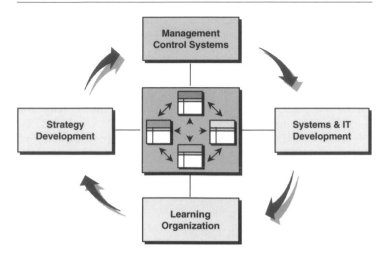

Figure 6.1 The balanced-scorecard process

in recent years with the introduction of customer-satisfaction indices and the like! Perhaps the director of personnel has also hired an opinion-research company to find out what employees are thinking. Thus, improving measures of performance has long been an important aspect of new developments in production management, market research, and human-resource management. Measures used for financial control have also been refined. Moreover, some of them have been used, with appropriate adaptations, at all levels of the company, where managers and foremen have kept informal notes separate from the system of formal reports.

As we see it, what is new is the *balance*, the comprehensive view, and the approach to the future. Successful efforts to reduce waiting periods or defects in quality show the value of temporarily focusing on specific measures. But at today's companies the total picture is also important. Determining what is right in the long run is not a matter to be left to a single executive acting alone; it calls for discussion. To that end there is a need to describe the business in a way sufficiently informative and clear to be useful to a substantial number of people. The balanced-scorecard concept can help us by showing:

- How both financial and other assets are being managed
- Both how others see us and how we see ourselves
- Both stocks and flows
- Both the short and long run

The comprehensive view brings out these trade-offs. The value of the balanced-scorecard concept is not in the key ratios themselves but in the discussion which the method entails. And this discussion is essential. While a few senior executives may feel that they understand the trade-offs referred to above, today it is not enough that only these few do. Many others at the company should also be discussing the current state and desired future of the business, and for that purpose the balanced-scorecard concept is a good tool. The reason for involving more people is that what they do may turn out to be of strategic importance for the company!

THE BALANCED SCORECARD AND OTHER METHODS OF CONTROL THROUGH MEASURES

We have emphasized how the balanced scorecard brings together different kinds of measures in a single comprehensive view of the entire business. It is important that this view describes what management actually wants to put in focus. Our experience has shown that developing this kind of scorecard and then using it in the ongoing exercise of management control is a good tool for strategic control as well.

The idea of presenting a number of different measures in a compact document is not new, and we do not wish to make too much of the difference between the balanced-scorecard concept and previous attempts based on key-ratio reports, measures of quality, etc. Measurement is a central element in a variety of concepts which have appeared in recent years, such as total quality management (TQM), business process management (BPM), European Quality Award (EQA), ISO certification, and others. Furthermore, personnel and marketing departments use measures more than before. Consulting firms, in particular, have contributed measurements of employee attitudes, customer-satisfaction indices, and the like. We will resume a part of this discussion in Chapter 7. Anyone seeking to develop better measures in a variety of areas will find a number of interesting ideas in the literature on TQM, business process redesign (BPR), etc.

The different theories surely reflect the same understanding of changed conditions at companies that led to the balanced-scorecard concept. Some of them are presented as comprehensive models for business management. Anyone whose experience with one of these models has been positive will surely ask what more the balanced-scorecard concept can contribute. Our own experience is insufficient for us to venture any general or final assessment. Among the companies which we have worked with or interviewed, and which have found the balanced-scorecard concept to be valuable, some also use TQM or similar models.

Xerox

Xerox has been one of the fastest-growing American companies of the post-war era. The business of the entire company is based on the xerography principle; that is, of making copies on ordinary paper. This principle was discovered by Chester Carlson, a descendant of Swedish immigrants. "Xerox" is derived from a Greek word meaning "dry writing".

In the early years Xerox had a monopoly position which enabled it to achieve a return on assets (ROA) of 25–30%. At the end of the 1970s, however, its patent expired. The Japanese entered the market, and in 1979 they introduced their first xerox-based photocopier on the American market. Because of its market position Xerox did not at first consider the Japanese products to be a major threat, but it soon found out that the Japanese products were being sold at a price equal to Xerox's production costs. Furthermore, the Japanese products were of superior quality. Consequently, the ROA curve dipped sharply, plummeting to a low of 4% in 1983.

In the mid-1970s Xerox made the fortunate move of acquiring 50% of the Japanese company Fuji Xerox, which in 1980 received Japan's highest citation for quality, the Deming Award. From 1979 to 1983, when Xerox was in the depths of its slump,

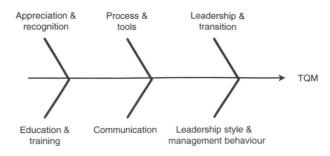

Figure 6.2 Six principal areas of strategic importance at Xerox

management tried to launch the expression "leadership for quality". Xerox then "benchmarked" itself against Fuji Xerox and was subsequently able to raise profitability to the current level of 18%. According to Xerox, this endeavour succeeded because management persisted in following the guidelines established in 1983. Not only did ROA improve, but the company's efforts were crowned with the Malcolm Baldrige Award (1989) and the EFQM Award (1992).

Once Xerox had introduced the expression "leadership for quality", management soon realized the necessity of creating a strategy for change. For this purpose, groups consisting of participants from all over the world were appointed to develop strategic guidelines for Xerox. Their work, which identified six critical areas in which a strategy was to be formulated, was subsequently documented in Xerox's "Green Book" (Figure 6.2). A further conclusion was that Xerox should focus on four priority areas: customer satisfaction, employee motivation, market share, and ROA.

One area where Xerox has become increasingly involved in recent years is the environment. Each year a report is sent to all shareholders on the company's progress in this field.

In retrospect, Xerox management believes that the attempt to implement "policy deployment" was a mistake. Everyone was supposed to have a "Blue Book"[1] after only one year. As it turned out, over two years had elapsed before everyone in the organization even understood the meaning of policy deployment. After this experience, Xerox would advise other companies to limit their efforts in the first year to the organizational level immediately below the top and to treat policy deployment primarily as a tool of senior management rather than use it more extensively as an instrument of control.

In actual practice, both the balanced-scorecard concept and other methods should be adapted to the needs of the user, so that no absolute comparison of the methods as such will ever be possible. However, we believe that the other approaches are generally viewed as more limited in scope. The evaluation system used for the EQA (and its national counterparts), while said to be equally appropriate for the provision of services and the public sector, has been most widely used in the engineering products industry. By the same token, measures of customer attitudes are seldom integrated with other ways of describing a business. What has happened here may explain why some approaches have never been adopted outside a limited circle of company employees. There is a lesson in it for those considering the use of the balanced-scorecard concept. It is not enough for someone to put together a collection of measures in a single scorecard. The discussion concerning the scorecard is what determines whether it will have any effect.

As early as the 1960s, it was suggested that critical success factors could be identified and then specified in the form of *key performance indicators*. In some companies such as General Electric, this would seem to go back several decades further. Then the studies of the 1970s on key ratios discussed what would much later be called *benchmarking*: in other words, comparing key indicators for certain aspects of a business with the corresponding numbers for other companies. In certain industries this practice was already well established through the efforts of trade associations. Similar thinking was involved when PIMS (profit impact of market strategy) soon afterwards began to collect measures of business performance for the purpose of inter-industry comparison of the relationship between profitability and different profiles of measurements describing market investments and the like.

Proponents often emphasize how their various methods provide a structure for using measures to improve business performance;

for example, the manual for the Swedish Quality Award emphasizes (Helling, 1995) that top executives themselves should be involved in gathering and analysing facts on how their business works, thus taking advantage of an opportunity for self-teaching. The measuring instrument used to determine who should receive this award consists of a set of questions based on fundamental values relating to involvement, participation, long-term approach, and continuous improvement. The starting-point for TQM is similar; it shows signs of inspiration by the Japanese style of leadership which became known to companies in the Western world starting in the 1970s.

The models provided by the various methods may be considered as valuable aids or as rather unimaginative, depending on the reader's temperament and situation. We would repeat what we stated above: the important thing is to find something that works for your own company. We have heard reports that the introduction of quality standards at some companies has served as an alibi for management to show that it is doing something, although little has actually changed. But the same programmes may of course work well at different companies. Right at this point a difficult question of principle arises. ISO 9000 is similar to a number of other standards (for military and nuclear operations, for example) in calling for documentation, task definition, specific qualifications for operating staff, the existence of certain procedures and adherence to them, etc. Ensuring that these criteria are met can easily degenerate into a routine check not requiring any real understanding of whether meeting the criteria will actually lead to the desired result. It may also deter creative thinking and the invention of new working methods. Would it not then be preferable to measure end results (outcomes) while granting complete freedom of action to those in charge? No, this option is not always open, either – the whole point of our discussion in previous chapters was that reports on the state of the business are needed long before the final results are evident, and that sometimes we may never be able to determine the connection between what a company does and how well it succeeds.

For this reason it is surely wise to begin by introducing one of the existing methods of quality assurance. However, ISO 9000 primarily includes criteria which are assumed to affect production, not criteria for administrative support systems. There is next to no information on much that we previously noted to be in particular need of better control. To fill this gap we must go on to TQM, EQA, and the like. These methods resemble ISO certification in that they involve "approval", but with the added feature that they take other aspects of the business into consideration and also evaluate the results. However, by comparison with our reasoning in previous chapters, we find less emphasis on the need for management to set the level of ambition for values like competence or customer service. Since this decision must reflect the chosen strategy, we reach the question of how the word "quality" is to be interpreted. Is it an absolute or relative concept? And in whose judgement?

Every distinction or award for quality is based on a kind of index which combines various measures of business performance. Like other indices, it is a summary of several measures in a single derived measure that permits comparison over time or among different objects. The measures on which the index is based must be comparable, and we must agree on a model for combining them according to their relative weights. An example is the consumer price index. This parallel also shows the possibilities for disagreement: some economists maintain that an annual increase in prices of a percentage point or so merely reflects an inability to correct the comparison for improvements in quality over time, and at present various alternatives to the consumer price index are being discussed. In fact every combined measure will be based on a set of assumptions about the cause-and-effect relationships which we have repeatedly stressed as a major subject for discussion in a balanced-scorecard process, and we will develop it further in Chapter 7.

The above-mentioned models for quality certification basically involve combining many different kinds of measures into a single one of "certified". Often, when a number of criteria must be fulfilled, the procedure is a kind of check-list. However, it may also include certain features of an index-like weighted average. For example, the European model for total quality management (published by EFQM, the European Foundation for Quality Management, 1998) apportions the total weight of 100% among different graded factors as shown in Figure 6.3. EFQM indicates

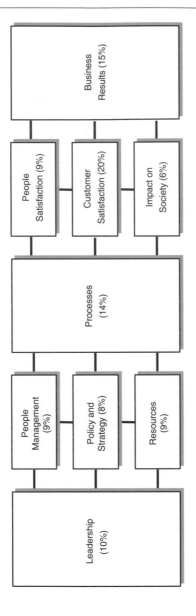

Figure 6.3 The measurement model of EFQM. Source: Adapted and reprinted with permission from *EFQM Self-assessment Guidelines*, European Foundation for Quality Management (1998)

that the model was created and percentages were established "after extensive consultations throughout Europe and is revised annually". It is apparent from EFQM's publication that the procedure began with verbal descriptions which were translated into numerical grades and then combined in a weighted average. The measures are based largely on self-assessment.

The first company to win the EQA was Xerox in 1992. The company's application for the award consisted of a comprehensive self-description, which presented measurement results and business processes for a long list of areas. The EFQM material describes different methods for this procedure, including forms which may be filled out, seminars, etc. Thus, in practice the company may choose its level of ambition in the various areas, but one difference from our previous reasoning is that no one has apparently realized that companies might intentionally try to give greater weight to process development or the environment, for example, than the percentages indicate. In our view, this practice would contrast with how we would like to see the balanced-scorecard concept applied.

Let us summarize. The emphasis of the balanced-scorecard concept on discussions about measures may remind us of a number of the theories of quality which have been presented over the past 20 years. We see no cause for rivalry between these and the balanced scorecard. However, in companies where both have been used, it is important to clarify the relationship between the two different methods:

- We recommend that the scorecard be designed to indicate the thrust of an appropriate strategy for the business. We suspect that certain quality-related projects tend to be based primarily on local conditions and on what different units of the business consider most important. (At the same time, of course, in conjunction with TQM we find attempts to encourage new thinking, sometimes even radical ideas like BPR.)
- ISO certification is one of a number of approaches that concentrate on those business processes which are most relevant to a company's near-term deliveries to customers. There is a significant need to measure and develop other processes within the company.

A dilemma always present when methods like these are used – indeed, whenever we are talking about quality – is how we can recognize a good business, in particular how we should reach agreement if there are several persons who should bring their influence to bear on the decision. Even though we may believe in rational choice and find logically reasoned strategies desirable, most of us need time to think about various alternatives before we are actually ready to decide whether we like them. This statement applies both to our personal lives (purchases, choice of job) and to our work with business strategy. But in the latter case several others should be in on the discussion. It is then important to make various possible conceptions of a business as concrete and explicit as possible, and all of the methods which we have mentioned can provide inspiration when a company is designing its own particular version.

NatWest Life

NatWest Life (National Westminster Life Assurance, NWL) is a young company. In September 1991, it was announced that NWL would be established within the National Westminster Group, and trading in the new company's shares commenced in January 1993. NWL markets life assurance, pensions, and long-term investment products in the UK. In the first four years of trading NWL has produced more than £200m. of retained earnings for shareholders and in 1997 had approximately 500 employees. NWL is a certified Investor in People, and was a finalist in both the European and UK Quality Awards for 1996 and 1997.

The initial strategy was set out in a business case developed by the NatWest Group to guide the management after the establishment of NWL in 1991. The case was prepared by the executive team in 1992, when the following statement of strategic intent for the company was formulated: "We will build the outstanding Life Company of the 1990s and will do so in a way that raises industry standards."

Once it had been decided what kind of company NWL would be, the vision statement was drafted in August 1992. This step was taken to ensure that NWL had a solid foundation on which to build business excellence in terms of staff employment and methods of operation. The first vision was set out as a series of commitments to the stakeholders. These commitments can be summarized as follows: "We will be a leading provider in our chosen sectors of financial services – first choice for customers throughout their lives for outstanding service, straightforward products and superior investment returns."

During 1996, as a part of their corporate transformation programme, the executive team continually reviewed the appropriateness of the vision statement and guiding principles, while also taking into account the feedback from the annual staff survey. This work resulted in a précis of the vision statement: "First Choice for Life." This new, shortened version serves three purposes:

- It responds to staff feedback, recommending an instantly recognizable statement
- It recognizes that the success of NWL's business will depend on long-term relationships between customers and NWL staff
- It reflects the nature of NWL's business

As part of the corporate transformation programme, the guiding principles were also reviewed. Based on the NWL philosophy, the guiding principles were developed to support key operating policies, to guide decisions, and to help create the sort of company where individuals want to work. For each of the nine guiding principles, there are expectations and responsibilities.

From the outset NWL were determined that the company should be built on the fundamental concepts of TQM. Management were convinced that quality performance in all aspects of the company's operations would be a suitable source of competitive advantage. With this underlying belief and to support the strategy consistent with it, NWL applied – successfully – for EFQM membership in 1992 before the company started trading; in 1994 NWL became a founding member of the British Quality Foundation.

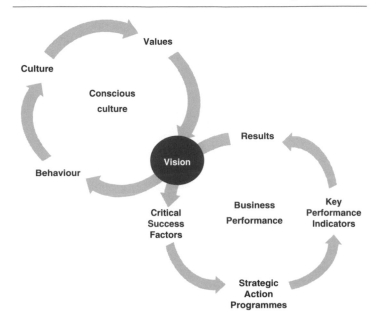

Figure 6.4   The virtuous circles of NWL

At an early stage NWL recognized that leading organizations typically concentrated both on "harder" measures of financial and business performance and "softer" developmental issues such as the creation and maintenance of an appropriate culture. This realization led the company to develop a model, the virtuous circles (see Figure 6.4), to help the organization maintain this balanced focus.

Since 1992 NWL has been using the balanced business scorecard, which serves as the structure for performance management in the NatWest Group. When the balanced business scorecard was to be developed, a project group was formed consisting of senior managers and members of the executive team (a total of eight people). The project group attended a workshop called "Vision into Practice". At this workshop four perspectives were identified: financial, customer, internal quality, and organizational development. The vision was then broken down into critical success factors (what should the business succeed at in the long run?) and key performance indicators, and actual measures were identified (what should the business measure in the short term in order to succeed in the long run?). This workshop resulted in one of the key documents in the development of the organization, thus establishing the basic policy for measuring and tracking company progress.

At this point NWL became the first major business unit in the NatWest Group to begin reporting in terms of the balanced business scorecard. During 1991/92, the NatWest Group had only carried out some experiments for the purpose of adapting their performance-management structure to the balanced-scorecard concept. In the early stages the balanced business scorecard was used mainly to understand the business, to cluster information into the four quadrants, and as a guide to organizing the business.

Later on, in 1992, the executive team were attracted to the business excellence model, which not only offers an objective method of measuring business performance, but also enables the company to benchmark its performance against the best practices of other companies throughout the UK and Europe, irrespective of industry. Therefore, the executive team decided to use the business excellence model as well as the balanced business scorecard in their ambition to create a demonstrably world-class business. NWL sets forth the relationship between the balanced business scorecard and business excellence model as follows:

Financial perspective
- Financial results

Internal quality
- Resources
- Processes
- Non-financial business results

Customer perspective
- Customer satisfaction
- Impact on society

Organizational development
- Leadership
- Policy and strategy
- People management
- People satisfaction

Both the vision and the guiding principles are very much alive at NWL and are continually reviewed in the course of the performance management process. As a part of the annual planning cycle, the executive team review and refine both the measures in the balanced business scorecard and the linkages to the business excellence model. In order to ensure that staff are fully aware of the business objectives, interactive discussions involving all staff are held each year.

The balanced business scorecard details all the key performance indicators for NWL and is used as a way of focusing the company's activities and measuring its achievements. An integral part of the strategy and planning process is to ensure alignment with the key performance indicators. The use of a strategic balanced business scorecard and an operational balanced business scorecard (the latter reflects the key themes of the former and includes more detailed operational measures) ensures a balance among short-, medium-, and long-term objectives.

According to NWL, their approach is not only systematic and integrated, in that it is tested against the vision and guiding principles; it is also tested for completeness against the balanced business scorecard and business excellence model (Figure 6.5). NWL has both an executive committee and a management committee. The former focuses mainly on strategic issues, while the latter is responsible for managing day-to-day operations, as well as ensuring that the KPIs (key performance indicators) in the balanced business scorecard are actually measured and analysed, and that action plans are developed. This work is reviewed in a management committee monthly report. Issues concerning the company's strategy are highlighted here and referred to the executive committee, which in turn ratifies the strategic priorities as being appropriate and in harmony with overall group aims. Once agreed on, the details are published and communicated down the line to all employees.

At NWL communication is considered an extremely valuable tool, provided it is used effectively. According to management, the company has had a strong culture of communication right from the start. For NWL communication is three-dimensional: upwards, downwards, and laterally – peer-to-peer.

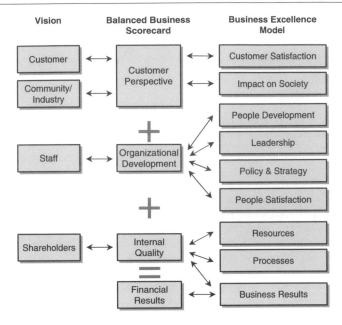

Figure 6.5 NWL's view of the linkages between the vision, the balanced business scorecard and the business excellence model

Upward communication is achieved through various channels, including the individual performance-management reviews, regular team meetings, satisfaction surveys, and "leapfrog sessions" – periodic meetings between different levels of the hierarchy. Information is transmitted downwards through the same channels as well as through an annual staff conference, in-house magazines, monthly team-briefing meetings, and e-mail. The process has been refined in the light of staff comments, which have expressed a preference for one-to-one meetings and team briefings for receiving important information.

At NWL the balanced business scorecard is not the pre-eminent management tool. On the other hand, the company has found that the business excellence model can be perceived as complex by junior staff. Therefore, the different models are used for different purposes. Since the balanced business scorecard is more simple, it is used, for example, to describe and communicate rewards at NWL, whereas management always uses the business excellence model for "hard" action planning.

British Telecom

> "Few companies have re-made themselves so completely as BT plc, the state owned company that was privatised in 1984. Since privatization it has cut costs, shed its slow moving bureaucratic methods and claimed a place as a dominant force in the world-wide telecommunications industry." (*New York Times*)

BT (British Telecom) is one of the world's leading suppliers of fixed and mobile communications services. In the UK, it provides over 27 million customer lines and through a 60% stake in Cellnet, a mobile telecommunications network operator, provides over 3 million mobile connections. Its main services are local, national, and international calls (with direct dialling to over 230 countries worldwide); and supplying telephone lines, equipment and private circuits for homes and businesses. BT considers itself at the forefront of the development and marketing of a comprehensive range of advanced data and interactive multimedia solutions and technologies for the future. It is one of the largest Internet providers in the UK, growing at more than 100% per annum. Multimedia is also growing fast with 10 million e-mails sent each day in the UK.

Its organizational structure comprises three divisions which deal directly with customers – Consumer Division, serving residential customers, Business Division, serving UK business customers, and Global Division, serving multinational business customers – and one large support division, Network & Systems, which operates the network.

BT has undergone substantial change since it was privatized in 1984:

- Turnover has more than doubled, from £6.9bn (1983/4) to £15.6bn (1997/98)
- Pre-tax profits have grown more than three times from £1.0bn to £3.2bn

- The number of employees has nearly halved, from 241 000 to 125 000 during the period.

BT views its transformation since privatization as a testament to its long-term commitment to business excellence. The company is one of the founder members of the EFQM and has been an active user of the business excellence model (cf. Figure 6.3) since its inception. It is the largest company ever to have won an EQA prize, achieving this accolade in 1996 and 1997. In addition, during 1997, two of its divisions won the UK Quality Award outright.

BT's continued success in the fiercely competitive climate of the global telecommunications market is due to a single-minded focus on achieving its vision: "To become the most successful worldwide telecommunications group". This vision is taken as the ultimate objective for BT's strategy, which in the words of its chief executive, Sir Peter Bonfield, is:

> quite simply to seize the opportunities for growth in the communications market worldwide . . . which means growing demand in the UK, moving into new growth markets, such as the rest of Europe, and maintaining our world leading position in serving the needs of multinational companies. Across all these markets we will look to take advantage of the explosive growth in advanced services, such as mobility, data, multimedia and the Internet.

Despite its size and the fast changing technological and competitive climate of the global telecommunications market, BT is held together by its focus on clearly articulated business objectives and by the widespread deployment of truly excellent business processes. To ensure its strategy is communicated, understood, and implemented throughout the company, BT has created a state of the art strategic planning and management system, a system recognised jointly by the American Productivity & Quality Center and the EFQM for its innovation and excellence.

In 1995 BT introduced SPAM (strategic planning and management). SPAM emerged from a business process re-engineering project, called Breakout. In-depth interviews, with senior executives across the business, highlighted the need to improve the

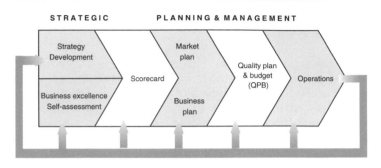

MONITORING

Figure 6.6   Elements of the SPAM system used at BT

linkage between strategy, planning, and budgeting processes (Figure 6.6). They also identified one of the key challenges for strategic planning – to develop and maintain clear linkages between individual, team, and overall business goals. The SPAM process was developed with precisely this challenge in mind.

The scale of the challenge for a company as large as BT is indicated by the range of inputs to the SPAM system – BT group, divisional, and unit specialists in strategy development, feedback from business excellence, balanced scorecards, business planning, market planning, budgeting, and operations. The SPAM system provides the framework to co-ordinate and integrate all the inputs and outputs of the individual sub-processes.

The purpose of the SPAM system is to ensure that the strategy of the company drives objective setting, planning, budgeting, and operational activities throughout the company. Balanced business scorecards emerged as the key element within SPAM, providing the framework for linking strategy to all the other activities. Scorecards are now deployed at corporate, divisional, and unit level, setting priorities in four linked areas: shareholder/financial, customer/key stakeholder, internal processes and organizational learning. These four areas create a "virtuous circle" of improvement: delighting customers helps generate revenue and satisfactory returns for shareholders, increased revenue helps fund investment in processes and learning, better processes and learning help people delight customers.

At an operational level, managers use scorecards as the organizing framework for setting and reviewing unit objectives. Traditionally, the focus would have been predominantly financial, whereas today, a more rounded view of performance is encouraged. By raising the importance of key non-financial measures, scorecards have stimulated a quest for a greater understanding of the underlying drivers, e.g. setting customer satisfaction targets has generated market research to identify the key drivers of customer satisfaction and dissatisfaction. In turn this has led to process improvements. Similar successes have also been achieved following the setting of employee satisfaction targets.

Unit, divisional and corporate scorecards provide the context within which managers set personal and team objectives – a process that encourages the alignment of operational action to corporate goals. Or, put another way, provides the foundation for passing the "elevator test" (if an employee in an elevator tells you one thing, but the management team has a different story, it raises questions about the true purpose of the organization and how this has been communicated).

As mentioned earlier, BT is a founder member of the EFQM and an active user of the business excellence model since its launch. The model is regarded as a powerful diagnostic tool providing a rigorous and structured approach to self-assessment – an assessment based on fact, rather than individual supposition. The model is used widely across the whole company to identify strengths and weaknesses to drive business improvements. When first introduced, it looked at first glance that scorecards and the business excellence model were competing frameworks which led to some confusion as to why BT needed the two approaches. Over time, BT has leveraged considerable benefit from using both approaches and has found considerable synergy. BT regards the business excellence model as an excellent tool for reviewing an entire business. It provides a "look in the rear view mirror" that tells you where you have come from, as well as an excellent assessment of where you are now. The rigour demanded of the model ensures the capture of benchmark data and historic trends for key performance indicators – information used as the base data for setting targets within the scorecard process. The scorecard is forward looking, describing exactly what the company needs to achieve if it is to be successful. The relationship between the two models is illustrated below with each focus area of the scorecard relating to one or more criteria of the EFQM business excellence model:

Shareholder/financial
- Business results

Customer/key stakeholder
- Customer satisfaction
- Impact on society
- People satisfaction

Internal processes
- Processes

Organizational learning
- Leadership
- Policy and strategy
- People management
- Resources

Since 1995 BT has developed a family of scorecards at corporate, divisional, and business unit level. These were created top-down – starting with a corporate scorecard, followed by divisional and finally, unit scorecards. The whole process was managed by a small team, initially comprising of external consultants and key BT people. By shadowing the consultants, the BT people absorbed their tacit knowledge and became skilled practitioners in their own right. This shadowing process was repeated to transfer skills to other groups across the company. From a knowledge management perspective, it was found that a full transfer of skills could not be achieved through academic research and do it yourself type activities alone. Some degree of handholding by expert scorecard practitioners appeared to be essential.

Figure 6.7 illustrates the major stages of the process used to introduce scorecards. For scorecards developed at the corporate and divisional level the main components of the process

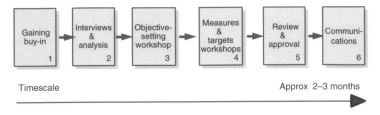

Figure 6.7 Building a scorecard: the full process

remained broadly similar, with individual components being customized to meet the requirements of the directors involved in each situation. Over time a range of fast track options were also developed to enable teams and subunits to create scorecards for themselves. These fast track options ranged from an approach involving a one day workshop to an abridged version of the main scorecard process. By experimenting with the approach used to introduce scorecards, the core team found that they were able to involve many more people and units from right across the company in a "scorecard experience".

Creating scorecards using the full process was found to have major benefits over the "fast track" approaches. Commitment and consensus to the agreed objectives, measures, and targets were found to be much greater. Communication of the scorecard was easier and more effective, because many more people had been involved. Creating and reviewing programmes and plans linked to scorecard targets were also conducted more systematically. The main downside of using a full scorecard process is the time and resource required.

BT has a very long history of performance management. Literally hundreds of measures are tracked across a range of different systems – hardly surprising in view of the size of the organization and the technological nature of its operations. This history meant that many of the measures required to populate the four perspectives of the scorecard already existed within the company. However, the measurement systems for the four perspectives covering customers, processes, financial, and organizational learning had been developed separately and at different times. Each was regarded as a discrete system of measurement, owned by different functional and operational units within the company. Top-level measures for each perspective were reviewed separately with targets often set at different times of the year. Performance against these top-level measures was managed by directors in the operational and functional units. All of this meant that it was difficult for senior executives to gain a holistic perspective of BT's performance and a clear understanding of enablers and results. Following the introduction of scorecards, three benefits have emerged:

- Performance reviews are conducted on a holistic, multi-perspective basis
- Executives focus on a small number of objectives, measures, and targets
- Executives understand the increasing importance of managing non-financial measures of performance particularly in the area of intellectual capital

Currently, within BT, scorecards have become an integral part of the way the company is managed. However, in the spirit of continuous improvement, BT is constantly experimenting and learning to capitalize fully on the benefits it has gained from the introduction of scorecards.

PREVIOUS EXPERIENCE WITH MANAGEMENT BY MULTIPLE OBJECTIVES

Applying measures of the kind used with the balanced-scorecard concept is thus hardly novel. Nor is it anything new to describe the mission of a business in terms of several different objectives, as has been done by companies in many countries, including the Swedish Post Office, which since the 1980s has declared its three objectives to be profitability, satisfied customers, and employees who enjoy their work. At times the profitability objective has been expressed as "adequate profitability", thus implying a discussion on the balance to be sought among all three objectives. Naturally, adequate short-run profitability combined with maximal customer satisfaction may be a way to achieve higher profitability in the long run than if profit maximization had been given immediate priority.

To measure customer satisfaction, the Swedish Post Office attempted in 1989 to develop a Swedish customer barometer, an endeavour which we will describe more closely in Chapter 7. Their model, which was designed by Professor Claes Fornell at the University of Michigan, has now been developed into an American Customer-Satisfaction Index (ACSI) for 190 companies (*Fortune*, 16 February 1998, pp. 83–88). As at many other companies, different tools have been used to measure employee attitudes. Simple measures relating to each of the three objectives have thus been found and used throughout the organization, and paying attention to all three has been a part of management responsibility.

In any business that runs on a timetable, the quality of service may be clearly the most important success factor. For employees in charge of operations, their responsibility emphasizes the finance focus (costs) and the process focus (being on time and other factors weighted according to their presumed effect on customer relations). In this way critical success factors are given visibility and priority. Adding measures for innovation and growth to complete the scorecard should not be difficult.

There are parallels which go back even further. Both German and Anglo-Saxon literature contain numerous examples of *Kennzahlen* and *key ratios* from the 1950s on (see Mossberg, 1977 for references). Their purpose was to provide systematic, concise information for management control. It is emphasized in this literature that the selection of measures was based on experience and hypotheses as to what was important, and that the person receiving the information must be able to understand it well enough to use it. The necessary understanding can be provided primarily in one of three ways:

- As an *alarm* which leads to closer examination
- As a *diagnosis* which may be included in such an examination
- As *accumulation of experience* on what constitutes normal values for the measures, thus furnishing a better basis for taking appropriate action in the future (Mossberg, 1977, pp. 40ff.)

From here it was a short step to the discussion in the 1960s and 1970s on hierarchies of means and ends, with a means at one level being an end at the next. However, it is not always possible or appropriate to reduce cause-and-effect relationships at a company to such a hierarchical model. To be sure, in our model, which we presented in Chapter 3, there is an attempt to do just that, and when successful it has its value in focusing the company's efforts. The cases in this book also include examples in which it was not possible to find measures which could be linked to overall objectives in a simple hierarchy.

Attempts at management by multiple objectives generally lost their momentum in the 1980s, but hardly because of the difficulties mentioned here. Rather, managers were searching for even more simplified ways to represent cause-and-effect relationships at companies: establishing intracompany market relations, with profit centres and company units transformed into subsidiaries. In our opinion, some of the experience of the 1970s should be revisited today.

THE BALANCED-SCORECARD CONCEPT AND OTHER THEORIES OF PLANNING

A logical sequence of vision–success factors–activity plans–measurable goals has been found in many theories of planning. This statement has been true in respect of companies at least since the 1960s, when the business world began to talk about strategic planning and to apply ideas which had been developed by the military long ago.

Several of these theories start with an environmental analysis to identify what customers would like us to offer them; from this analysis they then proceed to draw logical conclusions for our strategy and development. Two features distinguish the balanced-scorecard concept from previous theories of this nature. The first is that the starting-point for the balanced-scorecard concept is the suggestion that the scorecard be designed in a particular way. The four perspectives provide a "user interface" which is easy to understand. This matter may seem trivial, but in practice precisely this kind of compact but carefully prepared presentation of essential measures has proved to be of great value in leading to fruitful discussions about the business.

The second is the emphasis on clear strategic hypotheses about cause-and-effect relationships. As we have stressed a number of times, the perspectives in the lower portion of the scorecard highlight activities of long-term significance. These often concern creating a platform for doing business in the world where we expect to find ourselves tomorrow. It is quite conceivable that this subject will also be discussed when other theories of planning are practised. But these are often based exclusively on today's consumers and their situation. Persistent, persevering efforts to cultivate competencies and to position the business for the world which we believe will be here tomorrow is hard to justify by this kind of reasoning. It calls for the kind of strategic risk-taking which we spoke of in Chapter 2.

THE BALANCED SCORECARD AS A SUBSTITUTE FOR THE BUDGET

At least at conferences, the balanced-scorecard concept has sometimes been presented in recent years as a substitute for budgeting, which has been described as a rigid, antiquated, and bureaucratic form of management control. There may be something to this view if budgeting is considered as making ironclad decisions far in advance on spending limits for various accounts. However, modern budgeting may be designed in another way. As early as 1973, theoreticians in the field described budgeting as a programme for action based on explicit premises and assumptions expressed in financial terms, though not necessarily in monetary amounts. Just because we should stay flexible and keep our options open in the changing world around us does not mean that we can do without any form of programme for action. But perhaps a balanced scorecard may be an appropriate form for a budget?

For many people, the word "budget" is also more closely related to specific accounts and implies more inflexibility than the definition which we mentioned in the previous paragraph. They would prefer to avoid the word altogether in favour of business plans or the like. Of course the choice of words does not matter very much. What matters is to identify the areas where a company needs to make decisions and plans in advance of what should be done. In Chapter 2 we argued that decisions of this kind are required for a number of activities relating to a company's competencies and customer base. These activities are often better described in non-monetary terms, but they also have a cost in money and other resources. Some form of plan or budget is needed.

Critics of budgeting also tend to emphasize the risk that preparing a budget once a year will become a mere routine. Of course other intervals may be better suited to the natural rhythm of a business, and in some cases changes in the business environment may call for planning as needed rather than by the calendar. For the balanced-scorecard concept, too, a decision must be made on how often the process is to take place; Kaplan & Norton, for example, recommend an annual cycle similar to that of a budget. We believe that few companies are capable of thoroughly reviewing their business strategy more often than once a year, and that few can get by with doing it less often. However, these are practical matters which each company can best decide for itself.

If we choose to regard the balanced scorecard and intellectual capital as "supplements" to the income statements and balance sheets of financial accounting, we can draw the illustration shown in Figure 6.8. The arrows indicate how some of the costs which we see in the income statement are usually incurred to cultivate the company's processes and stock of customers, in the hope of increasing the value of the company's "intangible" or "intellectual" capital, with a favourable impact in the long run on revenue and profits.

In Figure 6.8 we have played with the image of a body of water. Conventional accounting shows what is visible above the surface. The balanced scorecard and intellectual capital are both attempts to capture some of what is concealed beneath.

In practice the balanced scorecards of companies often include certain measures of their intellectual capital in addition to measures of performance. Thus, the balanced scorecard becomes a balance sheet as well as an income statement. Assets would include market shares, the current situation with regard to competence, the stock of products under development, and other items, rather than

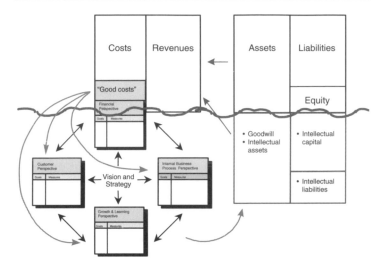

Figure 6.8 The balanced scorecard and conventional accounting

just changes during the period of measurement. Still, the perspective of the illustration is important. Traditional financial statements leave a gap. Expenditures to prepare for the future – R&D, training, purchases of programmes – are reported as costs. A few years later, if we are lucky, the actions taken will have a favourable effect on our income statement. Until then, they are not reported. There is thus a danger that significant assets will not be treated with the respect and care which they need and deserve.

These expenditures – provided we can agree that they have given the company assets of long-term value – should be reported as investments rather than costs. In Chapter 10 we will address the question of whether this practice should extend to the financial statements. We may choose to treat them as investments for the purposes of management control, even if we do not report them as assets in our financial statements. However, many companies are unwilling to change established practices. One reason is a desire for consistency between financial and managerial accounting principles. Another may be a belief that cost control will be jeopardized if we allow ourselves to report as assets what we spend

on capital which is usually immaterial, intangible, and – to use the
concept which we discussed in Chapter 2 – intellectual in nature.

These objections are not necessarily valid. If we report intellectual capital as an asset, we should of course keep track of it in
subsequent years, examine its effects, and hold people accountable
for how it is managed. Reformed *monetary* measures will then be
our primary instrument for improving control of the company's
preparations for the future. If we are unwilling to go this far, we
should at least try to treat these outlays separately as a kind of
"good costs", unlike costs of operation, which we should always
strive to reduce and avoid. Effective use of resources is obviously
also important in the case of good costs. But we should resist the
temptation to eliminate them for the sake of improving short-run
profits. Instead, we should try to show what we get for our money
by linking different cost components to their effects in the customer, process, and development perspectives. This is our purpose
with the arrows in Figure 6.8.

Volvo Car Corporation

The entire Volvo corporate group has undergone major change
since plans for the merger with Renault were cancelled in 1993.
Considerable time and resources have been devoted above all
to formulating visions and strategies for the various subsidiaries
of the Volvo Group. At the outset of 1995, Volvo Car Corporation
(VCC) presented its new vision: "To be the World's most
Desired and Successful Specialty Car Brand". Based on the
vision detailed strategies were formulated for each and every
part of the company. By means of activity-based business plans
these strategies are implemented throughout the organization.

During the process of strategy formulation, corporate management realized that the Volvo Group's budgeting and planning
system could not provide reliable forecasts. The system of
management control did not take proper account of the technology, products, and processes which Volvo needed to be a
competitive actor on the market. The company required a flexible instrument of management control which could simulate
scenarios and permit rapid response to changes in the business

environment. These considerations led to the introduction of what was called "the new planning process".

The new planning process is one of reporting and control in which the company prepares both *long-term* and *short-term* forecasts at least four times a year, while at the same time *focusing on objectives* and *current planning* of operations. The new planning process de-emphasized budgeting, even going so far as to pass on the message "no budget requested". According to management, budgeting had become a formalistic process, an annual ritual which impeded effective control of the business.

With the new planning process, Volvo wanted to change the focus from details to objectives. Volvo believes that decisions should be made as close to the customer as possible. This kind of delegation calls for a system of management control which provides early warning signals; as soon as reality begins to deviate from expectations, pro-active decisions should be taken to reorient the company towards established objectives.

Management control at VCC is to be exercised by measuring the various units according to performance indicators which are presented graphically on scorecards (Figure 6.9). Performance indicators should be relevant and easy to measure, and they should consist of monetary or non-monetary parameters. Further, they should be directly or indirectly linked either to financial performance or to capital employed, both short term and long term.

Objectives are set for each performance indicator. The objective-setting process should begin with a clear definition of the desired position of the unit; often this step has already been completed in the business-development and strategy-formulation process. The next step is to define the success factors which will drive the unit towards the desired position. The critical success factors are then translated into measurable objectives. It should be possible to effect achievement of the objectives, to understand them easily, to decompose them into subsidiary objectives, and to adapt them to different organizational levels. A deadline date should be set for achieving each objective, and it should be practicable to forecast progress towards objectives in the short and/or long run.

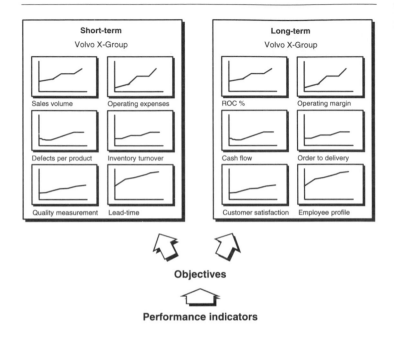

Figure 6.9 Graphic presentation of short-term and long-term performance indicators

Forecasts are made for each quarter, with short-term forecasts broken down by month for the current and subsequent year. Long-term forecasts are to be prepared for the coming two years. A total of five years, including two historical years, are thus in focus. In this way Volvo management can be alerted to trends and take pro-active decisions. During the course of the year, performance is monitored on an ongoing basis, and forecasts, control, and the future trend are discussed continually for each performance indicator.

The trend in the different measures is then presented in a number of documents:

- Business Plan – the Business Plan covers a four-year period and is updated twice a year. Trends in measures are presented and analysed once or twice a year. Most of the measures in this report are non-financial.

- VCC Performance Report – focuses on the business itself. The VCC Performance Report covers a two-year period and is updated 11 times a year. Trends in measures are presented and analysed each month. The measures in this report are largely financial, and trends are shown in the form of graphs and tables.
- Project Catalogue – shows the progress of decided and ongoing projects. The Project Catalogue is updated six times a year.

In addition to the above-mentioned documents, more or less standardized material, a document called the "Business Situation Package" is presented to management each month. Here an attempt is made to summarize the company's situation in the form of five financial measures and five "bullet" points, issues which management has chosen to emphasize because of the importance of related trends or future activities. In this way Volvo seeks to achieve a balance between financial and non-financial measures, but also between the short and long run.

The VCC Performance Report consists of reports submitted by the various units at VCC. Each unit is monitored on the basis of performance indicators on scorecards (indicators that have been determined in advance by the VCC controller). Together with the scorecards, comments are provided on trends, discrepancies, and noteworthy events; for any discrepancy, an action plan is also presented. This reporting is done not only in writing but also orally at monthly follow-up meetings with either the CEO or the CFO, one of whom calls the meeting. From the VCC Performance Report a number of performance indicators are reported to the management of Volvo Group, i.e. profit, customer satisfaction, quality, costs, and operating capital.

By continually measuring actual performance against the forecast, the company can always be sure that there are action plans to achieve established objectives. According to Volvo, this feature constitutes the principal difference between performance reporting and annual budgeting. There is, however, an extended objective setting process where it is important to note that short- and long-term objectives always remain fixed, whereas forecasts are modified continually as the situation changes. Thus, it is also possible to see how well remedial action plans are working.

According to Volvo, the VCC Performance Report is to be considered as an instrument of management rather than control. By measuring performance indicators as presented in scorecards, management obtains factual documentation which permits follow-up through remedial action programmes. Throughout, the individual manager can see what is actually being done in relation to what should be done, which in practice is what management is all about.

The aim of the VCC Performance Report is to provide a comprehensive view of the current status of VCC to the reader who can spare only 15 minutes of his/her time. The remaining pages of the document are for persons seeking a more complete picture of the company.

The picture of VCC which we have provided is based on talks with its management. At the local level, changes in the system of management control may of course be viewed differently. Some units decided to use existing measures of quality within the new planning system, and consequently in some places the difference may not be very great. Even if the message "no budget requested" is sent out, a local unit may still feel a need to budget in order to develop standard costs, for example. But there is a major difference in that the budget is then limited to that particular level, whereas scorecard thinking increasingly characterizes interaction on the divisional and corporate levels.

An important question is to what degree a corporate group should and can interest itself in scorecard presentations of its various businesses. A conglomerate group may find it natural to regard subsidiaries as financial investments and to be interested only in the return which they yield. On the other hand, if a search for synergy is part of corporate strategy, management would more naturally want to see a number of other measures and could also contribute to the discussion on future strategy. This consideration should of course affect not only the choice of measures but the entire system of management control.[2] But even the management of a conglomerate may find that measures other than financial ones have a value in providing earlier signals which may relate to future profits, thus perhaps enabling parts of the group to avoid overemphasizing the short run.

USING THE SCORECARD VERTICALLY OR HORIZONTALLY

Budgets are generally based on a vertical view of the business: budgets are submitted for approval by units higher up in the hierarchy. As an addition to conventional financial statements, the scorecard then becomes a kind of supplementary request from the business unit to senior managers to authorize funds for activities to develop intellectual capital.

By contrast, ABB has presented its balanced-scorecard model, EVITA, as part of a *horizontal* approach to the management process, in which units find the appropriate design for what they do in consultation with others involved in the same flows of value creation.

While there are arguments in favour of both approaches, they probably result in somewhat different scorecards. In many organizations, the vertical, more budget-like process serves to dimension and focus the business for the somewhat longer term. Profit requirements must be reconciled with the amount of "good costs" which may (should!) be devoted to cultivating the strengths needed for the business of the future. Moreover, this kind of decision will always be needed on such matters as the location of a business, the number of stores or offices, etc.

The horizontal approach has other purposes. Along the flow of value creation, it is important to agree on matters like the level of ambition for customer service, to co-ordinate the time spent on various processes, to develop competencies demanded by users within the company, etc. Here a shorter time frame is more likely to prevail.

Sometimes the horizontal perspective may extend to include other companies. We believe that the scorecard may serve as a good way to create a set of shared goals together with suppliers, for example. It may also provide an incentive for closer co-operation

– to guide collaboration towards the development of an imaginary organization.

We have not yet found any company which has fully resolved this balance between vertical and horizontal. What we see here is the fundamental problem of the matrix organization. However, it would appear urgent to seek the right balance and to adapt the scorecard and process to the actual importance of each dimension.

A good place to start is by asking what we would like to show with a scorecard for the unit. When there is a danger that traditional performance and budgetary measures, with their more narrow, short-term focus, will lead a company astray, they should be supplemented by a scorecard. Let us assume that a unit must meet requirements imposed by the hierarchy (vertically) and also by the process (horizontally). We have encountered such situations in an engineering products group, where a producer of semi-manufactures sends its products on to other group companies, and where time and quality affect the reaction of a remote final customer. But we have also seen them at the baggage service of an airport, where a traveller's overall impression depends on a long sequence of events at departure or on arrival. (The latter case is one where legally separate companies can be active in the same process.)

The principal reasons for having a scorecard in such a situation are:

1. Contributing (horizontally) to the success of others in the organization. Meeting time and quality goals is often hard to reconcile with the financial goals of one's own unit. Even sophisticated systems with rewards and penalties often lead to suboptimization which is harmful to the overall interest. The ambition should be to create a common focus on the success of the *entire* process and to direct it all along the flow of value creation. The scorecard could include measures of success for the entire flow. Responsibility for horizontal performance is then a complement to vertical profit goals, or even a substitute for them.

2. Investments in the future which are not reported as investments in the financial statements (primarily vertical). To succeed in its business, the unit must take proper care of its

competence, its physical assets, and its structural capital. Expenditures for this purpose are the "good costs" of which we have spoken earlier. This kind of long-term asset cultivation is a matter of interest to owners, and it should primarily call for the use of supplementary measures in conventional management control by hierarchy.

3. Collateral effects of current operations on customer attitudes, data bases, etc. (both horizontal and vertical). It is important that all employees take the time to document what they have learned, submit suggestions for improvement, correct mistakes made earlier in the flow, make customers happy, contribute to a good work atmosphere, etc. In this way beneficial effects are created in addition to the basic product or service. Measures of performance are often too imprecise to show these benefits. On the other hand, if the same areas are neglected, the damage will in time become apparent.

These three kinds of collateral effects from the activities of an operating unit show that scorecard measures in a matrix-like situation may send information both upwards (vertically) in the hierarchy and outwards (horizontally) along the flow of value creation. Process measures, including certain measures of quality in the eyes of the customer, relate primarily to horizontal co-operation along the flow. Financial measures, but also certain measures of competence and structure, relate mostly to vertical accountability. The dichotomy corresponds to the dualism found at many companies between a vertical dimension – "producing and cultivating resources" – and a horizontal one – "utilizing resources and delivering what is required". The scorecard should encourage us in our striving to find a balance between the two.

SCORECARDS AS A GENERAL CONCEPT IN MANAGEMENT CONTROL

We have emphasized how scorecards function as a language: a concise way to describe the mission of a business and how well it is succeeding. The process which we presented in Chapter 3 was about the development and use of the company's own "dialect".

This shared language, or dialect, is a vehicle for developing a shared view of the proper strategy for the business. On the basis of this view, missions are defined for the different units, in theory all the way down to the individual level. This process raises many questions relating to costs, profitability, and long-term profile, thus justifying our previous comparison with the budget. The process should relate to and summarize a number of tools and methods already used by most companies for management control.

When we began working with scorecards at a number of companies, we often found that a number of projects on the workflow approach, new types of control, etc. were already under way. The question was how to relate the balanced scorecard to these projects. We sometimes encounter distrust of three-letter abbreviations where TQM, BPR, ABC, etc. have already been tried. We then have to explain how scorecards can work as a general concept in management control.

For this purpose it is helpful to see how the various parts of the system of management control interact:

- Mapping out flows and activities (*process orientation*) is a natural starting-point for our search to find where to take measurements and for our attempts to describe the business.
- ABC (*activity-based costing*) identifies the cost of what is done and the "cost drivers", or underlying cause-and-effect relationships.
- *Capital-budgeting procedures* are important for managing the trade-offs between the present and the future. Our ambition should be to capture all consequences of a proposed investment for future cash flows. Many companies, therefore, also study the effects on indirect costs, like consulting fees, and on their own working time when new equipment is installed. However, we still commonly find that "intangible investments" not involving any obvious physical assets are not subjected to a capital-budgeting review.
- Certain indirect costs are difficult to relate to today's products and customers. Much staff work falls into this category. The traditional procedure for dimensioning these items is the budget process. While the aim of ABC is also to identify the drivers for this kind of indirect costs, there is always a

remainder which must be controlled through the budget. This item is sometimes referred to as *discretionary spending*.

- Responsibility accounting and control of costs and cash flow require prompt reporting, preferably supplemented by certain scorecard measures. There is a widespread tendency to transform financial reporting so that it emphasizes *forecasts*, continually updated accounting, and early warnings, rather than the rigid adherence to the budget period and the detailed accounting for discrepancies traditionally found in budget follow-up.

Several large companies are now studying how to implement a process approach to their business while at the same time obtaining a better picture of cost drivers. Some attempt to co-ordinate process-mapping with a study of cost drivers according to an ABC model on a corporate-wide scale.[3]

We have previously described how many companies today spend substantial resources on cultivating their capacity to meet the challenges of the future. One consequence, in our opinion, will be that when these companies review their business processes and use ABC to link them to resource consumption, they will be unable to find any meaningful connection between a large portion of their activities and costs, on the one hand, and *today's* products and customers, on the other. A major part of current costs are more like investments in future capacity to act or in short-term profile creation: "good" costs. In other words, they concern what we have previously designated as important areas for a scorecard. To make appropriate decisions here, a company must discuss how it wishes to dimension various urgently needed endeavours and to decide on the trade-offs among them. In our opinion, the score-card is a good form for describing these matters: what has been accomplished, and what has it cost? An investment perspective is needed both when these endeavours are decided on and when they are evaluated – are the long-term benefits which we expected worth the short-term sacrifice?

Kaplan & Cooper (1998, pp. 311–312) appear to view this inter-action in similar fashion, though they do not develop it further. They note how activity-based budgeting works best for activities "triggered by demands from products, services and customers. In addition . . . the budgeting team must also estimate the quantity of discretionary spending for the upcoming year. This spending will typically represent elements of product- and customer-sustaining expenses, plus spending at higher hierarchical levels." They also mention how the balanced scorecard can serve as a framework for setting priorities and identifying the processes which are most critical to strategic success (Kaplan & Cooper, 1998, p. 155).

This task is of course a delicate one. Both process-mapping and ABC projects may be seen partly as efforts to improve efficiency. Let us assume that in reviewing the activities and costs involved in a business, or an entire company, we find that a substantial portion of costs are not immediately justifiable for sustaining products or customers. Those in charge of the business concerned claim that these costs should be treated as investments in the future, intended to develop the company's intellectual capital. It can even be shown with various measures on the scorecard that these investments are paying off in terms, for example, of customer awareness of the company, the product range, delivery times, data bases. What does management then do when short-run profit targets must also be met?

There are several answers to this question:

- If management is convinced that these investments are reasonable and will pay off, it will be important to find financing for them by convincing owners and the capital market to share this view. IT is one industry where we find examples of companies that have been able to raise capital despite several years of continuous losses. At least within the company it should be possible to use the scorecard to describe what management would like to achieve and to determine whether it is worth the cost.
- If management is not fully convinced, or is unable to convince the shareholders, it will have to set priorities (find a balance) among different ambitions. Here it will prove valuable to have used process studies and ABC to identify the costs of different investments for the future. It should be possible to link these costs to the scorecard measures which they affect. In this way an appropriate level of ambition can be set and later followed up.

- It is conceivable that this kind of review will show that certain investments are not well co-ordinated, fall short of achieving critical mass, require actions to be taken in other parts of the organization, etc. In this case alleged "good costs" may turn out to be a meaningless waste of resources. The balanced-scorecard approach enables management to review this kind of "discretionary spending" and to give it greater focus, thereby keeping it within the limits of available resources.

Similar reasoning also applies to the discussions between the management of business units and their superiors at the corporate level.

We therefore offer the following prescription for co-ordinating the different aspects of management control:

- *Process-mapping.* We first need an analysis of the business. It may be possible to use descriptions already on hand; otherwise a brief, clear overview of flows and activities can usually be prepared quite quickly. The description is supplemented by a rough picture of cost allocation or resources used by different activities, and of the cost drivers. Increasingly often, this information will have been provided by previous ABC projects.
- *Business plan and budget.* Budgeting or business planning, usually on an annual basis, includes a discussion of the possibilities of improving efficiency or cutting the costs driven by products and customers. Of course, consideration should be given to collateral effects, for instance in terms of customer satisfaction or self-teaching, which as previously noted are important to show in scorecards. But the principal role of the balanced scorecard in this context is to describe investments in tangible and intangible assets, and the intended effects of these investments. This part of the process also includes dimensioning various physical assets and the resources to be spent on them. A fairly thorough review of what has been accomplished and of ambitions for the future should be made at least once a year.
- *Reporting during the current year.* During the year it is important to maintain a good grip on costs and efficiency. This

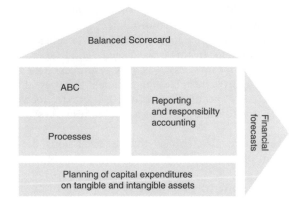

Figure 6.10   The building blocks of management control

purpose will be accomplished if there are clear lines of responsibility and prompt activity- and flow-related reporting. The
extent to which the measures in the scorecard will be involved
will depend on how often it is practically possible to take the
necessary measurements and how important it is considered to
keep watch on changes. As we mentioned above, this follow-
up may concern both the vertical and the horizontal
responsibility of a unit.

● *Continuously updated forecasts.* In order to anticipate financial
flows, foreign-exchange positions, financing, etc., the company
may often need a system of continuously updated forecasts.
Some companies have begun to prepare such forecasts more or
less separately from their business planning and responsibility
accounting. The purpose is to avoid tactical manœvring and to
obtain assessments which are as impartial as possible. The use
of scorecards may reinforce tendencies to separate these
functions.

The foregoing discussion may be summarized in Figure 6.10.

A critical question for the effectiveness of management control is
whether its different elements fit together in a well-functioning
overall system. In Chapter 9 we will return to how the system of

incentives can be linked to the measures used in the scorecard. In Figure 6.10, we attempt to illustrate how the financial forecasts required for planning cash flow and foreign-exchange positions can lead us in a different direction from the measures on the scorecard. In such cases it is important that the system of incentives and rewards encourage giving priority to the intentions expressed in the scorecard. The latter should of course take account of cash flow, but primarily as a restriction on the development of the company.

TO SUM UP . . .

The balanced-scorecard concept is an attractive one – but not entirely easy to apply in practice. Here are some thoughts on how it should be used:

- The strategic resources which we are discussing are affected by many employees of a company. A cardinal feature of the balanced-scorecard concept is that it permits comparison of different ideas on the nature of the business which we should be in. If management already knows best, then the balanced scorecard is a way to help many others to understand *why* important things are important. But management does not always know best.
- Once the scorecard has been created, the challenge is to use it for management control. Goals must be set, and follow-up must be provided for. Now we have to prove what we have been claiming. It is not enough simply to say that all measures are important. For the sake of balance we have to establish *how* important each one is. We are not talking about a permanent trade-off or weighting – management control would then be reduced to simple policies or to some form of success index. But top management must be prepared, for example, to indicate how much may be invested in competence development or in marketing to new customers, assuming of course that the "investment proposals" presented by those in immediate charge of the business are accepted. Budgeting with the balanced-scorecard concept will have certain features of a capital

expenditure review. Here, however, "intangible" investments throughout the company will be proposed and discussed: process improvements, customer-sustaining activities, competence development.

- Just because we call the idea the balanced-scorecard concept does not mean that it has suddenly become easier to find measures to describe every important aspect of a business. Usually, the only easy thing is to find *too many* measures – which still do not provide a complete picture. Here it is important to let well enough alone. The measures used should correspond reasonably well to what is considered to be of potential strategic importance. The fact that certain measures tend to be inadequate indicators does not matter so much. Remember to consider measures in the light of what we have just said: as a description of the business which should enable us to discuss it. This statement is just as applicable to goal-setting as it is to performance evaluation. The use of several measures will hopefully help us to avoid the danger of window-dressing: that is, of deliberately confining our efforts to being successful at what is measured.

NOTES

1. For further discussion on policy deployment and the Blue Book, see the section on Xerox at the end of Chapter 5.
2. This line of thinking is developed in detail by Nilsson & Rapp (1998).
3. For example ABB. This work commenced in the autumn of 1997 and is based on a programme supplied by the Swedish company ProDacapo. A similar procedure is described by Kaplan & Cooper (1998).

7

Measures and their Causal Relations

In this chapter we will examine measures which may be of interest for each of our perspectives, or areas of focus. We have already discussed measures in Chapter 5; for example, as when customer satisfaction is based on answers to a number of different questions on attitudes, addressed to many different people. Key numbers often relate different measures to each other in a way which conveys a comparison, for instance with last year's numbers, or a measure of cost-efficiency. In Chapter 6 we touched on indices of this kind when we compared the balanced scorecard with TQM and other measures of quality. Now we will examine more closely how measures are interrelated, a question which we must consider in our choice of measures or initial selection of possible measures.

This chapter is based on a number of criteria which we have found useful in determining what measures to use:

- Measures should be unambiguous and defined uniformly throughout the company.
- Taken together, the measures used should sufficiently cover the aspects of the business which are included in strategies and critical success factors.
- The measures used in the different perspectives should be clearly connected. A scorecard may be said to portray the business as it is, or as we would like it to be. The picture should be interpreted as a coherent and convincing report which clearly shows how the efforts described in the lower

portion of the card are logically justifiable for successfully attaining the criteria in the upper portion.
- Measures should be useful for setting goals which are considered realistic by those responsible for achieving them.
- Measurement must be an easy, uncomplicated process, and it must be possible to use the measurements in different systems like the company's intranet and data warehouse, for example.

We will further develop this last point in Chapter 8. The previous points will be discussed throughout the present chapter.

PERFORMANCE DRIVERS AND OUTCOME MEASURES

It is often emphasized that we should seek a proper balance between performance drivers and outcome measures – in other words, between measures which describe what we do and the effects achieved. We introduced this idea in Chapter 1 – cf. Figure 1.1. Strictly speaking, drivers and outcomes form a chain in which lower-level outcomes may be the drivers of higher-level results. Such chains of cause and effect may be very difficult to identify, one reason being that external variables often affect actual outcomes. But underlying every goal-directed action is some conception of cause-and-effect relationships.

It may at first seem preferable to be able to measure outcomes rather than performance or its drivers. But the scorecard should often aid us in discussing how today's actions can help set the stage for tomorrow. It may then be difficult to wait for the outcome. We may also want to reward employees now for their performance, e.g. for marketing campaigns which have made customers more aware of our company but have not yet led to increased sales, provided we are sufficiently convinced that the desired effects will ultimately result. Another reason may be that management assumes the risk of running a marketing campaign, whereas the staff who actually conduct the campaign may be considered to have done a good job even if the expected increase in sales – because of changes in technology or the state of the economy – fails in the end to materialize.

Therefore, the scorecard should probably contain an appropriate number of drivers. It may also prove easier to agree on drivers, since these have to do with something immediate and tangible. The mix of drivers and outcomes should probably vary among the different perspectives. In general, the more long-term perspectives, particularly the growth and learning perspective, are likely to include more drivers.

MEASURES FOR THE DIFFERENT PERSPECTIVES

We have mentioned that in each perspective there are a number of ways in which measures should "cover" the relevant success factors. For example, to the extent desired they should show how we see ourselves and how others see us, permit comparisons over time and with others, be linked together in a cause-and-effect relationship, and be appropriate for describing both stocks and flows. Often we want measures which themselves involve comparison, such as percentages, ratios, and rankings. Beyond this point, however, it is difficult to recommend measures. To a large degree, the situation and the strategy will determine which measures are "good". In addition, there will be more support in the organization for measures which have emerged through a process rather than adopted because recommended by experts.

Nevertheless, in the following sections we will consider possible and recommended measures in each perspective. To begin with, the same measures can be useful in describing different perspectives (areas of focus). This point is illustrated in a number of the examples provided by Kaplan & Norton (1996a):

- Measures suggested for the financial perspective include market shares for certain customer groups and capacity utilization for physical facilities – although these are measures which we may find more often in the customer or business-process perspective.
- The profitability of various customer segments is one of the measures suggested for the customer perspective – but these may of course be useful also as part of the financial perspective.

- Among possible measures suggested for the business-process perspective is the share of sales provided by new products – we have encountered this measure more frequently in the development perspective, but here it is described as a measure of the innovation process in a company where this factor is critical.
- Competence and process-improvement time (how long it takes to reduce costs, rejects, etc. by one-half) are mentioned as measures for the learning and growth perspective – we might expect to find them more often in the business-process perspective.

These examples show that discussing cause-and-effect relationships is very important. Competencies and capability of improving are factors with longer-term effects than the share of new products, which in turn is an indicator of the outlook for future profits. Such reasoning justifies the choice of perspective for these measures. To agree on cause-and-effect relationships, preferably as shown in simple graphs, is of course quite valuable, and we have emphasized above how they can be used for simulation purposes. We have not encountered any formal simulation of scorecards at the companies which we have studied, but informal cause-and-effect reasoning does of course exist, and it may develop into simulation when they gain more experience in working with scorecards. The same comment applies to breaking measures down for use at lower levels of the organization, for example by work teams. Lower-level scorecards are rarely linked in a formal, mathematical sense to higher-level ones. But of course there is an attempt to make the existing links logically persuasive. Here we may be talking about extremely specific objectives; for example, employees should try different kinds of work in order to develop their competence, certain data bases are to be built up, etc. Thus, ideally measures like these should also be linked in a clear cause-and-effect relationship to measures at an overall level.

When relationships among measures are made clear and are discussed by many people, a basis for learning is also created. It may be possible to establish mathematically the strength of the relationships and the length of time it will take before the effects become apparent. For example, studies may reveal that satisfied customers pay their bills more promptly. In that case, treating customers well will prove directly profitable even in the short run, while perhaps also raising hopes of new business in the long run.

At the end of the book there is a list of measures used in the different perspectives. At this point we will discuss the fundamental aspects of the measures used in each.

MEASURES FOR THE FINANCIAL PERSPECTIVE

The scorecards which we have seen use customary measures of profit/loss, return on investment, and the like. These are monetary measures, or measures derived from monetary ones. In the literature measures such as revenue per employee or profitability of different customer groups are included in this category, whereas we have sometimes seen related metrics in an employee or customer focus, for example. This classification is reasonable – the measures represent an understandable extension of classical measures of profitability; both measure something which has already occurred. However, we can also consider them as good indicators of success factors for customer relationships and business processes, so that they would also be appropriate in other areas of focus.

Financial measures need not always be taken from the company's regular accounting system. In the scorecard of a company listed on the stock exchange, the market value or price per share of the company's stock may be an important measure of success. If we can determine the value of the intellectual capital (see Chapter 2) of the company or business unit, the observed market value of this capital, and the changes in its value, are of course appropriate measures.

One step in this direction is to apply different rules for period costs and revenues in managerial accounting than in financial accounting. In Figure 6.4 we used the term "good costs" for indirect costs relating to development of competence and software, for example; actually, these costs should be considered investments.[1] It is of course fully permissible to follow managerial accounting principles which differ in this manner from the company's financial accounting, although many executives would like to keep such differences to a minimum. "Good-cost" investments are made with the expectation that they will yield benefits for a number of years into the future. If they are reported as depreciable assets, we will have a fairer picture of the business. Giving these assets such visibility also has a positive influence on the people who are to manage them. The drawbacks relate to the fact that the resulting measures of profit/loss will not agree with the income statement, but it should be possible to explain this discrepancy.

This point has been the subject of much discussion in recent years, particularly since certain American studies have found a better correlation between a company's profits and the market price of its stock when reported profits are adjusted by treating development outlays as investments rather than costs. The method for this kind of adjustment which has attracted the greatest interest is called EVA (economic value added) (Stewart, 1991). It has also been presented as a recipe for managing companies – if all managers must keep an eye on their contribution to the company's EVA, they will act in the best interests of the owners; for example, they will make investments in development which they might have avoided had they concentrated excessively on reported profits.

Advocates of EVA are not overly enthusiastic about the idea of a scorecard. If a financial measure can be used to reflect efforts to develop a company's future capability, it can then be maintained, of course, that other measures of these efforts are unnecessary. EVA proponents would like to award a bonus based on this kind of adjusted financial measure, in theory down to the lowest level of the company – a suggestion hardly consistent with using other measures to exercise control and perhaps also as a standard of reward-worthy success.

The relevant question may instead relate to the appropriate levels for using financial and other measures, respectively. We have found that the more concrete description provided by the scorecard is appreciated at the operating level, where a translation to even the most accurate of financial measures may appear abstract and mystical. At the top level of the company, the financial focus may predominate; many aspects of the business may be difficult to compare in any other way, and in view of the responsibility of top management towards the owners and the market, it may be natural to use financial measures. The more management can improve the accuracy of financial measures as a reflection of future competitive conditions, perhaps the further down in the organization it may be appropriate to change to the multi-measure approach of the scorecard. However, we ourselves are convinced that EVA (and similar measures) can be used within the framework of the scorecard to ensure that its financial portion provides appropriate measurements. Therefore, we would encourage companies to consider including in the financial focus other measures than those taken directly from the financial statements.

Sometimes we may want to give the financial focus an enlarged role as an ownership perspective on the business, since the expectations of owners may be more than just financial. This statement applies particularly to the public sector, to which we will return in Chapter 11. Trade associations and parts of corporate groups, for instance, may also be subject to owner expectations of this kind. An example might be building up to "critical mass" in a new business area or in a country where a company had not previously done business. In the case of a scorecard describing an entity whose owners expect it to produce other benefits than purely financial ones, our view is that it makes sense to include measures of its success in an enlarged "financial/owner focus". The alternative would be to regard the owners as customers, for whom these benefits are produced, and who are willing to provide the necessary financing. Our experience, however, is that broadening the financial focus to include the total impact on the owners is quite useful, and easily understood.

MEASURES FOR THE CUSTOMER PERSPECTIVE

For many companies, measures relating to customers are selected from those which are already available but have been developed for other purposes. Often a company will have already engaged a firm specializing in measuring customer attitudes and the like. Here it is also relevant to consider what we stated in Chapter 5: that the customer perspective could also be construed as a customer focus, so that we would provide measures both of how customers view us and of how we view our customers; that we could measure both flows and stocks – for instance, both how customer perceptions have been affected during the last period and what our ratings currently are; and that both attitudes and behaviour may be equally important to us.

Thus, the measures used may vary depending on whether we are asking ourselves Kaplan & Norton's original question, "How do customers see us?" (the customer's perspective), or "How do we see our customers?" (focus on customers). We find out how customers see us through their behaviour (e.g. complaints, repurchase frequency) and through attitude surveys. Our picture of the customer should also include our share of his/her total purchases, market shares in important segments, etc.

NatWest Life

The products that NatWest Life (NWL) markets (life assurance, pensions, and longer-term investments) are all supposed to provide value over a long period of time. Therefore, the customer relationship, and measuring it, becomes even more important.

At NWL various methods are used to monitor customer perceptions of products, service, and relationships. Examples are satisfaction surveys, transaction-based feedback cards, customer focus groups, and surveys of sales force satisfaction, non-buyers, policy cancellers and competitors' customers.

NWL has done some experimentation with transaction-based feedback cards, which provide a continuous flow of information between regular surveys. In the beginning NWL started off with small cards which were slipped in with documentation, the response rate was a modest 9%. Today NWL uses coloured A4 sheets, and the response rate has risen to 23%.

The results from all sources are analysed, and improvement tables are compiled; every trend and comment is logged, numbered, and allocated to an individual who is to take appropriate further action. For NWL there is little doubt that this approach produces results. The philosophy at NWL is that every item of feedback represents an improvement opportunity.

Electrolux

Unlike other companies, Electrolux does not know the identity of its final consumers. Also in the future the company must continue to rely on the willingness of its consumers to make voluntary registration with Electrolux of their ownership, providing comments and other information. There may be legal difficulties if consumers are not registered at the time of purchase. By experience only 10–15% of the consumers reply to questionnaires, and this sample is not representative of the average. Therefore, telephone interviews are needed to supplement this information.

Since the industry in which Electrolux operates may be categorized as in-between consumer and capital goods, it is particularly difficult to conduct customer surveys. The management of various business areas has begun to consider these problems which, however, do not concern certain areas such as forest and garden products, with its specific customer group consisting mostly of professional buyers. These customers are generally quite interested in influencing product quality.

Xerox

Xerox has had a corporate-wide objective of 100% satisfied customers. The present figure is around 98%. Since the same approach is used throughout Xerox, it is possible to "benchmark" the various parts of the corporation by comparing them with each other. In this way it can be found that companies with a high degree of customer loyalty also have a large proportion of satisfied customers. The category of "satisfied customers", however, comprises both "very satisfied customers" and merely "satisfied customers". Last year half of the 98% were very satisfied, and the target for this year is to increase the proportion of very satisfied customers to 70%.

MEASURES FOR THE BUSINESS-PROCESS PERSPECTIVE

The measures which concern us here are taken mostly from TQM and similar projects, as mentioned in Chapter 6. Examples would be throughput times, quality of production, and rejects. If we want to describe particular processes, there are many kinds of measures which we might use. Here are some examples:

- Productivity, usually measured as quantity in relation to time worked or to cost
- Quality, either the percentage of acceptable units or the opinion of some user (attitude questions, or complaints)
- Level of technology compared to the most modern methods
- Penetration: how many of the target users actually use the process
- Capacity utilization
- Delivery time, e.g. percentage of on-time deliveries
- Waiting lines and waiting time
- Share of resources or working time spent on the process, either within the unit concerned or as a part of a longer flow or an entire production process

Measures like these describe processes and in some cases what they accomplish. The effects of a process can be seen more readily in the customer or financial focus. However, even these measures make it possible to determine whether the processes:

- Have been improved – if we have comparable data for previous periods
- Are on a par with those of others – if we have comparable data for other units, ideally outside our company and recognized as good (*benchmarking*)

- Have accomplished their goals – if they are formulated in terms of these measures

The most common measures of business processes tend to be measures of flow; that is, they describe the business and the result it has achieved during the current period. But here we should also find measures of business-process capital such as documented procedures, data bases, and software for handling various routines. Items of this kind are not measured nearly often enough. Under the heading of "Measures for IT", we will return to the subject of what these measures should include.

British Airways

One good example of how Heathrow developed procedures and systems is the measuring of the manning at the check-in desks. During the summer of 1997, the check-in desks had frequent problems with very long queues, and customers were very dissatisfied. Because of this the director of customer service and operations ordered 100% manning of all the check-in desks, the whole working day. This was a very expensive move, but the manager saw it as a public-relations gesture. The question then was how this objective was going to be measured. The business manager of this area could not do so because the system at that point treated the check-in desk as unmanned if anyone with a ticket from another airline checked in. When the director of Heathrow got that answer he told the manager: "If the system is not able to do it, you will have to fix the measure by letting people walk around and measure it." So at first this measure was taken visually by letting one person walk up and down the desks, during peak time. The measure was then put on the business manager's scorecard. The director asked the manager when it would be possible to measure a whole day and when the system could be developed so that this kind of information could be captured.

What happened was that the measure was measured visually for one month. Then, in the second month, the system was in fact modified, so that today the measure is measured all the time. Before this measure was actually taken, the director was assured that they were 100% manned. Today, the director can establish that the desks are at the best 90% manned and worst of all, during peak-time, figures like 50% can appear. In other words, today the situation can be analysed and action taken in a different way than was possible before.

MEASURES FOR THE INNOVATION AND DEVELOPMENT PERSPECTIVE

In measuring this perspective (sometimes called the learning and growth focus), we quite often have to resort to "surrogate measures", for instance measuring the amount of resources spent on development or training rather than the results. Sometimes we measure the share of sales from products introduced most recently, as a kind of indicator of the success of the development process. But the actual ability to innovate, or the new learning that has taken place, is usually a rather elusive concept, particularly if we want to determine to what extent new development has been useful, or how it can be expected to contribute to future success.

Innovation, learning, and development can only be measured if we are clear about what these processes do and do not include. What do we obtain for our "good costs" in these areas? Knowing how much has been spent obviously gives us less confidence than would an indication of what has been accomplished. For this reason a growing number of R&D operations have long been searching for measures of the same quality as number of patent applications or – in the case of basic research – published scientific articles.

We believe it important not to forget that we are looking for a way to communicate the strategy of the business to other people within the company. Of course measures like those mentioned above may sometimes be good ones. But development may consist of broadening our range of competence, of conducting trial operations in new fields of business or on new markets, or of changing the organization or the management-control system (by introducing the balanced scorecard, for instance). Some examples of measures:

- Proportion of employees who use the Internet regularly
- Proportion of employees whose duties have changed during the year
- Number of co-operative agreements with new partners
- Average behind-schedule time of ongoing systems-development projects
- Proportion of orders received via the Internet

As with business-process capital, it is also desirable to have metrics that measure a kind of development capital. Examples might include the number of new products or solutions in the "pipeline" ready to be launched, or the number of employees with a university education. As we described above, measures are particularly interesting when they permit comparison over time, among different units, or with other companies.

MEASURES RELATING TO EMPLOYEES

As we described in Chapters 4 and 5, there are companies like Skandia and ABB which have adopted a separate human-resources focus. In justifying the use of this perspective, Skandia explains that it would like to emphasize that employees are a resource and that human-resource capital and business-process capital, for example, are mutually reinforcing. For success a high score is required on both.

In the discussion above we have primarily considered this interaction as a basis for measures in each perspective. Customer perception, well-functioning business processes, and innovation are based on both people and systems. While of course we may want to provide a thorough picture in regard to employees, the presentation of the other perspectives may be incomplete if we do so.

Studies of companies' business plans show that goals for employee learning and competence are seldom well articulated (Hansson, 1997). Human-resource accounting was introduced in the late 1960s and involved attempts to assign these items a monetary value. It tried to prepare a kind of balance sheet on the company's human competence, and through special calculations it was determined how employee absenteeism and turnover affected the financial results and position of the company. (For a current summary, see Johanson et al., 1998.) It is our opinion that some of these attempts go too far in their effort to adopt the language of accountants. It should be possible to use measures and indicate goals at a more basic level: attitudes, feelings, knowledge, and skill.

The scorecards which we have seen frequently appear to be based in part on attitude studies. Sometimes companies engage the same consulting firm to measure employee opinion and to study customers. But there is also a place for key ratios and measures in absolute terms. Trade-offs between the former and the latter are of course necessary. With statistical sampling it should be possible to obtain a fair picture of larger units with an inexpensive study. At companies where a large proportion of employees use e-mail and the intranet every day, questionnaires can be sent out and collected easily and quickly over the Internet. At many companies there are already measurements which can be used as indicators; for example, of what employees think of their bosses, of the atmosphere at the company in regard to a businesslike approach or opportunity for initiative. However, we find no reason here to discuss the measures and issues which are customarily involved in these situations.

Halifax

The Halifax project group spent considerable time finding relevant measures for the staff development and improvement perspective. It was easy to identify certain measures like number of training days, absenteeism, and staff turnover. But all these measures could be readily manipulated; objectives could easily be reached without showing whether the measure really reflected the company's progress (i.e. the development of competence in comparison to the company's needs). So what Halifax did was to design a series of opinion-survey questionnaires focusing on the performance-management process. Now Halifax actually measure how well the staff of a specific unit find that the unit manager is managing them. The four questionnaires concerned planning and setting objectives, ongoing management and coaching, appraisal, and training and personal development. Staff members receive one of these questionnaires each quarter. Some questions in the questionnaires are always the same. These questions concern areas which are considered to be of special importance and are therefore measured four times a year.

Electrolux

One of the non-financial measures in GIMS was employee motivation. At least for short-term purposes, this measure has been replaced by a measure called the employee attitude survey (EAS). This step was taken because measuring employee motivation was done by an external company and considered too costly. For the EAS, three times a year employees answer a less comprehensive questionnaire consisting of 16–18 questions.

Volvo Car Corporation

Each year Volvo conducts an attitude survey called "Insight". The purpose of the survey is for each unit to gain more knowledge and a deeper understanding of its own work and its employees. "Awareness" includes an evaluation of each employee's performance; it also indicates areas where improvement is needed and those where everything is satisfactory. The annual survey is corporate-wide and covers the following five areas:

- Motivation and commitment
- Leadership
- Work efficiency
- Customer orientation
- Total quality

MEASURES FOR IT

A report to a Swedish government commission (Olve & Westin, 1996) presented 500 measures which had been used or proposed for follow-up and decision-making on IT in organizations. Many of these would be appropriate in a balanced-scorecard process. However, in only one case had measures been used in an actual scorecard. It was the scorecard of American Skandia and was published in one of Skandia's supplements to their annual reports (cf. Chapters 4 and 10); see Figure 7.1 which shows how manage-ment has chosen to show the use of IT at American Skandia as a business in itself. Just as often, we will find IT described as a part of a more general operation. Certain measures of IT competence and performance may then be included in a "general" scorecard, particularly in the business-process focus, but also in the develop-ment focus and customer focus.

Most of the 500 measures listed in the Swedish report show the stock of computers, the number of companies and people active in the IT area, and the like. In our opinion, the picture should be completed with other measures, since experience without exception shows that successful use of IT is just as much a question of the information which is handled and the way in which people use the technology. Figure 7.2 shows the structure proposed by the report for what may need to be measured. In the case of American Skandia, we find primarily measures of hardware, IT employees, and certain direct internal consequences. Most are expressed in relation to the company's expenses. The measures in Figure 7.2 were found in material from other companies and in published national statistics. Their purpose here is solely to serve as examples of the different categories of measures which in our opinion should be considered. Whether these measures are good or bad depends on the context in which they are used. A measure of quantity may of course describe both stocks and flows. In the case of American Skandia, the two kinds of measures are used together; for example, in the business-process focus, various technical measures show capacity as a stock for the year in question, in combination with a monetary measure of flow.

In our opinion, there is an urgent need to present the IT operations of companies in a better way than is found at present

Financial Focus

IT expense/administration expense	19%
Value added*/IT employees	117
Investments in IT	2297

Business-process Focus

IT capacity (CPU & DASD)	
AS/400 168 300 trans./hour	47 GB
PC/LAN 14 044 MIPS	199 GB
Change in IT inventory	3639

Customer Focus

Number of internal IT customers	552
Number of external IT customers	14
Number of contracts/IT employees	1906
Corporate IT literacy	+7%

Innovation & Development Focus

IT development expense/IT expense	60%
IT expense on training/IT expense	1%
R&D resources/total resources	5%

* Value added means change in IT inventory
All amounts in US$ 000s

Figure 7.1 Example of a balanced scorecard for American Skandia. Based on numbers given in "Visualizing Intellectual Capital" at Skandia, supplement to the 1994 annual report

IT-dependent activities (Matrix A)

	Hardware	Program software	Data inventory	IT workers	Entire system
Quantity	Number of computers/person	Number of IT packages	Megabytes stored	Total number of IS staff	Total IS budget
Capacity	MIPS/employee	Program maintenance			Data centre operating hours
Utilization	Transactions per hour	Number of ATM transactions	Number of times customer data accessed by sales personnel	Function points/ man-month	Number of network users per .....

Consequences of IT-activity (Matrix B)

	Direct	Indirect
Internal	Number of computer-supported customer contacts	Profit per IT expense
External	Number of subscribers to electronic newspaper	Reduction in trips to work as a result of "teleworking"

Figure 7.2 Examples of proposed IT measures, assorted by structure for objects of measurement. Source: Olve & Westin (1996)

(Falk & Olve, 1996). The most important measures for encouraging the necessary discussion on how IT and information should be used are not the technical ones, but those shown in the cells in the lower portion and to the right of Figure 7.2.

ENVIRONMENTAL MEASURES

We have not recommended the environment as a separate focus, but environmental measures can fit naturally into several areas of focus, as can measures of IT. The difference is mainly that IT and information are found and used within the organization, whereas a large portion of the relevant environmental measures relate to the effects of the business on its surroundings. Jansson et al. (1997) shows that environmental measures may be used in a number of areas, including:

- Utilization and attributes of production factors
- Emissions resulting from production
- Product content and effects of product use
- Effectiveness and environmental consequences of various modes of transportation
- Residual products
- Administrative processes, such as the existence of environmental audits, litigation, etc.

It is apparent that most of these measures relate to the business-process focus. In addition, effects on the external environment may sometimes influence customer attitudes as well as entail costs; thus, they may be considered in the customer and financial areas of focus. If strategy includes such ambitions, the development focus may need special measures to show the company's progress in developing more environment-friendly products and processes.

Electrolux

Electrolux has developed an environmental measure known as "Green Range", which is also part of a broader measure, EPI (environmental performance indicators). Electrolux management emphasizes the importance of distinguishing between measures primarily for internal use in management control, and those which indicate how well the company is meeting the new criteria set by outside analysts.

CAUSE-AND-EFFECT RELATIONSHIPS AMONG MEASURES

The balance among different areas of focus and measures is an important element in the design of scorecards. There is often a more or less clear intention to agree on interrelationships and priorities among different factors:

- How urgent is it to increase computer literacy among employees?
- How important is customer service for repurchase frequency?
- Is it more profitable in the long run to concentrate on improving business processes than on lowering prices?

Thus, it is a natural idea to try to create a model showing how the different measures in our scorecard are interrelated. The model might indicate how certain measures are dependent on others: more satisfied customers buy more, thus increasing profits (cf. Xerox, p. 211). The model may also be a way of expressing the importance that we attach to different measures. For instance, the quality of a bank's branch offices may be described by a measure which combines a customer-satisfaction index, an audit evaluation, and timeliness in completing annual reports (cf. Nordbanken, in Chapter 9).

These relationships may be of two kinds. One comprises more or less *verifiable* relationships which may be revealed by experience and studies, such as the added productivity of a computer-literate employee, or customer response to the service received. The other kind of relationship is more an expression of what we choose to *assume*. For example, we may be convinced that more visitors to the company's home page will enable us in time to exploit new business opportunities, and that it will pay more to invest in the Internet than to use the money in some other way. Of course we can list the consequences which we expect, but no study can tell us yet whether we are right.

Therefore, when we are discussing relationships and the balance among different measures in our scorecard, we must both make use of studies and experience from which conclusions can be drawn, and realize that there will always remain a certain element of what we choose to believe.

Our reasoning on cause and effect proceeds in two directions. When we decompose the vision and strategies into measures and goals which support them, we start from the top with the vision and attempt to derive measures which will help us to fulfil it. When we then communicate statements of mission to various parts of the organization in the form of scorecards, we show how the measures form a chain leading to the vision. The interrelationships work in both directions through the different perspectives. Figure 7.3 is an illustration of this reasoning: the arrows in the figure also stand for a certain lapse of time. Improved values in human-resource and development capital should be a leading indicator of improvement in customer capital and also profitability. Certain consulting firms claim to have established these kinds of connections.

While we find such examples interesting, for many companies the particular one shown here would be far too incomplete, perhaps even dangerous. If the business is highly dependent on structural capital in the form of IT solutions, then the level of knowledge will be only one of the factors to be considered. The quality, accessibility, and utilization of the company's IT resources should perhaps be added to the factors which are measured. This illustration shows what we mean when we say that the measures chosen should provide a view which covers the significant aspects of the business reasonably well.

But must the scorecard describe how the measures are interrelated? Many scorecards contain several unrelated measures; this feature is even one of its advantages over traditional monetary reports. If we could relate all measures to each other, then we could "put a monetary value" on computer literacy or customer service, for example. Generally it is preferable to leave such

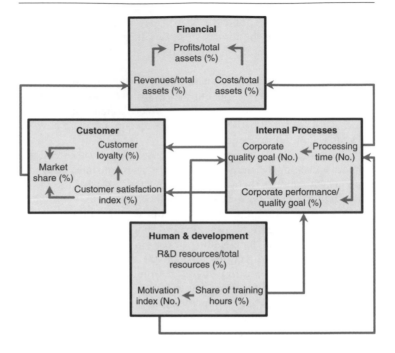

Figure 7.3 Cause-and-effect relationships between strategic measures

determinations to readers of the scorecard. The discussion on priorities is in fact one of the crucial aspects of the scorecard process. If we prefer one alternative to another, we will have chosen to attribute greater value to certain consequences than to others. For example, when we decide to improve customer service, we have passed over other options such as improving our business processes or lowering our prices. Our value judgements will be reflected in our actions, assuming our behaviour is reasonably rational.

The reason why we do not want to proceed too rapidly in reducing the number of measures is often that we want to benefit from what a large number of employees may know or think about the business. There should be an open discussion on how measures

Figure 7.4 Illustration of the cause-and-effect relationships among measures at Xerox

are interrelated. For measures which in some way can be established or illustrated through factual studies, it may be advisable to use formal methods of statistical investigation.

Xerox

Xerox focuses on four priority areas: customer satisfaction, employee motivation, market share, and return on assets (ROA). Xerox devotes considerable effort to these areas in order to guarantee and increase customer loyalty; a decline in loyalty is basically related to the degree of customer satisfaction, which in turn affects market share and ultimately has a considerable impact on ROA. At Xerox it is known by experience that an increase of 1% in customer satisfaction will produce an increase of 0.5% in customer loyalty. In other words, Xerox has been seeking to find the cause-and-effect relationships and links among the different measures (Figure 7.4).

Halifax

Even though the implementation of the balanced scorecard was very thorough – the process involved different workshops, the use of staff magazines and newsletters, training materials, etc.

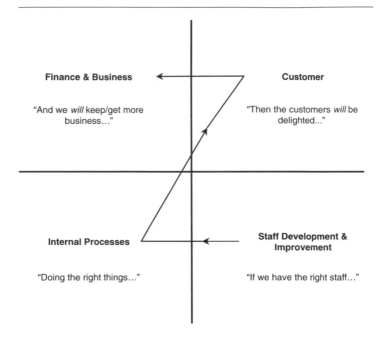

Figure 7.5 "Theory Z: To make it easy for our staff"

– Halifax found that people had a tendency to consider the different perspectives separately. Therefore, at the beginning of 1997, Halifax introduced what they called "Theory Z". The message of "Theory Z", addressed to the staff, was that all four perspectives of the scorecard were important all of the time (see Figure 7.5). The logic of "Theory Z" was as follows. If

- We have the right staff and they are well trained and motivated (staff and improvement)
- We are doing the right things efficiently (internal processes), then
- Customers will be delighted and customer loyalty will improve (customer)
- We will keep/get more business (financial)

The purpose was "to make it easy for our staff". In order to instil an awareness of this cause-and-effect logic, Halifax has made a "Theory Z" logo that is put on everything connected with the balanced scorecard. According to Halifax, the balanced scorecard did not really come to life until "Theory Z" had been introduced. Then people throughout the organization began to understand the importance of all four perspectives; previously, they focused mainly on financial figures and internal processes.

At present Halifax is dealing with the challenge of finding specific linkages between measures in the different perspectives. Hopefully this effort will stress the logic of how financial figures can be affected by actions in the different perspectives.

British Airways

At Heathrow certain cause-and-effect relationships have also been found. The measures within the internal processes category are those that the manager is trying to manage in order to get the customer measures right. In other words, the internal process measures are the drivers while the customer measures are the outcomes. At Heathrow the output measures are the most important to measure since they indicate whether or not the organization achieves success.

At Heathrow there are inputs such as resources, equipment, number of people, etc. Then there are outputs such as punctuality, customer satisfaction, etc. (see Figure 7.6). The challenge for management is to understand the complicated links that exist inside the box. At Heathrow they call it the "intellectual challenge of management". The director does not want to measure people on their inputs, but on their outputs. If there are failures on the output measures, the director starts to ask questions about the inputs. In relation to the balanced business scorecard, the output measures are in the customer box and the input measures are in the internal performance box. Then the manager and the director discuss what kind of links exist between inputs and outputs. The manager is not measured on the outputs until he/she is fully confident on what drives them.

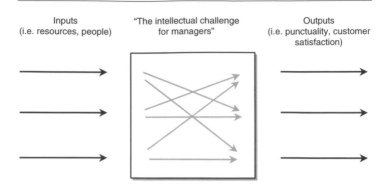

Figure 7.6 Input and output box

If he/she fails on any of the outputs, the manager is asked to analyse inputs and the links that affect the outputs.

Many overall, high-level measures and indices are based on a combination of assumptions and established relationships. Commonly used measures of customer satisfaction or human-resource capital are often quite simple combinations of questions on attitudes. For instance, scores on employee competence may be an unweighted average of a number of questions in a questionnaire study. Let us say the competence score is 80%, but we find that 75% of the staff agree with the statement, "I have the professional knowledge I need". As the score on this question has obviously lowered the overall competence score, it would seem an appropriate target for improvement. But is it necessarily better to have more employees agree with the statement? There are several possible reasons for answering "no" rather than "yes":

1. The employee in fact has certain knowledge deficiencies which he/she realizes the need to remedy.
2. The work is not well organized, or its organization is misunderstood, so that employees perform duties for which they are unqualified and which they should not be doing.
3. Employees are ambitious and would like to advance their professional development.

The last two explanations are quite plausible. If (2) is a major factor explaining the percentage of "noes", a programme of competence development is probably the wrong solution; it would be better to reassign duties or to review procedures. If (3) is an explanation, competence-development programmes may be appropriate, but possibly we should be pleased that 25% are not satisfied with the current situation. Perhaps 75% is too high, and we would like to see that more than 25% are dissatisfied!

This reasoning does not imply criticism of such studies in themselves, but only of the manner in which they are sometimes interpreted. It emphasizes our need to familiarize ourselves thoroughly with what we want to measure, and to consider carefully whether individual measures should be combined into a single overall index.

DIGRESSION: ON MEASURING ATTITUDES

In the first article by Kaplan & Norton on the balanced scorecard, the authors described the customer perspective as "How customers see us". Of course, questions of this nature have been the subject of study since long before the advent of scorecards. Firms specializing in attitude measurement are found in all countries, and it is natural to draw on their experience when we consider measures for the different parts of the scorecard. Moreover, these firms have long been searching for appropriate ways to combine several measurements into a single overall index, and for relationships between actions taken and measured results. Some firms are now developing services which to some extent meet the same needs as the balanced-scorecard concept in that they combine different kinds of measurements using methods similar to the scorecard.

An example is the customer-satisfaction index, a measurement based on a statistical model developed by Professor Claes Fornell at the University of Michigan and now used in a number of countries. Advanced statistical analysis is applied to measure not only the degree of customer satisfaction, but also how customer satisfaction is affected by various attributes of the product or

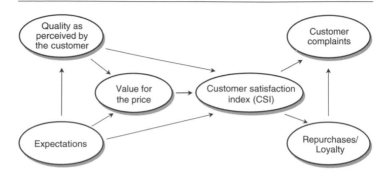

Figure 7.7 Relationships assumed to exist among measurements in the Swedish customer barometer

service. Drawing conclusions from the observed relationships, companies can adjust their strategies and refocus their business. For example, if delivery time for a mail-order product, or waiting time for check-in at an airport, is an important factor for the customer, we can reliably estimate how much customer satisfaction and loyalty may be affected by improving company performance on these points. An example of such relationships taken from Swedish studies of customer satisfaction is shown in Figure 7.7.

The customer-loyalty index is expressed as a percentage of the total number of customers and indicates the proportion of current customers who will probably patronize the company for their next purchase. This probability can in turn be related to the company's customer capital, defined as the average duration of customer relationship times the revenue generated by the customer. The measure provides guidance for developing the business, investing in R&D – or sometimes eliminating product features or even ceasing to serve customers when there is little benefit to be gained.

There is an urgent need for companies to form a clear opinion about interrelationships among the various components of "customer perception" – product, delivery, price, and service – and among customer perception, satisfaction and repurchases. Satisfaction affects loyalty, which in turn pays off in profitability, although customers may be satisfied without being loyal. What matters is that the customer comes back – it usually costs less to keep a customer than to attract a new one. Thus, it is most important to measure customer loyalty.

Customer barometers based fundamentally on Swedish experience are being developed in the USA, Norway, Germany, and Taiwan. Moreover, Directorate III of the EU is currently considering how to introduce measures of customer satisfaction – throughout the EU we increasingly find the same companies with customers in several countries.

Other indices are similarly based on confirmed and assumed interrelationships: Xerox claims that an increase of 1% in customer satisfaction leads to an increase of 0.5% in customer loyalty. The latter is in turn translatable into monetary terms; loyalty means that more customers will come back, with a direct effect on future profitability. We should also compare the cost of attracting new customers with the money spent on increasing the loyalty of our present customers, and we may find the latter alternative more profitable. According to Xerox, statistical evidence to support this line of thinking is provided by the company's extensive experience from selling comparable products throughout the world. Today a number of consulting firms follow a similar approach. In retail trade we find examples of studies showing how the customer-satisfaction index can tell us where to take market share from competing stores, as well as where our own store may lose customers.

By making such explicit assumptions as to how various factors are related, we will be able to assign a monetary value to customer capital. The likelihood of repurchase, together with our knowledge of how often customers make purchases and what we will then earn, may be used for a present-value calculation. We must always keep in mind that such calculations are based on assumptions, but if we dare to believe them, the resulting estimates are the product of a logical chain of cause and effect, linking what we invest in customer service, for example, to the long-term prosperity of the company. Encouraging discussions of this nature is one of our purposes in recommending a balanced-scorecard process. We may also simulate the effect of better service, for example, on customer capital – in other words, perform a kind of investment calculation. We will resume this discussion below.

Xerox

Xerox conducts practically all customer studies itself. Management wants complete control as well as the capacity to react quickly to customer complaints. All customer information is collected in a computerized system known as the LICA process (life care). The information is then grouped and broken down by product areas, service units, and individuals. This procedure provides continuous feedback to the person in charge of each product area, and a complete report on any given customer is quickly available throughout the company.

Information is obtained from customers by telephone. Within 48 hours after the product has been delivered, all customers are asked how they have been treated by Xerox. Any complaints are to be resolved within 48 hours. After 30, 90, and 365 days, all customers are requested to answer 15 questions. In addition, the same questions are sent at random to customers which the company has been serving from one to five years. Customer information is fed into LICA, and any complaints may then be traced to the person in charge and the process concerned. Once a year an outside institute is also engaged to assess Xerox's customer relations in comparison to those of competitors. Similar questions are used.

It is extremely important at Xerox to find out whether customers are satisfied with what the company is offering. Therefore, no one has ever suggested that too much time, effort, and money are being spent on these studies. If anything, the opposite tendency has been observed.

Smaller companies may have difficulty in performing this kind of measurement. There may be rather few customers, or the process may be considered too expensive. In the case of new services, there may be no one to ask; instead, the company will have to proceed on the basis of the other kind of relationship which we mentioned earlier in this chapter, the one which management assumes to exist. How will sales be affected by investing money in home pages on the Internet? For most companies the answer will not be known for years. Meanwhile, in the best of cases, we will be able to find out how much attention these home pages attract, how often they are visited, and how well they are appreciated. Possibly we may soon see the effects of our actions on such factors. But any conclusion drawn about consequences for the business will have to be based for some time to come on assumptions by the managers in charge.

SIMULATION USING SCORECARDS

As we have just noted, the relationships which experience has shown to exist between actions and their effects enable us to begin anticipating the consequences if we succeed with the ambitions expressed in our scorecards. We were then thinking primarily of relationships which were more or less proven. However, as we mentioned at the outset of this chapter, there are other relationships which people at the company have *chosen* to assume, such as how soon a particular investment in development will begin to bear fruit. If we can fully specify this point in time, we will also be able to calculate what we may expect to find in the scorecards of future periods. This sort of *simulation* represents an exciting development of the scorecard model, particularly if we bear in mind that many of today's expenditures are actually a kind of investment. In Figure 6.8 we reported these items as "good costs". They would include day-to-day improvements in efficiency, expenditures to develop a market, training, documentation of customer contacts, processes, etc., which at best may be recorded in some data base (structural capital) but are often only noted in the minds of employees, in the form of new individual experience and knowledge. Such investments must be based on some belief as to when they will pay off. If we dare to assume how different factors are interrelated, we will be able to simulate what will happen in the future. Computerized aids can help us to do so.

As an example, let us consider the "good cost" of developing and maintaining home pages where the reader of this book can learn about ideas which have subsequently emerged, find links to what others are writing, and perhaps – if the book is to be used in teaching – obtain tips on course programmes or examination questions. We believe that the customer focus in a possible scorecard for the book or its publisher may be affected in regard to reader appreciation both of the book itself and of the publisher's services in general. This appreciation will be an asset for the publisher in the form of repurchase probability; for example, university faculty members may require use of the book and thus ensure that it will be sold. If we know what the publisher earns on each additional copy, we can quite easily perform a kind of investment calculation for the home pages – provided we are prepared to estimate their effect on sales by attracting reader interest and attention. Such an exercise may appear difficult. But there is an implicit assessment of this kind in every attempt, for example, to put out a home page. Sometimes it may be useful to bring out the underlying assumptions for discussion and test the implications of what different people believe.

There are several computer programs which can be used for this purpose. For example, we have had experience with *ithink* (® High Performance System), an American program which is presently being developed for scorecard applications. With *ithink* it is relatively easy to build models which through simulation can help us to see which investments will pay off. This approach resembles what we usually learn from business games on investments in development and marketing. We can envision a number of interesting combinations of scorecard descriptions of a business and game-like simulation support for top-management discussions on the future. Verified and assumed relationships concerning the business would be built in. Assumptions made by different people could be compared. All major investments are based to some extent on belief, but it is an advantage if the judgements of several informed individuals are factored into the decision. We all know how the positions we take can be influenced by this kind of constructive discussion. The example of home pages for this book is just an illustration in miniature of the discussions which should be held on more critical investments – but which far too seldom take place!

SCORECARDS, "STRATEGIC CONVERSATIONS", AND SCENARIOS

What we would like to encourage by describing businesses in scorecard terms is the involvement of employees in what we might

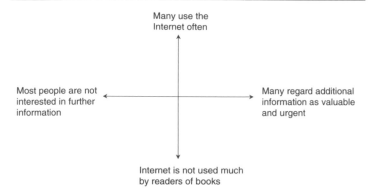

Figure 7.8   Example of a conceivable scenario diagram for decisions on a home page for products of a publisher

term "strategic conversations" on everything we do which cannot be justified on the basis of short-term benefits. Here there is a similarity to the scenario technique which promises interesting possibilities of combination. It is sometimes described (van der Heijden, 1996) as "the art of strategic conversation" – a way of thinking about the future. It does not refer to the rather forecast-like scenarios which we may choose to justify what we do, but to a kind of living concept of equally plausible courses of future development.

One usual method is to start with a couple of aspects of the future which are important to us and where we lack a basis to determine – or at least to agree on – what is most likely to happen. Using them we prepare a scenario diagram – see the example in Figure 7.8. There we have continued our mental experiment about this book. We may have difficulty in judging – or at least in agreeing on – how many of its readers will use it in a way, such as in courses of instruction, which will make it relevant for them to receive further information. Not necessarily via the publisher's home page, as above, but also on paper. Nor do we know how many people in the target group will use the Internet in the next few years as a preferred method of acquiring information of this kind. (For the present we are ignoring the likelihood that home pages about our book may also be a way of attracting the interest of people who have not bought it.) The four quadrants imply obvious differences in the "correct" course of action. We can even imagine follow-up products on paper as an appropriate response to a scenario in the lower right quadrant. (Further consideration of the upper quadrants would also lead us to ask how interesting books will be as a future form of distributing information, but that question would lead us beyond the scope of the present discussion.)

The purpose of thinking in terms of scenarios is to bring out the issues on which decisions should be taken *now*, and to encourage us to think about how these decisions relate to different scenarios, all of which are equally conceivable. Which of the things to be done now are just as urgent in virtually all conceivable scenarios? Which are so dependent on one or more particular scenarios that we should not at least go through with them without hedging our bets in case events turn out differently? Often the person who has suggested a course of action is completely convinced that the appropriate scenario is the only conceivable one!

In the example which we have considered, checkpoints may be included to alert us to early signals of what is to come, so that we can adjust our course as necessary as soon as a clear picture begins to emerge. Material for possible future home pages may also be used in other ways if one of the lower scenarios turns out to agree better with what is actually happening.

The link between the balanced scorecard and scenarios is included in the discussion on interrelationships. When we concern ourselves with the lower squares on the scorecard, we do so because we believe in a business logic that will reward us for what we develop there. We want to benefit from what several people may contribute to the discussion. Scenarios can be a stimulus for this kind of "strategic conversation". They may also make us more discerning in our selection of critical success factors; for example, they may help us to identify which early signals of market acceptance or solutions proposed by our employees we should follow more closely and be prepared to act on.

Thus, if we are to make the right decisions about our strategy and communicate them to the organization, we must first try to link together the different measures in our scorecard and to determine how they are interrelated, on the basis of either previous experience or assumptions made. This step will also prove useful when our scorecards are later used to monitor the business and to act as needed to keep it on course. When we see how developments are proceeding, we can compare outcomes with expectations. Previous experience and assumptions will be continually reviewed in the light of new experience. Our conception of relevant relationships will be adjusted accordingly. In this way the discussion concerning the scorecard can provide a platform for learning, a subject to which we will return in Chapter 9.

SIMULATING EFFECTS ON SHAREHOLDER VALUE

If a complete model could be specified, along the lines of Figures 3.12 or 4.7 (Coca-Cola), it would of course be possible to simulate the effects on shareholder value from all kinds of actions which may be considered. So is this the ultimate goal? Although we believe this kind of discussion to be fruitful and would encourage it, we still have some doubts.

Most of the organizations we have worked with are of course concerned with long-term shareholder value. But an essential aspect of their current interest in the balanced scorecard is the benefits of having a *multidimensional* view of a business. For business firms there is a likely implicit belief that the desired "balanced" development of several measures will ultimately improve shareholder value, but the exact shape of these causal chains is something not often discussed. It is even doubtful if such a discussion would be felt to be so important; different managers or stakeholders have different long-term world-views, but they are able to agree on what should be done short term.

It may be argued that a discussion of what is likely to lead to long-term shareholder value is then needed, but in many cases the value of simulations could lie in establishing and manipulating a multidimensional representation of the business and its environment, rather than establishing a unidimensional "value".

This is even more so with the many applications of scorecard thinking in the public sector, or for parts of a corporation where its utility for the whole is multidimensional, e.g. an administrative department. For many firms a relevant description of the company is likely to recognize that a business can create value *of different kinds* for different stakeholders. The shareholders are no longer pre-eminent!

It follows from what we said in Chapter 2 that an alternative perspective on the stakeholder balance in a business is quite possible, where the really interesting resources are not bought, except in the sense that companies of course pay wages to their people, and enter into commercial relationships with their partners. Considering a business from this perspective, what matters is how it mobilizes the intellectual capacity and goodwill of these and their customers. Succeeding in this, a company may create a much larger pie to be shared. Ultimately, this could be called shareholder value maximization. But as the financial capital will play a role of decreasing importance in it, it could be argued that it should not be stressed too much.

Does this make simulations less interesting? Not really. To compare views and, if possible, agree on the views held on how for instance customer satisfaction relates to future sales, is quite as important if the ultimate goals of the business are perceived to be a constantly changing balance between those of different stakeholders who contribute in different ways. But to some of them it would seem off-putting and a waste of time to try to trace relationships with the outcome for just one of a business's constituencies.

Simulation can be regarded as a system dynamics approach which links in interesting ways to current ideas about knowledge management (see Chapter 9). An interactive use of simulation software should make it possible to make partially explicit the implicit mind-maps that managers have and which guide their intuitive perceptions aboutl which actions are desirable. To compare such mind-maps would seem to be an important part of utilizing and leveraging the knowledge existing in the organization. The idea of a balanced scorecard is essentially about creating a language for communicating about a business; adding simulations would seem to be a good way of provoking people to explicate and share their differing views.

This could not be expected to lead to any ready consensus on relations and causal chains (performance drivers, outcomes, etc.), at least not all the way to an agreement on shareholder value.

It may yet be valuable in order to improve and agree on the assumptions underlying the actions of a business.

SUMMARY

In this chapter we have discussed questions relating to measures and measurements. When we choose measures within a particular focus, we should consider how they may be related by cause and effect to measures in other perspectives. We noted that:

- Careful thought is required in choosing measures and combining them appropriately, and it is often useful to hold a discussion on how people believe that various measurable factors will be interrelated.
- The experience of different firms which have conducted studies may be useful for this purpose, and it may sometimes be necessary to engage these firms if more extensive measurements are required as a basis for scorecards. At many companies, studies are already available for use.
- As already emphasized in Chapter 5, every measure presented stands for a choice to emphasize certain conditions while not considering others. Even though scorecards are based on reasoning about critical success factors (see Chapter 3), we must be observant about underlying assumptions of what is "obvious" in the picture presented.

Simulation and thinking in terms of scenarios are methods which we think should be used together with the balanced-scorecard concept. The following is a short checklist summarizing some of the questions which we have raised:

- Do the measures cover different aspects of the business, or does one aspect predominate?
- Have we considered what is most important to measure: stocks, capacity, utilization, or effects?
- Is there an appropriate balance between stocks and flows in the measures we have chosen?

- Are the measures related to what we have previously measured, or will they require new measurement procedures?
- Can we relate the measures to other measures, either by gathering experience on how they are actually related or by developing clear hypotheses as to cause and effect?

There will always be a need for a number of measurements and key ratios outside of the scorecard. We have seen that certain companies use substantially fewer measures. But when we choose a smaller number of measures, we still believe that the questions which we have raised will encourage consideration of measures other than the most obvious choices.

NOTES

1. See Falk & Olve (1996) for a detailed discussion on this point. In Chapter 10, we will touch on the same question as it concerns a company's financial statements.

Part III

Implementing a Balanced Scorecard

8

Systems and IT Solutions for Scorecards

In this chapter we discuss how a balanced-scorecard project can progress from a strategic process to the implementation of a management-control system in a more operational sense. In this respect we address issues relating to the balance between manual and automatic systems of measurement, the balance between cost of measurement and the utility of knowing what is measured, and entrusting employees far out in the flow of operations with making decisions based on the non-financial measures in the new management-control system.

What tools are needed to ensure that all information shown to be important in a scorecard is obtained? Should a balanced scorecard be introduced as a permanent system of management control, and should its use be part of normal operating procedures? The answer to these questions depends on what we expect will give us the most for our money; of course, we will have a hard time proving that our expectations are correct. The costs of following a balanced-scorecard approach relate less to developing systems and software than to the work that the approach entails. It is not enough for someone at the company to put a few selected measures into a scorecard diagram, or to produce these measures in existing systems and to generate reports. What determines whether the method will be of any benefit is our dialogue about the measures and how we reason in choosing our strategy. The ultimate test is surely not to be found in any cost estimates, but in whether we find the benefit sufficient to justify continued use of the method.

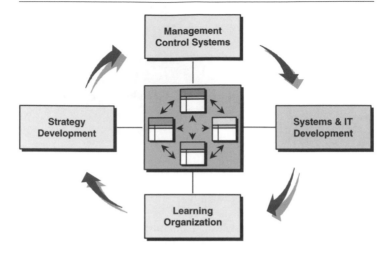

Figure 8.1 The balanced-scorecard process

Figure 8.1 is repeated from the beginning of Chapter 3, where scorecards were seen as enablers of a circle of learning. In previous chapters the emphasis was on scorecards for strategy development and management control. We now move on to systems and IT development as enablers of practical scorecard use.

KEEPING A SCORECARD ALIVE[1]

An effective balanced scorecard must be continually updated with current, operationally relevant information if it is to play a natural part in the company's strategic discussion and learning process. A well-designed scorecard shows a company's strategy and the logic of its business. The link between the various measures and the company's strategic aims may be regarded as a hypothesis about the essential relationships – of cause and effect – between what the company invests today and what pays off in the long run. A company active on a highly dynamic market should continually analyse and evaluate the different parts of its scorecard. But will doing so be enough to keep the scorecard alive?

Of course a company's vision and its strategic aims are vital to its future survival, but unless they are communicated to all levels of the organization, it will be difficult to bring about the changes which are desired and required for the company to stay competitive. Thus, a crucial question for the company is how to establish procedures and systems of measurement which not only collect operationally relevant information, but also communicate it to employees and partners so as to influence their behaviour in the desired direction – that is, towards realizing the shared vision. The balanced-scorecard model in itself provides only a structure for describing the company's vision and strategy in terms of specific goals and measures. If the scorecard is not followed up with the help of specific systems and procedures, there is a clear danger that the development of employee competence will be neglected. It will then be difficult for the company to bring about certain changes in behaviour which may be required if it is to remain competitive.

The development of strategy and strategic control are the foundation of the scorecard; we have treated these areas extensively in previous chapters. Sometimes it is also said that these are the aspects which are primarily involved and which matter in a balanced-scorecard project – the project being concluded once existing measures have been placed "in the four boxes". In our opinion, there is an immediate danger in taking this view, for only in subsequent phases, as shown in Figure 8.1, do the effects of a balanced scorecard arise. These phases are essential if employee competence is to be developed, behaviour changed, and hypotheses about the future tested.

If a scorecard is to be kept alive, there must be systems and procedures for collecting relevant information and conveying it to employees and partners. A company is not ready to introduce an IT solution until the quality of the information in the scorecard has been ensured. This step consists of two elements:

1. *Analysis of measures* – here the measures which have been developed are analysed. Are they clearly and uniformly defined? Do they reflect the company's strategy? Is it evident how the different perspectives are interrelated?
2. *Ensuring the reliability and validity of systems and methods of measurement* – the company's capability of performing the

necessary measurements is analysed. How adequate are today's methods and systems of measurement for what they will be required to do in the future? Is it economically justifiable to measure everything? At what intervals should the different measurements be taken? What person or persons should be responsible for the respective measures?

British Airways

When the measures were identified at Heathrow, approximately 75% of them were already tracked by existing procedures and systems. It is important to mention that none of the measures had targets. Today, the philosophy is that everything that is measured should also be targeted.

Heathrow estimates that they have procedures and systems for measuring approximately 90% of the measures that were identified as critical. But 100% of the output measures are measured. According to the operations at Heathrow, these are the most important measures to track, since they indicate whether or not the organization is succeeding.

To secure measurements, Heathrow used the following three ways:

1. Put in a new measurement system and run it all the time – often quite expensive and therefore used at Heathrow only for certain measures.
2. Audit a sample of the population – for very complex problems the audit will not provide enough information. Not often used at Heathrow.
3. Batch sampling of 100% of the population over a certain time period – expensive if it is done frequently, but very informative since it covers everything during the chosen time period. Very often used at Heathrow.

ANALYSIS OF MEASURES

No matter how appealing the vision is perceived to be, or how clearly and communicatively the scorecard is structured, these factors will not bring about the necessary changes in the organization. The changes will only occur when each employee is shown tangible evidence of what he/she contributes and how it helps the organization as a whole to achieve its defined goals. The employee's contribution can only be made clear and will only be found interesting if it is based on day-to-day operations. For these reasons, we believe that the success or failure of a balanced-scorecard project depends on the reliability and validity of the systems which describe the performance of every individual, group, and department in terms of what the organization as a whole is trying to achieve.

When the scorecard has been defined – that is, when the vision has been established, the strategic aims have been formulated, and the critical success factors and measures have been derived from the vision and strategic aims – the next major phase of the project begins, a phase which is often forgotten in many organizations. Everyone is so happy now that the groundwork has been done, and so eager to start measuring, that the organization neglects the need to review and analyse the measures and the structure which the project group has produced.

The measures, which are the specific expression of the company's success factors, strategic aims, and vision, are seldom unambiguously defined as they stand. More likely, the measures used will be unclear in nature; often they have been chosen for precisely that reason. If defining the right measures and performing the appropriate measurements had been a simple matter, the measures would surely have been identified without the necessity of going through a balanced-scorecard project.

In systems and information theory, defining the meaning of various concepts has long been an important area. The purpose of conceptual modelling is to define the characteristics of concepts, what they represent in a given domain, and how they are interrelated. Many organizations have discovered, belatedly, the costs generated by various sets of concepts. An everyday example is illustrative: a corporate group would like to compare its subsidiaries in regard to administrative expenses per employee. Each business unit reports its data, but using different definitions of the concept. One unit reports the number of man/years of engagements, another the number of individuals, a third the number of administrative positions. The aggregate material is unusable, since each unit has prepared its data on a different basis. Not only that, but it has proven unreasonably expensive to prepare data using a single definition for the entire corporate group. In effect, no comparison is possible!

The need for a clear set of concepts is even greater when organizations begin to measure the performance of their operations in non-monetary terms. No organization can assume that all of its units – let alone all of its employees – will attach the same meaning to everyday terms such as invoice, customer, voucher, minutes of meetings, etc.

A uniform set of concepts is essential if the ongoing measurements inherent in the idea of a balanced scorecard are to have any meaning. If the control desired is to be possible, the cause-and-effect relationships among the different measures must be validated. One benefit of clarifying the internal logic of the scorecard is that employees will be able to see how they contribute to the financial result (see Figure 7.3). If employees do not believe in the relationships which are assumed to underlie the scorecard in question, they will not act in accordance with the non-monetary measures. In that case, the balanced-scorecard project will have little impact on the business. We must clearly show the link to the comprehensive vision, and thus to long-run profitability, if we are to give the organization the self-confidence to make decisions on the basis of the non-monetary measures in the customer, process, and development perspectives.

ENSURING THE RELIABILITY AND VALIDITY OF SYSTEMS AND METHODS OF MEASUREMENT

Much of the information on which the measures in the three new areas of focus are based is difficult to obtain from the company's existing administrative systems. If a basis for these measures had been available previously, surely the variables which they express would have already been measured.

One effect of formulating new measures of performance is that the organization will have to put in place new systems of measurement, systems which initially may entail a lot of work which will have to be done manually. Thus, our theoretical cost of measurement will be understated; we must constantly analyse the new information for decision-making and weigh its utility against the additional cost of preparing it. Here, too, we can use a simple example to illustrate our point. At a company which sells capital goods, sales personnel believe that the number of longer conversations with prospective buyers visiting its shops is correlated with the number of definite purchases. Naturally, it is impossible to register automatically the number of "longer conversations". The organization then faces the choice of either manually registering the number of conversations with customers or continuing as before – that is, remaining ignorant of how this critical success factor ("longer conversations with customers") is developing and changing as the company proceeds with other activities, such as massive TV advertising. (Does TV advertising generate more conversations with customers?) The company decided to register manually the number of conversations with customers; after each conversation the salesman places a token in a box behind the counter. Each week the number of tokens in the box is counted, thus generating information about the flow of customer conversations in the store. This registration takes time which could be spent on something else, such as talking with another customer. The salesman who must go to the counter and put in a token to record his conversation will always lose a few short seconds in the store; the loss can be regarded as inefficiency. Therefore, the company must let employees know why it is important to measure these factors and show how doing so will ultimately help the business to get where it wants to go. Since the weekly summary also generates additional administrative work, it is important that the company develop measurement systems which are as easy as possible to use. Manual registration, in the midst of the flow of operations, must be extremely simple, so as not to "steal" time from core activities.

It is preferable to use existing digital information to its greatest possible extent. For example, instead of measuring intensity of communication by registering the number of physical letters or telephone conversations, the electronic communication in the company's e-mail system may be used as a surrogate measure. By a simple operation the mail system can be made to generate a logbook which shows the flow of communication without the necessity of registration by the users themselves. To reduce the administrative burden on the organization, management should utilize every source of digital information which may be assumed to be correlated with the source which requires manual measurement.

IT SOLUTIONS FOR SCORECARDS

The balanced-scorecard model only gives a company a structure which expresses its vision and strategy in concrete terms of goals and measures. The company still faces the considerable challenge of building up a system which both collects relevant information and communicates this information to employees and partners. In order to obtain the behavioural change which is usually desirable, the information must also be:

- Presented in a *communicative* manner – in numbers, figures, diagrams, or multimedia which facilitate an overview
- Presented in a *user-friendly environment* – simple, familiar interface
- *Easy to access* – the person who needs the information must be able to obtain it wherever he or she is
- Collected and measured in a *cost-effective* manner – measures of "soft" data often require new instruments of measurement. The cost of measurement must not exceed the utility of the measures

Another question in choosing an IT solution is: For whom is the information intended? Sometimes management would like to see widespread distribution of scorecards in order to provide a shared view of different businesses, and in other cases the scorecard may contain very sensitive information.

There are three main categories of IT solutions to be considered for use together with the balanced scorecard (Figure 8.2). They reflect three different levels of ambition and are presented below, the first representing the lowest level of ambition and the third, the highest.

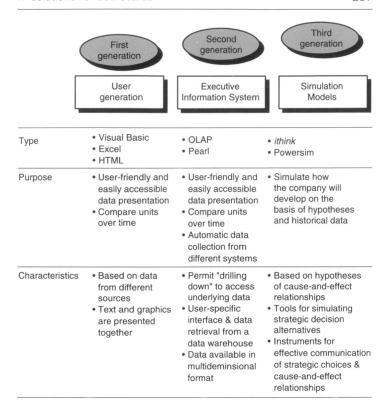

	First generation User generation	Second generation Executive Information System	Third generation Simulation Models
Type	• Visual Basic • Excel • HTML	• OLAP • Pearl	• *ithink* • Powersim
Purpose	• User-friendly and easily accessible data presentation • Compare units over time	• User-friendly and easily accessible data presentation • Compare units over time • Automatic data collection from different systems	• Simulate how the company will develop on the basis of hypotheses and historical data
Characteristics	• Based on data from different sources • Text and graphics are presented together	• Permit "drilling down" to access underlying data • User-specific interface & data retrieval from a data warehouse • Data available in multideminsional format	• Based on hypotheses of cause-and-effect relationships • Tools for simulating strategic decision alternatives • Instruments for effective communication of strategic choices & cause-and-effect relationships

Figure 8.2 Overview of possible IT solutions for the balanced scorecard

1. *User interface* – in other words, a manner of presenting data and of permitting comparison among units and over time. The suggestions which we have seen resemble instrument panels. Such a system may be based on data from several different sources, from both manual and automatic systems.
2. *Executive information systems* – in addition to the form of presentation, the system provides for automatic data collection from various other systems already in place. For a more sophisticated scorecard, the number of such systems may be large; we recommend letting the interface of the management-

information system be inspired by the balanced scorecard, rather than building up a special balanced-scorecard application. Such a solution can also make it possible to "drill down"; that is, the user can examine the underlying data to find out why the numbers shown in the scorecard have developed in a certain way. Here web technology may open up new possibilities.

3. *Simulation models* – here we can project the company's scorecard into the future or simulate the effects of changes in the measures. To do so we will have to make assumptions, e.g. of how long it will take for an investment in development to bear fruit, and of the resulting effects on financial measures. In Chapter 7 we briefly discussed simulation. Here we will attempt to express our ideas in terms of specific models and tools.

The IT solutions which we have encountered are primarily of the first generation. To provide data from a management-information system (second generation) in the form of a scorecard is largely a matter of report design and of ensuring the quality of data not found in existing systems. So far we have only seen a few third-generation solutions as described above. The difficulties in creating the new systems which are required fall into two categories:

1. Combining different sources of data – the problem may just as well be with the logical aspects of the data, ease of understanding, frequency of data collection, etc. as with the technical compatibility between different computerized systems.

2. Aggregation of data values through their respective hierarchies – the issue here is that many of the values measured in the scorecard do not lend themselves to simple arithmetical summation, or that an aggregate value becomes meaningless from a management perspective.

First Generation: User Interface

The introduction of the scorecard usually begins at the operating level. One purpose of IT support here is to provide a good comprehensive view of the measures defined in the scorecard. By user interface we mean that the data are readily accessible and presented in a user-friendly manner. There has to be an underlying data base, but applications can be developed with simple PC tools such as Visual Basic, Excel, Lotus Notes, Delphi, HTML, etc. The principal requirement is that the tool permits easy integration and presentation of text together with graphics, and thus comparison between units over time. One source of suggestions for user interface is the EVITA project at ABB.

ABB

With the aid of a presentation-support system which the company has developed itself, performance in the five perspectives is communicated by PC in a clear and well-organized manner to all employees of the unit. This effect is obtained through visual presentation of the various control metrics in diagrams and on indicators designed like automobile speedometers. The control metrics provide figures for the current period and a comparison with the preceding one. Short-term targets are shown in relation to long-term goals. It is also possible to see the action plans which have been developed for each control metric. In other words, the presentation-support system is intended as a simple and attractive way to show how each unit is doing. Examples of the presentation viewed on the screen are presented in Figure 8.3.

Second Generation: Executive Information Systems

Management-information systems involve linking the presentation-support system and analytical tool and data base to the systems which supply them with data. The nature of the data will depend on the measures to be included in the scorecard, but usually include accounting data and data for the order and production-control systems. It is not unlikely that data on employees and customers, particularly attitude measurements and the like, will be available in a form that permits linking them

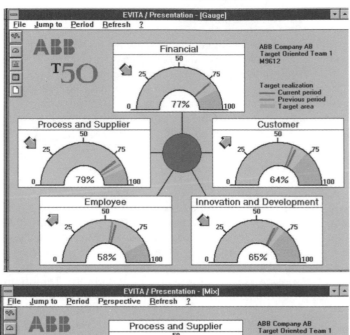

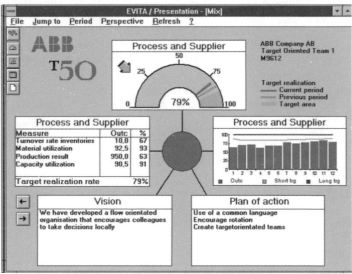

Figure 8.3 Examples from ABB's presentation-support system

directly to the system. Here the company may consider establishing other or alternative measurement systems and procedures, while still using the same system for presentation (see the section "Keeping a scorecard alive" p. 230).

There is actually nothing to distinguish this type of management-information system from other *executive information systems/ decision support systems*. The connection with the balanced-scorecard concept lies in the selection of information and the design of the interface.

When a balanced scorecard is introduced throughout an organization, the systems solution will be subject to certain requirements. There will still have to be an easily manageable graphic interface, but with the flexibility to permit variations in design according to the specific needs of different organizational units. The data needed to calculate the values of measures on a more detailed level may be voluminous and multidimensional. While much of the basic data will be the same for all units, aggregations and computations may differ from one department to another.

The solution chosen must offer each unit its own specific user interface, while at the same time permitting data to be stored in a common data base so as to ensure consistent and correct data. The client–server architecture in the variant called Co-operative Processing (see Figure 8.4) meets this requirement, since the part of the application which operates the data base and governs the rules for computation may be located in a company-wide server, whereas the client software which runs menu systems, for example, will be in the client environment.

There is little added benefit in using IT solely to present information. When various kinds of measures have been computed and presented, the user will naturally want to ask questions about trends or forecasts. To provide answers calls for a more sophisticated solution than one simply involving storage and presentation of data. The most appropriate technique is OLAP (on-line analytical processing). With OLAP, data are accessible in a multidimensional format similar to an ordinary spreadsheet but in more than two dimensions. Statistical calculations may then be performed to provide trends or forecasts.

An interesting application for the balanced-scorecard concept is to balance the various measures against each other so as to create

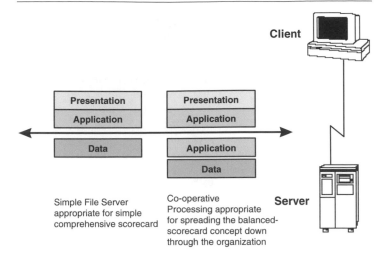

Figure 8.4 Architecture for functioning of client–server solutions as IT support for a balanced scorecard

a model showing how they are interrelated. The OLAP technique may be used for this purpose. Models which simulate how customer satisfaction and profitability affect each other, for example, can provide a basis for identifying optimal combinations of the two measures. For example, it hardly makes sense to aim for 100% customer satisfaction if the model shows that profitability declines at customer-satisfaction levels over 90%. The company should then improve its business processes so that profitability increases even when customer satisfaction exceeds 90%. OLAP makes it simpler to combine different business dimensions as desired and thus to simulate and optimize.

With the intranet this kind of IT solution becomes even more interesting; then we need not store software on our client computer but can download it as needed, or run it in a window using our web browser with the help of technologies like Java. A major advantage of using the web is that it has become a language and a communication platform which users have readily accepted. IT companies have responded by making many or all of their programs web-compatible. It has thus become possible with the web to:

- Report, cost-effectively and simply, data not retrievable from other existing systems
- Enable automatic data collection from different systems, as well as a certain degree of "drill-down" to different levels of data
- Provide a user-friendly, easily accessible vehicle for data presentation
- Present results and trends for data in a balanced-scorecard structure as well as comment on the trends and indicate what action should be taken

Figure 8.5 illustrates how different IT solutions (OLAP and Web) can be integrated into one system. Through the web interface the user can both enter and extract data. It is also possible to access the system through the OLAP client. With the OLAP it is possible to perform more extensive analyses in different dimensions, but here it is not possible to enter data into the system. The different systems, OLAP and Web, are connected both to each other and to the data warehouse. The data warehouse is also connected to other systems, i.e. accounting data systems, administrative systems and production systems.

Halifax

At an early stage, the project group realized that further development of the existing systems was necessary. One phase of the project dealt with complex questions such as creating appropriate data-feed procedures, and the need for a "PC-system" that would show indicators from all four quadrants of the balanced scorecard on an entry level. The system should also be accessible at different levels by different people. For instance, each branch outlet needed to see the details on its own performance alone, while area managers would want to view consolidated data for their territory, and so forth.

To develop a new system, Halifax hired external consultants. The system that resulted is based on a commercial OLAP software. Since a large number of parameters were to be measured, the nature of the system solution evolved as the

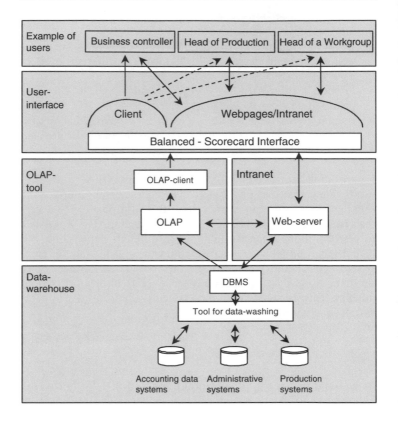

Figure 8.5 Structure for IT support for the balanced scorecard

measures were designed. According to management, Halifax did not fall into the usual trap of only measuring what could then be measured. Instead, the company created processes to ensure that the system would have measures of what should be measured. Putting it right from the beginning was more important than putting it in place at a certain cost.

Today, Halifax retail network branches have a PC-based balanced-scorecard solution (see Figure 8.6) which is accessed

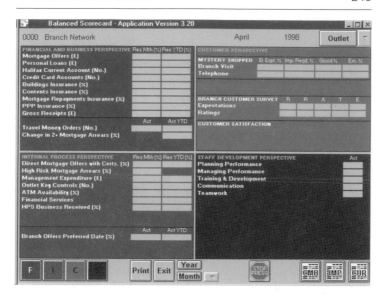

Figure 8.6 A screen view of the OLAP system at Halifax

from desktop computers at each Halifax branch and service centre, and from notebook PCs used by area and regional managers. The system is accessible by the entire staff of the branch. There are no restrictions, passwords, etc. Every employee can see an up-to-date status report at any time. The systems-entry screen displays the current development of measures from each of the four quadrants in the balanced scorecard. A further 60 screens can be accessed; these provide increasingly detailed data on aspects of the balanced scorecard. The information is furnished on a monthly basis in a user-friendly format to help managers understand the performance of the business.

Since the system is built on a planning-science, multidimensional OLAP data base, it is possible to "drill down" on every top-level measure in different dimensions. The various measures are stored in several data warehouses. Some measures – including many of those relating to customers – originate with outside companies, which unfortunately are not connected on-line to Halifax; these measures are updated by disc. With the present system, simulations are not possible. According to management, however, simulations would be relevant primarily in the strategic planning process, so that Halifax has not found any need for them at this time. Soon today's system will be integrated with a web-based intranet.

The new system was implemented towards the end of 1995 through a series of regional briefings in which some 1400 people were involved. Each manager was given a comprehensive presentation package, and the system was introduced on Halifax's own business television network. During the period from the end of November 1995 until the beginning of 1997, the old and new systems were running in parallel. Network managers were thus able to gain experience in using the new system prior to its formal introduction. It was also easier for managers to focus on closing the gaps that became evident when results were compared between the two systems.

When the new system was actually launched early in 1997, members of a small team visited every manager in the network to explain how the balanced scorecard worked, how plans and objectives would be set, and how these would be followed up. Since then the system has been modified a number of times because of the feedback from users.

In retrospect Halifax management found the timing of the "balanced-scorecard project" to be perfect, coinciding as it did with the Leeds merger in mid-1995. Since the two companies had been managed very differently, there was a great need for a common management system. For the people in both organizations, the balanced scorecard – as a new system for managing the business – met that need. Tension was thereby reduced; both organizations had to start from scratch. From this standpoint, the scorecard could not have been introduced at a better time.

NatWest Life

At NWL, it was possible to monitor the balanced business scorecard and all the key performance indicators through the executive information system, as early as 1994. The system was updated daily, and it was possible for every authorized person to "drill down" on any measure to see whether he/she was on target.

The system was very useful during the first year for teaching the people how to run the business and how to obtain useful information from the system. But NWL found that this method of management was unnecessarily expensive when measures were updated so frequently; a large number of measures did not change every day. Consequently, many functions in the system have been dropped, and today the progress of different measures is reported largely on paper. According to NWL, this method is more practical than before and not as costly. It is important to stress that NWL is still tracking the same data; the company is just no longer presenting them live on screen.

Another reason for dropping the "live system" was that it tended to lull employees into a false sense of satisfaction when all targets were being met. NWL would merely like to emphasize that the landscape is only as precise as you have been able to define it. According to company management, it was important not to underestimate the true complexity of the business. Therefore, it is important to conduct frequent reviews of the critical success factors, the key performance indicators, and the outcomes of the measures.

Volvo Car Corporation

In the automotive industry it is necessary to measure certain parameters. However, it is most important to measure trends. At present Volvo measures hundreds of performance indicators which in time will be automatically reported to a central data warehouse on a continuous basis. Today some of this information is processed manually, at considerable cost. With the new automated information system, VCC would like to establish a facts-oriented culture, in which data are available to anyone at any time. Facts are indisputable; you can never really dodge them, according to Volvo management. Hopefully it will also be possible both to use the parameters and to adapt them to the needs of different people in different situations throughout the world. Inculcating this way of thinking is what management would like to accomplish by measuring hundreds of parameters and making them available in a central data warehouse. Today only the VCC Performance Report is published on the company intranet. Even then, the document is not completely accessible by all employees; there are various levels of authorization. It is not updated automatically, but must first be processed by the central unit for financial planning and control.

British Airways

Most of the operational performance measures at Heathrow are followed in an IT-based support system that the unit has developed themselves. Here it is possible to follow measures in real time and "drill down" on certain dimensions. The system does not use the format of the balanced business scorecard, which is still under development. Almost everyone has access to this system. For instance, a computer is installed in every rest room throughout the organization.

Third Generation: Simulation Models

The third form of data support, simulation models, can use the aids available today to describe cause-and-effect relationships. Here it is important to remember a fundamental feature of the balanced scorecard: it helps us to consider several perspectives and measures simultaneously and to avoid being permanently tied to a particular manner of weighing them together. As we argue in Chapter 7, simulating what will happen to different measures over time should be regarded primarily as a means of encouraging discussion and consensus on central basic assumptions. What effect should we assume that marketing will have on sales, and in what time frame? What will happen if we speed up our deliveries or introduce more new products? Today there are various aids for using simulation tools with the balanced scorecard. One example is the *ithink* software, which is based on systems thinking and can be integrated with parts of the balanced-scorecard concept.

The heart of system dynamics is about recognizing the coherent patterns concealed in the complex structures of a business, where others see only isolated events among the myriad of details, events, and tendencies. In other words, systems theory is a discipline which seeks to capture the totality inherent in the various subsystems with which we come in contact. Systems theory provides us with a method and a technique for modelling, studying, and co-ordinating holistic relationships over time. It thus helps us to perceive and understand how different phenomena are interconnected, instead of viewing each in isolation, and to see processes of change and patterns instead of still shots (Senge, 1990).

By integrating the ideas underlying the balanced scorecard and systems theory, we can look at a business more dynamically. It is of course impossible to predict future events and results. But we can make better decisions for the future by using systems theory and the tools of simulation to test different decision alternatives as a basis for discussing how the future might look. To put it briefly, integrating these two fields provides us with:

- A structure which encourages and helps us to understand how to identify cause-and-effect relationships among strategic aims and measures, and how to achieve a balance among them
- A simple test of future results, or simulation, of the measures identified in a balanced-scorecard process
- A foundation for learning in the form of multidimensional strategies which reflect the company's competitive situation and operating reality
- A basis for discussion on how to develop operational action plans which lead to value creation

Ithink and Powersim are both computerized simulation tools based on systems thinking. Using *ithink*, which is based on a simple modelling language, we can build simulation models and visual maps. The program can structure and control complex multidimensional systems. Without the help of a computer, it is difficult to control a system and to obtain an overall understanding of how it works with respect to its internal cause-and-effect relationships. The simulation program clarifies and illustrates specifically how an action taken will affect different variables in the system.

The program consists of three different system levels. At the highest level, we can develop a user interface which makes it easier to simulate the models developed at the intermediate level. In the simulation, certain variables in the model are changed, such as how much a product should cost, how many employees the company should have, or how much should be invested in marketing. With the help of the user interface, we can clearly see the effects of the simulation in the form of tables and graphs. At the intermediate level of the program, as noted, we develop cause-and-effect models (see Figure 8.7). To develop these models, we draw simple flow charts consisting of stocks – that is, accumulated quantities – and flows in and out of the stocks. At the lowest level of the program, we can introduce into the model the equations which will then generate the outcome of the simulation.

SUMMARY

If a scorecard is to play a natural part in the process of strategic discussion and learning at a company, it must continually be updated with current, operationally relevant information. Thus, an important question for the company is how to establish procedures and systems of measurement which not only collect operationally relevant information, but also communicate it to employees and partners. The chapter discusses the importance of ensuring the quality of data, and it illustrates three different levels of ambition in regard to IT support for the balanced scorecard. The lowest level of ambition is limited to providing a user interface for presentation. The next level is to use the form and content of the scorecard to make management information available, e.g. with EIS or web solutions. The third level is to include the cause-and-effect relationships among the measures and thus make simulation possible.

Not until we reach this part of a balanced-scorecard project does our organization obtain a basis for action. The preceding phases focused primarily on the actual process of developing a

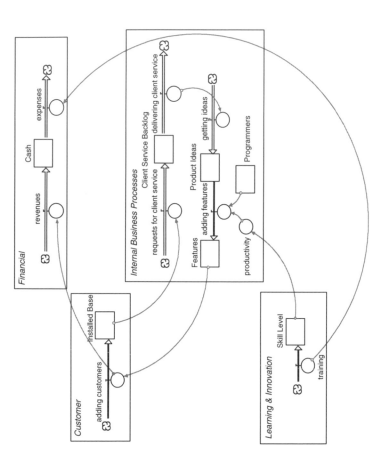

Figure 8.7 Cause-and-effect model drawn in *ithink* to illustrate the fundamental relationships in the system

comprehensive scorecard. By ensuring that there are reliable systems and procedures for collecting relevant information, we enable ourselves to question our hypotheses about the future (as formulated in the company's strategy). In other words, it is not enough simply to fill a scorecard with a number of measures and then link them to different systems. Only when we conduct a dialogue on how our measures are developing, on why we have chosen our strategy, and on how we can learn, can we reap the benefits of using a balanced scorecard.

NOTE

1. Based on an article by Westin & Wetter (1997).

9
Towards a Learning Organization

One of the main purposes of a balanced scorecard is to develop a learning organization. An organization which is constantly developing and changing in a way that will keep the company competitive in the future. The balanced-scorecard model itself is a structure for describing a company's vision and strategy in tangible, understandable terms. It serves as a language for discussions within the company, a means of interface between people who are jointly developing their view of the company in which they have a common interest. Transforming visions and strategies into specific action is done by people. The process often calls for behavioural change, development of individual competence, etc. In this chapter we will discuss the importance of a learning organization and how the balanced-scorecard concept both as a process of creation and of implementation can serve as a tool to enhance organizational learning.

SCORECARDS, STRATEGIC DEVELOPMENT AND LEARNING

Figure 9.1 is repeated from the beginning of Chapter 3, where scorecards were seen as enablers of a circle of learning. In our model for creating the scorecard (Chapter 3), we emphasized the role of the process in the *development of the company's strategy*. The use of scorecards contributes to discussions within the company which lead to explicit visions in terms of strategies,

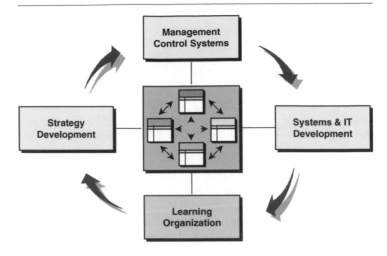

Figure 9.1 The balanced-scorecard process

measures, and action plans. There are many different opinions on the degree to which strategies may be planned. Mintzberg (1994, pp. 286ff) refers to strategies as emerging patterns, and views the development of strategy as a process of learning. He compares strategies to weeds which take root and gradually "proliferate to pervade the behaviour of the organization at large". This process may be managed but need not be – to manage is to "recognize their emergence and intervene when appropriate".

While recognizing that this view of strategy development is an extreme one, Mintzberg (1994, p. 289) does not find it more extreme than what he terms the pure planning model: "The two define the end points of a continuum along which real-world strategy making behaviour must lie." Whether we prefer a more traditional view of strategy formulation as a process that involves planning, or sympathize with Mintzberg's ideas of strategy as emerging patterns, it is important to communicate what different strategies mean, as well as the assumptions on which they are based. In our opinion, the scorecard method encourages an organization to draw on the ideas of its many employees and will speed development in this direction.

In the cycle shown in Figure 9.1, ideas on strategy are followed up through control of their implementation. The role which scorecards may have as *management-control systems* has received the greatest attention up to this point. In Chapter 6 we discussed how scorecards can broaden our conception of management control to one of focusing the attention of company personnel on what has been identified as important. Included here are the balance between short-term and long-term ventures, and how the company will develop competencies, markets, systems, etc.

In Chapter 8 we noted that technical solutions are required if scorecards are to be used permanently and regularly, and that these solutions must become a part of customary procedure at the company. *Systems and IT development* can prove decisive for success. Only then can the company monitor developments on an ongoing basis and thus obtain specific measurements often enough to be capable of acting on the experience which it is acquiring. For comparison, let us look at traditional management control. Merely discussing the ambitions expressed in the budget, and occasionally conducting special studies of what is happening, will not provide the focused attention which we want. For this reason considerable effort has been devoted to establishing a system of rapid and regular reporting. Not until this kind of reporting is used for scorecards can we expect them to be taken just as seriously.

We believe that the scorecard method can contribute to *organizational learning* in this way. We are thus back at reassessing our strategies, particularly if we adopt Mintzberg's view of strategy formulation as a continuous, ongoing process. While it may be practical to link strategy formulation to some form of routine business planning in the company's annual cycle, what a company learns may well lead it to reconsider more often what needs to be done. In this chapter we will more closely examine this possibility, as well as the question of who at the company should be put in charge.

LEARNING – A QUESTION OF KNOWLEDGE MANAGEMENT

"The learning organization" is one of the many concepts used in recent management literature. According to Garvin (1993, p. 80), a learning organization is "an organization skilled at creating, acquiring, and transferring knowledge, and at modifying its behavior to reflect new knowledge and insights". In other words, a learning organization improves a company's ability to react to, adapt to, and capitalize on changes in its internal and external situation. The use of the word "learning" is intended to underscore the focus on knowledge and competence – compare our previous discussion on intellectual capital. We would caution against believing that in the learning organization it is primarily individual employees who learn (increasing human capital – cf. Figure 2.5). While individual learning is important as a foundation for collective learning, in the long run it is of limited value to the company. What is learned should also be accessible to others at the company and preferably tied to it in a more lasting manner (structural capital).

The learning organization needs practices and mechanisms which among other things will:

- Capture what is happening in the business environment, perhaps especially through the many contacts of its employees with customers, new technology, suppliers, partners, and prospective candidates for employment
- Enable those who receive this information to relate it to what others are observing and to analyse it in the light of the company's previous knowledge
- Document both information and analysis and make them available to others at the company, and also for subsequent use
- Measure the organization's rate and level of learning in order to ensure that gains have in fact been made

The above has also been called "knowledge management". The term "knowledge" alone gives rise to conceptual problems. What are data, what is information, what is knowledge? There is no need to distinguish these terms for the purposes of our discussion. We find it sufficient to use roughly the same definition of knowledge as Davenport et al. (1998, p. 43): "knowledge is information combined with experience, context, interpretation, and reflection". Manville & Foote (1996) define knowledge management as a systematic process for the purpose of collecting and controlling employee resources and abilities, just as a company controls its inventories, raw materials, and other physical resources. Manville & Foote term this approach "post-modern re-engineering", in which technology plays a very important part in improving processes and the quality of organizational learning.

Sveiby (1997) refers to two tracks, or theories, of knowledge management. These can be related to two different professional categories: one views knowledge management as *managing information*; the other, as *managing people*. Professionals in the former category usually have backgrounds in computer sciences or systems theory. To them, knowledge consists of *objects* which can be identified and processed in information systems, and they consider the concept to be relatively new. At present, this group is growing rapidly and has close ties with new IT solutions.

Professionals in the latter category have generally studied philosophy, psychology, sociology, or organizational theory and management. To them, knowledge is equivalent to *processes* consisting of complex and dynamic human capabilities, behaviour, etc. all of which are constantly changing. To influence learning is traditionally regarded as a matter of dealing with individuals at a company. This view of knowledge management is nothing new, and its adherents are not increasing so rapidly.

The form of knowledge management to which Manville & Foote (1996) refer, and which is in focus for the first of Sveiby's two categories, is the one more closely associated with computers; it is also more frequently the subject of numerous books and articles, even new periodicals. The subject is presented as so simple in computer publications. We have "data warehouses" where we can find new knowledge through "data mining". But are stored data the equivalent of company knowledge? Can they be reviewed and managed, perhaps even evaluated – so that the company makes the right strategic decisions?

There are several reasons why we are now talking increasingly about the strategic importance of information. Technology has given us new possibilities, while also forcing us to seek competitive advantage in ways less easily imitated than close physical proximity to customers and our tradition of being good at what we do. With the use of robots in production and automatic task management, electronics is taking over in areas where we have previously earned a good living. If the societies of the industrialized countries are to have any reason to continue paying high wages to employees, these will have to do something which is not done equally well by computers and robots or increasingly better educated people in the Third World. What companies can do is to create structures around people: arenas for interaction, in combination with procedures and stored data.

Throughout history mankind has increased welfare in precisely this way. What distinguishes us from animals is primarily our capacity to foresee, to communicate, and to use external memory in the form of text and other records. These factors give enormous leverage to the rather limited capacity of our minds. Even when tribal elders by word of mouth transmitted to the next generation how things had been done before, we had an example of knowledge management. Today we have tools for more sophisticated varieties of what is basically the same thing. But it is also becoming increasingly clear that organizations are having difficulty in finding a way to use the tools. (For interesting suggestions, see e.g. Davenport & Prusak, 1998 and Quinn et al., 1998.)

WHAT THE BALANCED SCORECARD CONTRIBUTES TO KNOWLEDGE MANAGEMENT

The first question to ask for a company in search of a more conscious policy of knowledge management must be, "What do we want the knowledge for?" The assets of a company run for profit are worth the present value of their effects on expected streams of future payments. When a company invests millions of dollars in a data warehouse, it does so in anticipation of improving its profits: that is, of lowering costs and/or increasing revenues. How do we describe the link between expenditure and benefit? Before we spend our money, we should try to agree on why we are doing it.

We are not talking about proving these interrelationships; that we cannot do. But what we *believe* about interrelationships should be made explicit. Otherwise we will not make an effort to achieve the desired effects. The data in themselves will not do it. Results will come from what we do with the data. And "we" are the many employees, and sometimes also partners and customers outside the company, who are to handle the data which the company has stored: feed them into the system, analyse them, and use them as a basis for making decisions and doing business.

The investments in systems and training which will make everything happen are growing more and more costly. Even the recruitment of new employees affects how we can expect to use our data. If we are to reach agreement on why we are making these investments, we will have to join together in discussing the future strategic role which we expect knowledge to play. We have been talking about this kind of discussion throughout this book. For this purpose, scenario analyses, for example, may be very helpful, but even just comparing the ideas of senior managers and other employees in a structured fashion is a good start.

What can top management then do to develop these ideas further? As noted above, Sveiby identifies two "schools", one focused on data and information, the other on people. We would maintain that both are important, but so is a third factor.

The first school, we repeat, emphasizes the work of handling data, data which have not yet become information – still less knowledge – but simply consist of facts which we store and make available in computers and in other forms. Systems theory, which has long been concerned with defining concepts, has shown that we often define seemingly simple terms like customer status so vaguely that trying to analyse our data is pointless. Certain authors even hold that the sole justification for the existence of companies lies in how they integrate data which considered separately are also available to others. Grant (1996) maintains that there is a hierarchy of knowledge, with simple building blocks of knowledge (such as a description of a simple operation involved in an installation) at the bottom, and ranging upwards to management of major construction projects; in his view, a company's capacity for integration is what makes it unique. The building blocks need not even be located within the company; what matters is that the company can integrate the necessary knowledge so that we can understand how data, information, and knowledge fit together. Another American researcher, von Hippel (1994), refers to information as being more or less *sticky*, not easily removed or transferred elsewhere in the organization, where it may be needed.

The other school, as we noted, emphasizes people: training, skills in using IT tools, a culture which encourages sharing knowledge rather than jealously guarding it as a power base. Knowledge, especially in the form of skills rather than facts, is often intuitive or unspoken, perhaps even unconscious. Many of those who write about learning struggle with the question of how we are to communicate what has not been articulated. Do we destroy something important if we try to express intuitive insight in words and numbers? We believe that putting into words what our intuition tells us is part of a professional approach. Only then can people in the organization feel confident that they really know how something is done, that they can do it the next time as well – and perhaps even explain how they do it and be able to teach the method to others. Professionalism involves being able to do it, to know that we can do it, and to know how it is done. In the long run it is better for our self-confidence, and for our sleep at night, to understand how we do it than just to know that we usually succeed!

The third school to which we would like to call attention focuses on the structure surrounding people and data. What tools, what infrastructure, do we provide for people? What incentives do we offer to encourage them to contribute their knowledge? Do we publicize success stories which show the value of sharing knowledge? Fewer writers and projects appear to have focused on this area. The writers whom we have found emphasize what Davenport (1997) has termed *information ecology*: the totality of the environment and the conditions under which we live is included in the treatment of data and knowledge by the company.

In theory it is all quite simple. Everyone at the company is bombarded each waking moment by a mass of sensory impressions, of which we are only conscious of a minuscule portion (the number 10^{-7} has been cited). How do we control:

1. Everyone's focus of attention – what impressions do we have a chance of absorbing?
2. What each individual chooses to share with others or to document for future use?
3. How these data are used by each person himself and subsequently by others?

As a practical matter it is of course virtually impossible to find a formula for managing all of the above. The term *knowledge management* turns out to comprise all aspects of the lives of people at the company as well as a portion of what happens in our computers. At the same time, however, these matters are those which most urgently need top-management attention. The point of the company's work on its strategy is precisely to create something unique and difficult to imitate. It is not supposed to be easy! Top management must have a deliberately chosen conception of what it wants to achieve.

We believe that the formula must include data, people, and structure – all three. We must build on a conception of the possible futures for which we are preparing ourselves. Whether we should develop one data base or another, particular skills or information ecology, depends on what we expect to need. Since almost all employees are concerned, it is important that this matter be discussed.

Here the balanced scorecard has a natural and perhaps essential role. In it the development of employee competence, stored data, and the structures surrounding both are reviewed in the light of our intentions at the time when we chose our strategy.

"Knowledge companies" and "intelligent enterprises" are nothing new – all companies have been founded on knowledge, always. But if management is to control the interplay between people and data in a consciously designed structure, it must put on the agenda a number of questions which may not have been previously considered so important, or for which no appropriate language exists. If management does so because talking about knowledge management is the thing to do, they should be encouraged. But these conversations should not only be about investments in data bases or training in how to use the intranet. We need scorecards which give everyone a balanced picture of what we want to do.

INFORMATION SYSTEMS FOR KNOWLEDGE MANAGEMENT

The underlying cause of change is the shift of focus towards the core competencies at the heart of the processes and away from the

process flows themselves. This change also imposes new requirements on company information systems.

Manville & Foote (1996) hold that today's information systems
must meet three main requirements:

1. *A new information architecture* – which provides new languages, categories, and metaphors for identifying and
   measuring the company's competencies and skills.
2. *A new technical architecture* – which is more social in
   character, such as the Internet. In other words, an architecture
   which is more transparent, open, and flexible, and which
   shows respect for the individual and impels the user to change
   and develop.
3. *A new application architecture* – which emphasizes problem-
   solving and presentation, rather than results and transactions.

Traditional "re-engineering" is usually taken to mean gathering
traditional company information in newer, cheaper, or simpler
ways so that it can be made available more rapidly to more people.
Core competencies are based on learning and experience; here we
usually find that traditional data-warehouse solutions have little to
offer. The challenge is thus to build up information systems which
see that company employees share both their information and their
experience, and which help them to do so. In these systems people
and their needs come first, before technology. Manville & Foote
(1996) describe the difference between today's information systems
and those of the future as shown in Table 9.1.

British Telecom

For BT, the SPAM system has resulted in two benefits – effectiveness and synergy. The system provides improved cohesion
between the subprocesses compared to the business planning
process it replaced. This cohesion is a result of improved communication that informs individuals across the process why the
information they produce is important, when it is needed and
how it is used. The introduction of scorecards has ensured
everyone has a much better understanding of what BT is trying

Table 9.1

Today – systems which support processes	The challenge – systems which support competencies
• Transactional processes • Integrated logistics • Work flows • EDI	• Communication-building • Conversation and learning at work • Networks connecting people • Structures for interchange of experience

to achieve from its strategy. Synergies are created because a common base of information is used, shared, and discussed between scorecards, self-assessment, strategy, planning, and operations. Clearly, pooling knowledge has been a major benefit. The introduction of leading edge communication technology has spread these benefits faster and further. For instance, in addition to corporate and divisional scorecards, many units also share their scorecards via the BT Intranet. Intranet technology has proved to be an excellent way of spreading best practice and nurturing communities of interest.

INCENTIVES, MEASURES, AND REWARDS

In a company atmosphere that encourages new initiatives, groups and individuals on their own can compare their present course with the commitments which they have made, either in existing plans or in the continuing dialogue on the business. Information on performance and current status is needed primarily to enable employees themselves to assess their progress, and should only secondarily be considered a tool enabling management to ensure that different parts of the organization and individuals are acting in accordance with the overall strategy. For an employee to see his/her own progress is a reward in itself. Suppose you are a golfer and you are playing a round with your friends. You keep your score and can see how you are doing in relation to your capacity. You can do so because each hole on the golf course is assigned both a par (indicating the length of the hole) and a handicap (indicating the difficulty of the hole in relation to the other holes). In addition, every golfer has a handicap which reflects his/her level of skill. In other words, there is a structure and a system which permits measurement of an individual's performance. The purpose – in a business context – is to focus the actions of individuals (groups) on areas which are important for remaining competitive in the future.

In Chapter 5 we touched on the matter of individual scorecards. Here we return to the question of rewards in a more general sense. Of course, this subject can include the manner in which a group or department is rewarded for running a successful operation. But what is success? Achieving desired levels on all measures? Or are trade-offs permitted? One problem with rewarding performance in terms of the scorecard is that the dynamic balance among several different measures may be destroyed when these measures are combined into a single index of benefit. Such an index is necessary if we want to award bonuses based on performance. In the final analysis, what counts is naturally the amount of an employee's bonus, and for that there is a one-dimensional measure: money.

This statement is true at least if we simply weight together different measures. Often certain threshold values must be attained as a requirement for a bonus. Different measures will be considered quite important, and perhaps receive the greatest attention, as long as they remain below their threshold values, particularly if they reflect conditions which are fairly easy to influence. Once they have reached a certain level, it is no longer interesting from a bonus standpoint to improve them further. Sometimes this effect is a rather fair reflection of the desired "balance" among the different conditions reflected in the measures.

NatWest Life

According to NWL the ability to fulfil the business plan is critical to the company's success. Therefore, achievement in relation to the business plan is one component of performance-based rewards to staff. For this purpose the target level of achievement was initially set at 85% in 1993.

The performance management system at NWL is designed to link individual, team, and corporate performance. An important part is played in this connection by the performance-related reward scheme. In this scheme, targets are set for corporate performance on a number of key measures closely related to the balanced business scorecard and the business excellence model. In addition, a level of funding is established for distribution of bonuses to staff according to performance in relation to the target.

The scheme, which was established in 1993, was first tried on all managers; with their relatively large base salaries, a higher proportion of their total compensation would be at risk. After review in light of this experience, the performance-related reward scheme was extended to include all staff in 1994.

Progress on the measures is reported to staff at regular intervals, typically every month, through team briefs. These meetings strengthen staff understanding of how they can influence company performance. The measures included in the scheme are carefully selected by the executive committee to produce a balanced performance scorecard so that everyone focuses on the need to develop the company in a balanced way.

Each year management reviews the performance indicators. The balance of focus on results is also adjusted to reflect annual priorities; the adjustments are made in the weighting of the different scorecard components (Figure 9.2).

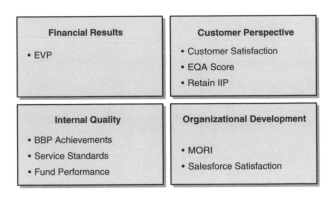

Figure 9.2 The performance indicators in the bonus calculation scorecard (1996)

Halifax

Every individual at Halifax has a personal performance plan for all four perspectives of the scorecard. In other words, the score-card is not only for the branch office, but is also broken down to the individual level. The actual performance of the individual is later the driver for his/her pay increases and bonuses. Halifax intends to improve the link between the individual scorecards and the reward system in the future. Every individual has a monthly coaching session with his or her manager. At these sessions the outcomes of the measures are reviewed, as are the employee's progress in comparison to personal objectives, and possible future actions are discussed.

At Halifax some managers had been very successful even though they only considered measures in the financial and internal-process perspectives. When the new system was implemented, these managers found it hard to adapt to the new way of running the business, and many of them left the company. Today everyone who joins the organization knows how he/she will be managed and how individual performance will be assessed. In other words, the way Halifax recruit people today has been influenced by the new system.

British Airways

At present, the link between the managers' scorecards and the reward system is not very sophisticated. There is a perform-ance management system based on the overall performance. Some of the measures in the scorecard, though, are used as key performance indicators for the individual. At the end of the year some of these measures are then related to the bonuses (the bonuses in operations are not very large, approximately 5% of the annual salary). Approximately 60% (depending on the person's position in the company) of the bonus is based on non-financial figures, and the rest is based on personal devel-opment, how well the person is working as a team member, etc.

Xerox

To be able to intervene in important activities at an early stage, Xerox has developed an incentive system for the entire organization. For salesmen the model is based on customer loyalty. Each salesman and team of technicians knows its own number of machines at the outset of each quarter. Through a point system in which the number of products and their value are added, different quarters may be compared. Salesmen who meet their established targets receive a bonus.

Xerox trains all its technicians itself; in Sweden there are approximately 160 of them. They are divided up geographically and into teams of 6–8 people. A team is responsible for its own customer area. When customer satisfaction is measured, it is broken down team by team, so that it may be monitored for each team. Teams which meet their established targets receive a bonus.

Through this arrangement Xerox delegates decisions and greater responsibility for customers to those in the organization with the closest customer contact. When the system was implemented in Sweden, Xerox made the mistake of not stating clearly who was responsible for what and what had to be done to achieve established targets. The company has attempted to solve this problem through training. For example, only if the technicians of a team are certified at three levels are they authorized to call themselves a certified "empowered workgroup".

Once a year Xerox measures the satisfaction of its employees, since satisfied employees are naturally assumed to be more productive. The degree of employee satisfaction is based on the answers to 15 questions which the employees are asked. The result is what Xerox terms the OSI (overall satisfaction index), which is then used as basic data in the management process.

For the last decade management has had a bonus system based on customer satisfaction, employee motivation, and business performance. The bonus amount is 30% of the annual salary, with customer satisfaction and employee motivation each counting for 6% and ROA for 18%. These percentages may vary from year to year, but only marginally. However, there is a threshold; 100% of the individual targets must be met.

Individual salaries are never tied to overall company profits. According to management, this policy automatically provides an incentive to focus on the various parts of the company.

For salesmen 8% of salary is based on their loyalty targets, and 3% of the technicians' salaries are based on their individual targets. Every supervisor is also required by company management to improve employee motivation by 5% over the previous year. If this target is met, the supervisor receives a fixed amount as a bonus.

Nordbanken

The Central Region of Nordbanken, one of the leading Swedish banks, use a sophisticated system to encourage giving operations the right focus (see Wennberg, 1996)[1]. Though not a balanced scorecard in the formal sense, the system is quite similar to it. Bank offices compete in what is termed "the Championships", in which there are four "events":

- New business
- Quality
- Strategy
- Profitability

The overall standing of an office in the Championships is computed by adding the rankings in each event by comparison with comparable offices and dividing the total by four. However, the procedure for measuring the ranking in each event is much more complicated. For example, "quality" is a non-linear combination of customer attitudes, submitting annual reports on schedule, and the audit rating of the office. As a practical matter, it is impossible to make up for poor performance in one area with outstanding results in another.

There is no link between "the Championships" and the formal system of rewards at Nordbanken. "For most people, just being in the competition is a reward," says the regional manager.

Experience also shows that the attention attracted by measurement and publication throughout the organization is often enough to influence behaviour, even without a bonus. Still, most people probably reason, "They have seen what I can do, and if I stay with the organization and we have bet correctly on the future, I will get my reward."

RESPONSIBILITY FOR THE SCORECARD

As the scorecard is developed, a number of different issues relating to responsibility should be addressed and resolved:

- *Responsibility for the operation covered by the scorecard.* The scorecard functions as a plan, providing for follow-up and documenting goals and results. The person responsible for these is, of course, the head of the division in question, although in certain cases a team is jointly responsible for the operation.
- *Responsibility for the design and use of the scorecard.* This responsibility concerns scorecard use as a "technique": i.e. terminology, process design. Particularly when scorecards are used throughout the company, it may be important to establish a deliberately chosen set of terms based on the accumulated experience of different parts of the organization. This duty is a part of controllership, if we interpret "management control" in the broader sense which we have used previously. However, we do not mean that the entire responsibility should necessarily rest with the company's controller – see below. In addition, at least at the outset, a special co-ordinator may be appointed for the scorecard project. As we have seen, this solution was adopted at KappAhl.
- *Responsibility to see that measurements are performed and that the results are made available.* Here the responsibility is for a system, since measurements and reports, or dissemination of data, generally call for IT solutions – a subject which we discussed in Chapter 8. We do not consider this function as a separate responsibility requiring specially appointed personnel. Rather, it should be one of the duties assigned to operators of

the company's information systems. However, there is another aspect to this issue. The systems do not always provide for automatic measurement; often employee action is required. As we also mentioned in Chapter 8, creating the necessary interest and involvement here is an important part of the scorecard process and may also be considered a part of controllership.

- *Responsibility for giving proper consideration to scorecards in management control.* Whether scorecards will actually be used may depend largely on the presence of incentives to do so. Traditional forms of control may have to be altered somewhat, so that success is no longer measured solely in terms of meeting the financial budget. Sometimes the bonus system should be changed, but equally often there will be a need to influence the way that success and what should be rewarded are viewed in the company culture. Meeting this need, too, is often a function of controllership.

- *Responsibility for learning.* In this chapter we have viewed this matter as the ultimate aim of the scorecard process. It takes time to reflect on the experience that has been gained, and this process, too, may be viewed as an area of responsibility. Here it is more difficult, however, to single out a particular individual as responsible. Perhaps the controller has an important role to play in this regard as well, although learning in the final analysis should be the responsibility of line managers. Their responsibility should be formulated in the process of developing the scorecard of each unit.

We have repeatedly referred to the controller's role in the scorecard process. How this role has been developing deserves a closer look.

THE CHANGING ROLE OF THE CONTROLLER

We have previously noted that we would be glad to see accountants in their role as controllers actively promote the introduction of scorecard thinking. This message has also been put forward in recent years at a number of well-attended conferences on subjects like "The controller of tomorrow", where the balanced-scorecard concept has often been presented as a substitute for traditional planning and budgeting. The discussion on this issue is useful, even though it has sometimes been carried too far. We mentioned this point in Chapter 6.

In Scandinavia and Germany, people began to use the English word "controllers" in the 1970s to underscore a more active role for accountants and business economists, one less constrained by the bookkeeping system and more focused on supporting company decisions. The trend reflected a belief, correct or not, that companies in English-speaking countries envisioned a more active role when using the term "controller".

Briefly, what this kind of controller does for a business is to make it more controllable. He/she does so by affecting the information which managers and their subordinates receive. Information is made available by the company's own systems, is collected from the business environment, or arises when data are processed locally, as in a calculation using a model designed by the controller. Another responsibility of the controller is to see that company practices and incentive systems encourage the people concerned to pay attention to existing information. In a corporate culture where it is natural to analyse a situation before action is taken, the controller may have to be involved in training and internal information. Today we see before us how internal networks are revolutionizing the basis for much of what the controller would like to achieve. At many companies calculations and analyses are being performed less and less by accountants themselves. The new role of accountants is to suggest, design, and install tools of control: everything from integrated, comprehensive information systems to new measures and calculation models, which will then be used by the people in charge of operations. Some controllers have also told us that a growing proportion of their work consists in managing change projects to develop these kinds of tools for control.

The debate on budgeting as something which could be superseded by scorecards should be viewed in this context. Many see the budget as an inflexible and possibly even misleading instrument of control. Svenska Handelsbanken, a leading Swedish commercial bank, claim to have abolished budgets 25 years ago. They maintain that budgeting was a costly and time-consuming process of producing detailed plans that were outdated from the start and thus of little actual use in the business. In recent years a number of Swedish companies, including major international enterprises like ABB and Volvo, have expressed a desire to replace budgeting with a new kind of business planning; see, for example, our description of Volvo's new planning process in Chapter 6. Handelsbanken, however, envisioned a more radical change, with much more limited planning than before and a stronger emphasis on adaptability to changing conditions, flexibility, and control based on forecasts. Still, not even Handelsbanken deny that certain business decisions call for advance preparation and thus for some form of planning. The degree of planning required may vary from one industry to another, and it may involve decisions not only on massive, costly investments but also on matters like the hourly rate which a workshop charges other company units. Thus, even companies which deny that they use budgeting still have some form of planning that resembles a budget. It sometimes appears as if "budget" had connotations which make people want to avoid the term rather than the process itself. Instead of limiting the budget process to one that produces rough estimates at modest cost, and concentrates on matters that require advance planning, people say that they have abolished the budget – and then introduce some new form of business planning which amounts to exactly the same thing!

Here we find the connection to scorecards. If we set goals in scorecard terms, or use a scorecard process in deciding on our activities for the next operating period, what we are doing may quite properly be considered an advanced form of budgeting. Classical definitions of budgeting (e.g. Anthony et al., 1992, ch. 9) describe the budget as a "financial plan, usually covering the period of one year", containing an element of management commitment and structured by responsibility centres. Although it is stated in monetary terms, these amounts may be backed up by non-monetary amounts. The difference is that the commitment, the economic mission of using resources efficiently, now includes both monetary and non-monetary measures. If communicating in non-monetary terms give us better control, then of course we should do so. For many employees and in many situations, monetary terms may be overly indirect and even confusing.

Table 9.2

Financial focus	Scorecard control
• Difficult to understand, thus providing a power base for specialists	• Everyone has an opinion, less obvious need for experts
• Compulsory, thus providing controller with arguments against sceptics	• Voluntary, and can be designed in many ways
• Measures can be consolidated and constitute a closed, well-established logic	• Measures usually hard to consolidate; links and value statements a matter of business strategy
• Foremost benefit: stay out of trouble and avoid business disasters	• Foremost benefit: helps business to be successful

For companies which decide to use scorecards, the time will therefore come, sooner or later, to begin gradually integrating the scorecard process with budgeting and traditional reporting. In Chapter 10 we will discuss the possibility of using scorecards to help describe the business in the annual report. Accountants and controllers must then ask themselves how they would like to view their professional role. How interested are they in the new measures? A simple comparison with our traditional financial figures gives us the picture shown in Table 9.2. The left-hand column lists certain advantages. It may be attractive for a controller to concentrate on the financial focus, because it is obviously necessary as well as familiar. The connection with the Accounting Act and the possibility of reconciling discrepancies help in maintaining management's attention and interest, although much of the information retrieved is for internal use and thus has no obvious links to legislative requirements or generally accepted practice. For the controller, the left-hand column has the advantage of limiting information to accounting data, thus giving him/her a power base and a ready answer to any difficult questions. Many others may also prefer a kind of control whose main benefit is that it avoids hard questions; particularly in times of losses and cash shortages financially oriented accountants usually tend to get everyone's attention at meetings of the executive team and in similar circumstances. With scorecards, on the other hand, everyone will want to take part in the discussion, and it will no longer be possible to hide behind the excuse that information must be presented in a particular fashion.

In the long run, however, this situation is unsatisfactory, even untenable. We think that the balanced scorecard is good for business. Maybe not so much this year, when established profit goals will do. But if we want to be in business next year and the years to follow, we need the ideas of the scorecard! Then even accountants must be open to a broader discussion and to new measures. We view this obligation as part of their professional responsibility for the controllability of the organization. In our opinion, monitoring and discussing measures other than money are necessary if a company is to benefit from the informed views of different people. Actually, dialogues like these have always been sought, e.g. in connection with traditional budgeting. It is the responsibility of accountants to promote the use of any better methods which we may find for ensuring that the discussions take place.

PERMANENT ROUTINE OR "AD HOC"

The balanced scorecard should thus be treated as a part of a company's planning. Now we have also considered the relationship between scorecards and the budget. Do we then have to include the balanced-scorecard concept in our routine planning, or will it suffice to have it available as a method for occasionally reviewing the state of the business? Should we then use it on the entire company, or can we – should we, perhaps – apply it selectively? Is it equally necessary everywhere?

In reality, not very many companies have advanced beyond applying it on a limited basis. Thus, not much experience is available so far, and there is little basis as yet for predicting what may happen. Many previous methods resembling the balanced scorecard have proved to be no more than passing fads, although they may have benefited companies by leading them to reassess their businesses. When they were introduced, however, they certainly were intended to prevail longer. This statement applies both to more budget-like instruments, such as zero-based budgeting and methods for focusing strategy, and to management by objectives (MBO). Once they are actually in use, however, there is a danger that they will lose their novelty and become largely a formal ritual in which certain headings are used when requests for resources are submitted. Perhaps we require new planning models from time to time to meet the need to inject vitality into a company by claiming that we now can do what we could not do before.

However, we dare to believe that some form of scorecard thinking will also be called for in the future. Then the interesting part will not be the four or five perspectives. Rather, it will be the communication on strategy in a form which is structured, though not to the extent of confining the dialogue to an overly limited number of measurement units. By comparison with the past, more and more people in the organization should partake in its "strategic conversations" (compare Chapter 8). What we must do is to design our language for that purpose.

In that statement we also find the answers to the questions just raised.

Few businesses can go through a scorecard process and then rest satisfied with the strategy that results. Both we ourselves and our environment change. Of course the discussions will be more extensive the first time, especially if no discussion of that nature has ever been held before at the company. By comparison with conventional budgeting, we believe that the use of several measures should remove some of the tactical manœuvring and monotonous routine when the process is repeated, although we have hardly any experience as yet to substantiate this statement.

If we establish the scorecard process as a normal procedure, we will have to decide on the resources to devote to IT solutions. We need not measure everything equally often. Perhaps the company's competence develops rather slowly, whereas customer attitudes may change rapidly in certain industries. So may employee attitudes. If we want to benefit from the focused picture provided by the scorecard, it may help us to be reminded of the more long-term measures on a monthly or at least a quarterly basis, though perhaps without taking new measurements and reporting new figures so often.

In most businesses there are probably some activities where we will find a scorecard to be of limited use. This statement is particularly true of functions which we might purchase from others, which we have no ambition to develop, and which we do not consider to be of strategic value: a purchasing function, an internal transport function, or the like. Perhaps such functions may be measured in strictly financial terms. But if we carry our thinking one step further, we will probably always benefit from early information on future changes. This information may be provided by certain process measures, descriptions of contacts between a unit and its internal customers, its suppliers, etc. Such measures will be interesting at least to the unit concerned.

Thus, our conclusion is rather that we need scorecards for certain operations more than for others, and that of course it may be appropriate as a practical matter to begin with these units and not to jeopardize the success of a scorecard project by biting off more than we can chew.

One difficulty with this partial approach is how to find for these units the visions and strategies required for proceeding further. Many a large company, when correctly starting its scorecard work with one or a few selected units, has found that it needed to develop a clearer vision for the role of these units. There is always a benefit from this discussion on strategy, though it will often be more comprehensive and not just concern the selected units. Without it, there will be confusion at the unit about the desired strategy, since the overall strategy must be clear if the unit is to determine its own contribution to it.

For this reason the method is sometimes termed a top-down process. We believe that it is more a question of alignment *upwards* and *downwards*. Alignment allows good suggestions from below to come to the fore. But the objective must be to create a communicable purpose for the entire enterprise, in which everyone in the organization has a clear role. Then top management cannot avoid responsibility for making its position clear.

In summary, the balanced-scorecard concept is a natural and appropriate part of the management control which is the controller's responsibility, but the process itself should be conducted by the managers in charge of operations. At certain companies we have also been told that accountants should not play too large a part in the process, on the grounds that they may fail to see the need for using measures other than financial ones.

WHERE WE STAND NOW . . .

The balanced-scorecard concept is an attractive one – but not so easy to apply in practice. Here are some thoughts on how it should be used:

- The strategic resources which we are discussing are affected by many employees at a company. A cardinal feature of the balanced-scorecard concept is that it enables us to compare different ideas on what kind of business we should be in. If management already knows best, then the balanced scorecard is a way to help many others to understand *why* important things are important. But management does not always know best.
- Once the scorecard has been created, the challenge is to use it for management control. Goals must be set, and follow-up must be provided for. Now we have to prove what we have been claiming. It is not enough simply to say that all measures are important. For the sake of balance we have to establish *how* important each one is. We are not talking about a permanent trade-off or weighting – management control would then be reduced to simple policies or to some form of success index. But top management must be prepared, for example, to indicate how much may be invested in competence development or in marketing to new customers, assuming of course that the "investment proposals" presented by those in immediate charge of the business are accepted. Budgeting with the balanced-scorecard concept will have certain features of a capital-expenditure review. Here, however, "intangible" investments throughout the company will be proposed and discussed: process improvements, customer-sustaining activities, competence development.
- Just because we call the idea the balanced-scorecard concept does not mean that it has suddenly become easier to find measures to describe every important aspect of a business. Usually, the only easy thing is to find *too many* measures – which still do not provide a complete picture. Here it is important to let well enough alone. The measures used should correspond reasonably well to what is considered to be of

potential strategic importance. The fact that certain measures tend to be inadequate indicators does not matter so much. Remember to consider measures in light of what we have just said: as a description of the business which should enable us to discuss it. This statement is just as applicable to goal-setting as it is to performance evaluation. The use of several measures will hopefully help us to avoid the danger of window-dressing: that is, of deliberately confining our efforts to being successful at what is measured.

- The allocation of responsibility for moving the process ahead should be carefully considered. Often it will be natural for controllers to play an active part, but we must not allow scorecards to show the business only through the eyes of controllers. As we have emphasized, measures, goals, and action plans must be actively discussed by line management.
- Scorecards may be viewed as a more advanced form of budget, in which commitments are expressed in non-monetary terms. However, we do not believe that comprehensive, routine scorecard planning throughout the company is necessary for the method to be of any value. Rather, we would recommend caution at the outset before gradually integrating other planning methods with the scorecard process.

NOTE

1. Nordbanken has recently announced a merger with the Finnish bank Merita.

Part IV

Additional Uses

10
Using Scorecards to Inform Outside Parties

In Chapter 2 we noted that outside parties may also have a need to understand our business. Does the quoted price of our stock reflect some omniscient assessment of the company's prospects by market actors who somehow have all relevant information? Hardly, unless we have deliberately helped them by publishing data on our business. The trend in generally accepted practice for financial statements is towards greater disclosure. Would it serve a useful purpose to provide a balanced scorecard as a complement to other information to outside parties? In this chapter we will refer mainly to Skandia, a Swedish insurance company and one of the few enterprises so far to adopt this practice.

THE BALANCED-SCORECARD CONCEPT IN ANNUAL REPORTS

In a way, the role of scorecards in the company's information to outside parties is a question of finding a balance between financial and other measures; we discussed this subject in Chapter 2. The company's management has an obligation of stewardship. As far as the owners are concerned, this duty is of course about managing money. But the money invested by the owners has already been transformed into other assets. How much do owners (and other interested parties) need to know about these assets, aside from their book values? One benefit of giving market actors a picture of the company in balanced-scorecard terms is that different people can evaluate the company according to what they think will happen. For instance, is the company's focus on customers and its efforts to develop competence consistent with the future in which this particular evaluator happens to believe? Even so, a number of credibility problems remain in regard to outside parties. The auditor's report (as yet) covers only the financial figures which are formally subject to audit.

Skandia

Skandia may be the only company in the world to have made such a massive effort to present itself publicly in balanced-scorecard terms. Will future annual reports contain this kind of information? Skandia maintains that what has hitherto been published as a supplement to annual and interim reports may in time become the principal report, with the annual report in its present format as a supplement. Management also notes that the US Securities and Exchange Commission (SEC) is urging listed companies to experiment by following in the footsteps of Skandia.

Skandia began its work with intellectual capital before the balanced scorecard had struck a responsive chord. As the term "intellectual capital" suggests, the principal purpose from the beginning was to describe assets not shown in the balance sheet rather than to "keep score" in various parts of Skandia. But even in the 1994 supplement, the presentation emphasized how the balanced-scorecard concept was coming into use at various Skandia units. As previously discussed, this system was called the Skandia Navigator: It added a fifth focus, for human resources, thus harmonizing the balanced scorecard with the categories of intellectual capital which we have previously presented. The various reports contain examples of scorecards for different Skandia units.

What has been Skandia's experience with its published score-card material? According to the company, the supplements have attracted considerable interest, even among financial analysts, and are distributed about as widely as the annual report itself. The more detailed view of the company provided by the supplements is appealing to investors who look to long-term sustainability. The risk of divulging too much about the company's intentions is not considered serious. What is important is to stay in the lead at all times. This kind of accounting reveals the dynamic forces which give the company's stock its market value. It provides both internal and external stakeholders with information that will give them a better understanding – and sooner – of Skandia's future earning capacity.

Here a number of questions arise. This kind of information, if the market is to understand it and feel confident about it, must be relatively compact, use understandable measures, and be possible to verify in some way. The limitations of today's financial statements are due to these factors and to the legal reality that the person who owns the company's capital also owns the company. The capital to be reported is the capital which is legally controlled by the owners; it has nothing to do with either customers or employees (aside from the rights arising from transactional and employment contracts). Can we agree on a scorecard which meets these requirements while still being relevant to a particular business?

Verifiability is a special question. Will the next step be to appoint independent reviewers – perhaps not the auditors of today, but a more specialized firm?

On this point, if a company today must invest heavily in training or processes, for example, it should be easier to find financing if management can explain why these investments are necessary, how they are progressing, and what benefits they are producing. Companies may be apprehensive about releasing information of this kind or making it available to reviewers. The assets which are being created are, of course, intended to produce future business benefits, and once known they may appear easy for competitors to copy. But companies in the industrial era could not conceal their investments in factories from competitors. Is the difference so great? And perhaps Skandia's supplement at least conveys a management attitude which in itself may appeal to investors.

SJ

SJ (Statens Järnvägar) is the Swedish State Railways – or more precisely, the operator providing transportation, as the infrastructure of rail and track was split off as a separate company in 1988. SJ has followed the lead from Skandia in also issuing a supplement to its annual report entitled *Renewal and Development at SJ – What the Balance Sheet Does Not Tell You.* The principal purpose is to provide additional information to fill out what is not contained in the annual report and thus to present a more complete picture of the company. It is too easy to look only at financial key ratios and to forget other aspects of company performance, according to SJ management.

The measures used are largely those which are also found in many other reports by boards of directors. For example, the following measures are included under the heading of "Employees":

- Distribution by age and sex
- Years of service at SJ
- Employee turnover
- Number of employees
- Number of university graduates in various operations

THE PURPOSE OF A BALANCED SCORECARD FOR OUTSIDERS

In both the text and in notes, the annual reports of companies have long been furnishing information in terms of non-monetary measures (see Johanson et al., 1998). A form of expanded annual report, in which several measures would be used more systematically, was emerging in the 1970s in the form of a so-called social audit,[1] but interest in it soon declined. More recently, there has been a renewed focus, particularly on the environmental impact of company operations. Auditors have begun to consider not only environmental audits, but also environmentally driven business development, environmental management systems, etc.

> Environmental accounting is considered a way for a company to communicate what it is doing about the environment, and to give the company a profile. It also provides information on the company's current status in regard to the environment, and it should constitute additional documentation for the purposes of valuation (Nilsson et al., 1996, p. 22).

The company may be particularly interested in informing business partners, environmental organizations, and the media, but also people who live near by and various authorities. Concerning measures which may be appropriate for this purpose, see Chapter 7. Today we seem to find that annual reports most frequently tell what companies are doing about emissions and waste disposal. The aforementioned supplements of Skandia and SJ represent the only systematic attempts which we have found to draw together these reports in a more complete picture consistent with the balanced-scorecard concept.

While internationally most of the discussion has actually concerned the development of financial accounting, if we want to improve the valuation of intangible assets, for example, we will first have to identify them and describe them using other measures. In 1991 the American Institute of Certified Public Accountants formed what has subsequently been referred to as the Jenkins Committee. The committee interviewed users of accounting information in the USA, primarily investors and lenders. In their report, the committee proposed that companies report, among other things, "high-level operating data and performance measurements that management uses to manage the business", (AICPA, 1994, Chapter 5, Exhibit 1), since this information may be used for assessing the company's prospects for the future. The information should pertain to the business-level segment of operations and may be used to:

- Analyse separately such segments
- Understand the nature of a company's business segments
- Understand the linkage between events and activities and their financial impact
- Identify trends affecting a business
- Understand management's perspective

Ideally, the information should of course be reliable, relevant, and comparable. The Jenkins Committee notes, however, that users give higher priority to following a company's progress over time than to making comparisons between companies. Anyone wanting to make such comparisons may add the necessary adjustments on his/her own. This observation is consistent with another: including intangible assets in the balance sheet was not deemed critical. The task was considered too subjective and difficult, and in reality the effect of these assets on future cash flows is more important. There is more of a need for information on the nature of the intangible assets, their origin, and the length of their useful lives. The Jenkins Committee cites the following examples of business measures that would serve this purpose:

- Statistics related to activities that produce revenues, such as quality; market share; customer satisfaction; defects or rejections
- Statistics related to activities that result in costs, such as the number of employees, and the volume and prices of materials consumed
- Statistics related to productivity, and to the time required to perform key activities
- Statistics related to the amount and quality of key resources, including human resources, such as the average age of key assets
- Measures related to innovation, such as the percentage [of] units produced in the current year that were designed within the last three years
- Measures of employee involvement and fulfilment, such as employee satisfaction
- Measures of strength in vendor relationships, such as vendor satisfaction (abbreviated from AICPA, 1994, Ch. 3)

These questions have also attracted the interest of the SEC. One of its members, Steven Wallman (1996), discusses the diminishing relevance of accounting and financial reporting to user needs because of difficulties in answering the following questions:

- *Who* is the company? In other words, how do we define its outer edges: virtual firms, as well as other entities, are critically dependent on other companies

- *What* are we measuring and reporting? "We attribute no value in financial reports to something as obviously significant as Disney's Mickey Mouse."
- *When* to report? With the "rapid acceleration of events", even quarterly reports are out of date. Will we need real-time reporting?
- *Where* should our financial reporting be directed, and *how* should it be presented? Sophisticated users are devoting considerable effort to disaggregating information which companies have previously aggregated, also at great effort. Should much greater quantities of data be distributed, and to a much larger extent in raw form?

Wallman compares today's financial statements to a black-and-white picture with no scale showing different shades of grey. Despite our notes and the written report on the business, we need to move away from today's black-and-white representation towards one in colour, even though not all "colour" layers of various kinds of information may be equally well verified.

By contrast to fresh ideas of this kind coming from the accounting profession, other studies reveal a more cautious attitude among information users. Many do not believe that non-financial information can be made comparable; they especially fear that it can be easily distorted into an excessively rosy view of the company. However, these studies are based largely on statements by major investors and financial analysts, who surely have additional sources of information. Perhaps it should be considered ethically unacceptable to arrange information meetings for specially invited analysts, as so many companies are in the habit of doing, since this practice may be regarded as improperly favouring these privileged invitees. Do other parties also need more extensive information? If they do, are they capable of interpreting it? And how do we solve the problem of verification?

Every time we select some measures, we exclude others. Thus, when we provide a description, we influence the user, no matter how accurate the information which we convey. Compare Chapter 5 on measures. Our accounting conventions are supposed to reduce the risk that information to users will be misleading. When we provide a more varied picture, as in the form of a scorecard,

our intention is to enable the user to furnish his/her own interpretation. Of course, there is still a danger that the user will be
misled, even if the data reported have in fact been verified.

However, the alternative – accepting the far less complete
picture provided by conventional financial accounting – is certainly no better. And if we include more intangible assets in the
balance sheet, we also transfer the responsibility to the person who
has determined their value. As far as we can see, a more detailed
description, with multiple measures – in the scorecard format, for
example – is the only solution. It leaves the reader free to assess
the information using any model desired. It would of course be
helpful if management provided some guidance by indicating the
future scenarios which it finds relevant and uses as a basis for its
actions. It is questionable, though, how explicit management can
be in this regard – sensitive information on strategic issues might
be disclosed. This kind of description would also require more of
the user.

VALUATION, GOALS, AND INFORMATION FOR
DECISION-MAKING

In the section on financial measures in Chapter 7, we mentioned
the recent proposals on reformed monetary measures, such as
EVA. If the metrics used in the financial focus could be changed
so as better to reflect future earnings, there would be less need for
the other areas of focus in the scorecard. We might even be able to
say that financial statements would then serve their intended
purpose: to provide a credible and reliable view of the company's
position, appropriate as a basis for decision-making by financiers,
business partners, and other parties.

We could then, for example, include in our balance sheet a far
greater proportion of the intangible assets developed by the
company. This change would be quite natural in the company's
internal, managerial accounting. There is still considerable vari-
ation in the generally accepted practice of different countries as to
what can be reported as assets in a company's *external*, financial
accounting. For example, the following statement is found in the

1997 annual report (Note 24) of Ericsson, the Swedish telecommunications company:

> In accordance with Swedish accounting principles, software development costs are charged against income when incurred. Under US GAAP (=Generally Accepted Accounting Principles), FAS No. 86 *Accounting for the Cost of Computer Software to be Sold, Leased or Otherwise Marketed*, these costs are capitalized after the product involved has reached a certain degree of technical feasibility. Capitalization ceases and amortization begins when the product becomes available to customers. Capitalization amounting to SEK 5,232 m. has increased income, and amortization amounting to SEK 3,934 m. was charged against income for the period when calculating income in accordance with US accounting principles.

The net effect on profits was an increase of more than US$ 160m., which after taxes probably amount to about 10% of annual profits.

However, at Ericsson there are other development efforts and expenditures with an impact on the future which could also be considered investments in intangible assets. In our opinion, a large proportion of such outlays should be treated as assets for the purposes of management control. We are more cautious, though, when it comes to information for outsiders. When such reporting is not provided, the reason is probably related to difficulties in establishing whether these assets exist and who controls them. Differences of opinion on their current value to the business need not be more problematic just because the assets are intangible – think of all the specially furnished facilities and equipment with virtually no market value, but which still would have to be replaced at great expense if they were destroyed.

Here is actually one of the principal reasons why a balanced-scorecard approach would have a natural role as a complement to the annual report. The ideal valuation for balance-sheet purposes would require a forecast, accepted by all parties, of the company's future. Since the future is of course uncertain, the determination would be a kind of discounted present value of expected values. Everyone receiving information in the form of this measure would have to accept a long list of assumptions;[2] one of these would be that they share the view of money as the ultimate measure of the benefit provided by the company, and of the value of money over time.

In itself the market can be said to fulfil the role of resolving divergent assessments of the future. Parties with different goals may choose to invest in different companies, depending on how well these suit their preferences. But investors frequently lack the requisite knowledge, and there is often no smoothly functioning market in the shares of many companies. At best the balance sheet can be a picture which is based on convention and which those familiar with convention may believe they understand; it does not fully show what a company is worth. Additional information would be useful, though companies choosing to provide it will have to deal with issues of possible insider information, as we have previously noted. For example, should financial analysts be favoured with special information from companies, or would that practice violate the ethics of the market?

For what sort of decisions would it be helpful for companies to furnish more detailed information in the more structured form of a scorecard? We can think of a number of possible users. These are not so much the major institutional investors, who have other ways of obtaining the information which they need (although they too might find it easier to interpret the more structured presentation of the scorecard than today's information, which is often provided in a rather *ad hoc* fashion). And the small investors with highly diversified portfolios would probably not be able to absorb more information. Rather, we believe that the primary beneficiaries would be the *medium-sized shareholders* who look to public sources for more information on a company and how it views its situation. These users might be interested in the presentation of the company provided by the scorecard, and they would have the time to give it their attention. *Major lenders* might find the scorecard useful in assessing their risk exposure. For *employees* and *business partners*, the scorecard could help them to answer the question, "Is the company's strategy in line with our own thinking, and does the company seem to be investing enough to suit our purposes in the long run?"

The relative lack of interest noted above should be regarded in light of these factors. What we nevertheless consider important is to present a simple overall picture of the company's situation – or that of the entire corporate group, as the case may be. The presentation should reflect the extent to which the company's investments in recent years have actually been in intangible assets (intellectual capital), and it should show the areas where these investments have resulted in assets of long-term value, *in the judgement of management*. Examples might include superior processes, control over a customer base, and IT capability, among others. It should be possible to present these assets as credible even though "hard measures" may be difficult to find.

One dilemma may be that information on such investments is sensitive from a strategic standpoint. Kaplan & Norton (1996a) mention a managing director who expressed no worry about leaving the company's internal accounting information behind on an aircraft, but added that it was a different matter with the balanced scorecard: to a competitor, it would immediately reveal the company's strategy. Actually, however, the situation is no different in principle when companies invest in certain countries, hire certain researchers, or build factories for a certain type of production. The only difference is that these actions are more visible. And potential financiers (via the stock exchange or in other ways) should also have an opportunity to decide whether they want to help the company to invest in software, training, new products, or any other intangible assets. Therefore, these investments should be described, and perhaps also commented on in the annual report, with an explanation as to why the "soft" assets acquired are needed for the future.

ADDITIONAL INFORMATION IN THE ANNUAL REPORT – WHO UNDERSTANDS A MULTI-OBJECTIVE REPORT?

Long before people were talking about the balanced-scorecard concept, many realized that service companies, at least, needed to present a fuller picture of their business. Social audits and environmental accounting were tried in the 1970s, human-resources accounting in the 1980s. Around 1990, some companies in Sweden began to provide more information in their financial statements on matters such as employee experience and environmental impact. Sveiby (1997, p. 185) furnishes some examples, noting that "even the world's largest computer companies, such as computer consultants EDS and Cap Gemini Sogeti, provide no more than a few hints that they employ human beings", so that what we are discussing is still not commonly encountered.

While we favour this trend on the whole, we do have reservations. The measures presented by some companies may be considered variants of the scorecard, if one takes a charitable view. However, these measures have their shortcomings and have been used only to a limited extent over the years. The principal objection is that they fail to meet the need noted above for management to justify investments in various kinds of intellectual capital in relation to the possible futures facing the company. Perhaps we would need new so-called rating institutes to provide a reasonably impartial opinion of the validity of such reasoning. But who would give such an institute its mandate? Probably the company's own management, who would have an interest in persuading outside parties, just as management pays the company's auditors (although these are formally appointed by the annual shareholders' meeting). Perhaps what is needed is a more thorough familiarity with the company's plans and systems than any outside party could realistically be expected to possess.

A sort of proposal to perform this kind of audit is contained in a new publication by KPMG, one of the major auditing firms: "Today's auditor should place more weight on knowledge about the client's business and industry, and its interactions with its environment, when forming an opinion about the validity of financial-statement assertions" (Bell et al., 1997). The focus thus continues to be on the financial audit. But KPMG states that the auditor's review should encompass, among other things, internal processes, the company's knowledge of its customers, and employee attitudes as measured in surveys. These aspects of the audit should be related to the needs that follow from the strategies articulated by management. One reason is that companies whose competitive strength is highly dependent on what we have previously called intellectual capital may otherwise have trouble convincing the market that the company is an attractive investment. Those companies most heavily dependent on their intellectual capital may lack visibility and thus have difficulty in using the stock market to obtain financing. The more a company uses special measures, the more it is essential to know how and why they have been developed. Of course, this requirement poses no problem for a limited group of investors. Perhaps for that reason the scorecard is most appropriate for an inner circle of fairly large shareholders, partner companies, and employees. We expect to see scorecard-like presentations of companies in situations where it is possible to furnish somewhat more information, as in company home pages on the Internet. Particularly when presenting different parts of a major corporate group over the corporate intranet, management may find it interesting to design the presentation like a scorecard, with further information naturally available by clicking a few more times. Similarly, information presented over an intranet can function as the "glue" holding an imaginary organization together (Hedberg et al., 1997), a subject which we will now consider.

SCORECARDS FOR THE INTERACTION BETWEEN PARTNER COMPANIES

A borderline case between internal and external use of the balanced scorecard is in relations between independent companies. This application is a natural one in view of a number of current developments:

- With increasing frequency, when we want to co-ordinate flows with the help of the balanced-scorecard concept (cf. Chapter 5), several companies will be involved. Companies engage subcontractors to a growing extent, and are often links in rather long chains of value creation, where the performance of each link in regard to quality and timeliness will affect the final result in the eyes of the customer. The reporting which we are trying to create with the scorecard will thus be of interest to several different companies.
- Often this reporting will even be more or less permanently embodied in the design of the enterprise. We are referring to *imaginary organizations* (Hedberg et al., 1997), groups in which one company, the leader enterprise, relies on, and seeks to influence the development of, resources and competencies possessed by other companies. The balanced-scorecard concept may be a natural part of such an arrangement.

- With the growth of the Internet, web technology is also being used increasingly to disseminate information within companies, particularly for enabling units in different locations to communicate when the company lacks a network of its own. In the last year or so, most such companies have developed web pages with access limited to employees, a so-called intranet. There is also a strong interest in extranets: i.e. web pages open to partners as well as employees. Extranets can of course be utilized to make the imaginary organization more tangible.

Thus, what we have in mind is assuring co-ordination of imaginary organizations largely through frequent employee observation of selected measures relating to the operation in which they form a link. In this way, information can provide an effective but subtle means of influence in situations where formal authority is limited.

The measures should focus partly on jointly created value for customers, partly on any special success factors for the joint enterprise itself, such as the number of joint projects, the amount of personal contacts, or contribution to shared data bases. If we can also show how these pay off in the form of new and more lucrative joint business, we are probably on the right track.

SUMMARY

In this chapter we have noted that opinions differ on whether it is necessary or possible to provide owners and the market with the more thorough picture which the scorecard is intended to furnish. However, it is easy to imagine situations where this kind of reporting would be appreciated:

- Companies with a few dominant owners, who require a more extensive description and are able to use it
- Companies with substantial intellectual capital and wishing to influence their valuation by the market
- Companies in close collaboration with others and seeking to provide their partners with a description of themselves and of their relationship

NOTES

1. For a description from that time, see Ljung & Oftedal (1976).
2. For discussion on measures requiring agreement, see Chapter 5.

11

Scorecards in the Public Sector

One fundamental idea in the balanced-scorecard concept is that financial measures do not always capture what is important. Therefore, the model is particularly suitable for operations where profit is not a primary objective. This is especially true of the public sector. We will describe the approaches which have been taken, while noting that here some adjustments in the model may be needed.

SCORECARDS WHERE PROFIT IS NOT THE OBJECTIVE

The balanced scorecard is a complement to a purely financial picture of an operation. Consequently, the need for it is least in companies where the predominant objective is to maximize short-term profits – as in certain kinds of trading. But even there it may be interesting to see what kind of learning is cultivated, and what kind of supporting systems are being developed. We believe that scorecards are needed most in operations with a longer-term perspective, and where benefits are not immediately visible in the form of short-term profits. Such is the case with service and development units at companies, even though the ultimate objective is to contribute to profits in the long run. So, too, is the case with voluntary associations and interest organizations, where key measures may relate to the activities of the members themselves.

What we are saying is particularly true of national and local government. As a provider of services, the public sector has many of the same needs for management control which we have previously examined. Above all in the USA, there has been considerable discussion on performance measurement and policy analysis (determining the success of public-sector operations) ever since the 1950s.

The balanced scorecard is currently being used on a trial basis at certain units in both local and national government, but we know of no case where it has been introduced on a broader scale. In this chapter we will discuss some of the differences which may arise – for instance because activities are financed by taxes and decided on in political processes.

LOCAL GOVERNMENT

Various measures of performance and ways of describing operations using key ratios have long been tried in municipal and county government in Sweden. About 20 years ago there was considerable talk about *zero-base budgeting*.[1] The idea was to describe different levels of ambition for each area of operation; programme managers and politicians could then choose the level which they preferred. For this purpose a form of capital-expenditure proposal was needed; it would show the consequences which various levels of appropriations would have for operations. However, it proved difficult to agree on the measures to be used.

In recent years, various forms of *purchaser–provider* models have attracted substantial interest in Sweden (Davén & Nilsson, 1996). Using tax revenues, a purchasing or contracting unit procures the services which the public needs. In order for this unit to consider itself free to reconsider the extent of various services and sometimes even the choice of provider, it is relieved of any responsibility as service provider. This responsibility is transferred entirely to the administrative units performing the service. For example, the county health-services administration can be divided into a purchasing unit and one or more service-providing units. The idea is that who does what and how it should be organized in detail should be regulated as much as possible through contracts between purchasers and providers. The aim of the purchaser is to obtain the best possible service for the taxpayers' money. This objective calls for specific contracts and measurements of the services performed. While both purchasers and providers were already evaluated by monetary measures of results, in some counties monetary objectives were clearly combined with performance commitments with regard to the quality of the services provided to the population. If the service provided has not measured up to that commitment, a positive monetary result cannot be considered satisfactory. In this connection several counties have also had studies done on their "customer satisfaction" using the same methods as those mentioned in Chapter 7.

A balanced scorecard could be used both by various service providers – departments of streets, schools, or hospitals – and by purchasers responsible to local authorities and to the public for the quality of the service. It can be one way of specifying in advance the resources to be used and the expectations to be met. It can also be used to establish what has been achieved.

A number of Swedish municipalities are in fact using various forms of scorecards. In some cases, municipalities have for several years been using the same key ratios and performance measures of a kind which might well be developed into a scorecard process. Much of the usefulness of these scorecards is said to come from active comparison, or *benchmarking*, which should be easier to do for municipal operations than for privately owned companies. Similar activities are conducted in many localities. There is no problem with disclosure, and it should be easy to find comparable municipalities among the many throughout the country.

Materials from Swedish city governments refer to key ratios which describe *resources*, *activities*, *and perceptions*. In other words, the measures follow a pattern which we customarily call an input–output model (see Figure 1.2).

Usually it is easier to measure the left of the model – in other words, resource inputs and activities rather than effects. This fact is regrettable, but users familiar with the company's situation can still find valuable information in what they see. The measures used are what we call *surrogate measures*. However, in various parts of Sweden, major efforts have been devoted to developing better measures of what people think about the quality of municipal service, for example. And advanced statistical methods can be used to study how schools, for instance, are evaluated. In addition, there are traditional attitude questions on how happy students and teachers are with school life, whether certain students are picked on, etc.

The measures and ratios between measures which are compared by the Swedish municipalities are well defined and in some cases designed as unit costs. Care has also been taken to sort the measures for use at different levels: city government, administrative units, and operations. Comparisons and trends are considered especially indicative; for example, differences in the number of cases handled by each official have had a direct impact on budgeting decisions.

Measures appear to concern primarily the quantity of existing facilities and equipment, and the annual costs of service.[2] The total mileage of the road network, and the number of traffic lights and lampposts, are among the measures found in describing the former, while costs are often expressed as key ratios by relating them to some physical unit or quantity, e.g. cost per lamppost. Which description is most appropriate depends as usual on the way in which the measure is used. However, we believe that there are interesting possibilities for starting to divide such measures among the different perspectives. One advantage of these measures is that measurements and comparisons are available for a number of municipalities and previous years.

Several municipalities are testing such alternatives. These run from a more *ad hoc* use of measures in discussions on cut-backs or other changes, to variants of the scorecard. An example is provided by the Board of Child Welfare and Education in the Swedish municipality of Västervik;[3] here the scorecard is more like a stakeholder model (Figure 11.1). In Västervik the board has developed a prototype using the Excel program to present status and performance figures in the different perspectives. The principal measures are as given in Table 11.1.

The measures are a mix of ratings on a five-point scale (most of the ratings which concern students and staff), percentages (financial measures), amounts (money spent on IT), and numbers (new educational programmes). Approximate, easily understood measures have been deliberately chosen.

We find all of these trials interesting. Surely what is true of scorecards for other kinds of operations is also true here: the measures should focus operations on the vision rather than seek to cover everything. There will always be a need for a large number of measures and key ratios at different levels of more complex operations, both in scorecards and separate from them.

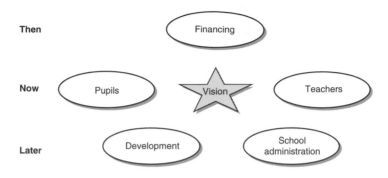

Figure 11.1 Suggested areas of focus in a balanced scorecard for the board of education in a municipality

Table 11.1

Perspectives	Measures
Finance	• Results compared to budget (several different percentages)
Students	• Quality (knowledge, sense of security, development)
	• Satisfied students
	• Problems
	• Parent involvement
Teachers and staff	• Competence/commitment
	• Co-operation
	• Job satisfaction
	• Competence development
Development	• Competence development
	• IT investments
	• New teaching methods
	• New educational programmes
School administration	• Efficiency of board
	• Efficiency of administration
	• Staff development
	• Evaluations

THE BALANCED-SCORECARD CONCEPT IN NATIONAL GOVERNMENT

In the 1970s the Swedish National Audit Office (hereafter referred to by its Swedish initials, RRV) adopted a view of performance measurement which focused on the use of several separate measures to *describe* performance (RRV, 1994). Reference was made to the figure similar to Figure 1.2. Moreover, the discussion was in terms of structural capital and of measures which indicated desirable social effects rather than actually measuring them. This approach has been emphasized now that management by objectives has been adopted at national government agencies; in their requests for appropriations and annual reports, they are to use measures of various kinds to describe their performance and the effects of their activities.

> The results of a government agency's operations are defined as . . . either its performance or the effects thereof. . . . We define *performance* as what the agency produces in the form of services and other products, normally those which the agency ultimately delivers (end products or services). We define *effects* as developments or changes which would not have occurred but for the efforts of the agency. . . . By *follow-up* we mean that the agency identifies and describes its performance and/or the course of events which the agency has attempted to influence through its work. By *evaluation* we mean that we also judge and attempt to explain the agency's performance and the relevant course of events (RRV, 1994, pp. 41ff).

The agency is to establish methods of measurement and measures of results for following up its operations and reporting its results. Such measures are quantitative and qualitative measures of what has been achieved during a certain period of time. They are used for comparison, for giving signals in the exercise of control, and as a basis for learning and change. A number of mutually complementary measures of results must be used at the same time in order to illustrate different aspects of the agency's results.

> . . . Often measures of results are used only as indicators, approximating relationships of broader scope than what the measure normally measures. Indicators are used when it is hard to measure the results of an operation – the results are difficult to obtain or imprecise, or measurement calls for methods which have not yet been fully developed. In such cases we must be satisfied with indicators which only give us an approximate picture of the

results of operations. It is essential that users and receivers of information agree on the indicators and their relevance. . . . Therefore, how the information is used is often more important than the measurement itself, and the approach and attitudes taken toward measurement are more important than measuring everything using the right technique (RRV, 1994, pp. 41ff).

In times of budgetary restraint there is a great need to indicate clearly what can be achieved through variations in the long-term endeavours which should reasonably be made. Both those in direct charge of operations, and their superiors in the decision-making hierarchy, should understand what is happening and what might happen. Our previous discussion on municipalities is also applicable here.

RRV has also issued a publication (1996) which describes a balanced-scorecard method very similar to the one we have presented. However, it is emphasized that certain adjustments must be made when the method is used in the public sector. For example, the starting-point for the scorecard process is the overall mission of the unit as defined by the government. Three fictitious cases are described, in which the four perspectives become areas of focus that should be considered more relevant by the agencies concerned. See Table 11.2 (RRV, 1996). An outward and an inward focus correspond here to the customer and process perspectives. RRV has adopted the idea of a time dimension, and instead of a financial perspective refers to a backward focus. A forward focus corresponds to the growth and learning perspective. These areas of focus are then described in greater detail, which varies according to the nature of the agency's operations.

Of course, the areas of focus and the measures must reflect the strategy deemed appropriate by the agency itself in the light of its mission and its analysis of its own situation. For this reason it is difficult to form an opinion on the three cases. An interesting example is that of a court, for which a legal rights focus is analogous to the customer perspective. The effects to be achieved by the proper administration of justice cannot be seen by looking at any group of immediate beneficiaries. One measure which has been proposed is the number of cases reversed on appeal by a higher court. This measure may be viewed as an indicator of the quality of the lower court's work.

Table 11.2

| Area of focus | Agency | | |
	Museum	College	Court
Inward	Exhibition focus	Teaching focus	Adjudication focus
Outward	Visitor focus	Student focus	Legal rights focus
Backward	Finance focus	Finance focus	Finance focus
Forward	Renewal focus	Course-development and human-resources focus	Development focus

Since the purpose of the balanced-scorecard concept is to encourage communication concerning the choice of strategy and the success of the operation, we should not take a negative view of problems of interpretation or difficulties in agreeing on appropriate measures. We are convinced that it is possible to initiate an extremely constructive and productive discussion at a government agency through the scorecard process.

A DIFFERENT SCORECARD FOR THE PUBLIC SECTOR?

Both the local government experience and the RRV cases are similar to the approaches to the balanced-scorecard concept taken by various companies in the business sector. However, certain changes may be necessary to adapt the scorecard to the requirements of public-sector operations.

First, the logic of the balanced-scorecard concept is dominated by the notion that the balance among different perspectives and measures should promote long-term survival and profitability. For a municipal or national government agency, the goals are different. Perhaps a substitute should be found for the financial perspective.

Second, the decision-making processes where scorecards are relevant differ from the rather rational choice-of-strategy discussion described in Chapter 3. Researchers (Brunsson, 1985) have questioned whether the term "decision" is at all suitable for describing what politics is about.

Let us examine the first point: are the usual four perspectives appropriate for the public sector, or should we make more substantial changes than those in the RRV cases, for instance? Some of the illustrations previously used in this chapter are of course examples of what might be done.

In the public as in the private sector, it should be appropriate to divide the balanced scorecard into sectors of "yesterday–today–tomorrow" as is done at Skandia; in other words, we regard the finance focus as a review of the past, and the other areas of focus as indicators of how well we are preparing for the future. This has also been done at RRV. But instead of a finance focus, an official agency should perhaps describe the results of its work, or of its performance, in broader terms: its effects, according to the input–output figure (Figure 1.2). The "owner" of an agency is society at large, as represented by its legislature and government. What they want the agency to produce is not primarily revenue but some benefit to society. Usually this benefit is broader in scope than what is delivered to any particular clients which the agency may have. For a school, for example, performance might be measured in relation to its graduates: their number, quality, subsequent occupation. How graduates as clients regard and evaluate their education is relevant to a customer focus. The interest of society is in assuring that there will be enough people with the necessary skills, that the nation will be competitive, that the labour market will function as intended, and other effects of this kind. How schools contribute to these objectives would be properly described in an owner focus. Measures like those indicated are probably preferable to monetary ones, even though colleges and universities are now paid by the national government for each degree conferred, so that it would be possible to calculate a monetary result.

The customer focus could perhaps be replaced by a relationship focus. The customer base is of critical importance for a company's future business. The municipality has its "customers" – the inhabitants – as long as they do not move away. It may of course be interesting to measure how many people are moving into and out of a community, particularly for companies, and to find out how attractive it is as a place to live and to locate a business. We would want to include such data in this focus. But in our opinion, relations with local business and associations, suppliers, citizens, etc. should not just be viewed as a delivery of services (performance)[4] which are more or less appreciated. By broadening the

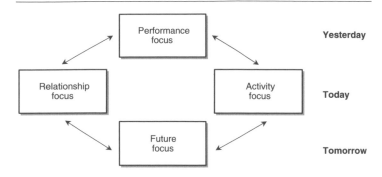

Figure 11.2 Generalization of the balanced-scorecard model to the public sector

customer focus to a relationship focus, we show what is happening with the relevant environment for the municipality's activities in a way which better balances the process focus, which has to do with the internal situation of the municipal government.

In Figure 11.2 we prefer the term "activity focus" rather than "process focus", since here the different municipal activities are described. Although the process concept of industry has been used increasingly in other areas, we do not think that public services should generally be viewed in terms of flows and processes.

Finally, the future focus matches the learning and growth perspective. Here we find the basis for tomorrow's operations, as with an ordinary company. What will the municipal infrastructure be like? For example, we should describe future needs for road and street maintenance, even (or perhaps especially) if no activities or performance have been noted during the year.

The other question which we posed above was: Are the decision-making processes involving the scorecard different from the rational discussion on strategy which we have described? In other words: will political decision-makers accept the well-articulated positions taken and trade-offs which are essential elements in the scorecard process?

Underlying this question is a suspicion that sometimes it may be politically expedient to avoid the clarity required by the score-card when priorities are set. We cannot yet know for sure. The description provided by the scorecard does not in itself mean that clear goals must be set for all its variables. However, even the clearer picture of an operation provided by the scorecard may prove embarrassing if it turns up in the headlines of the local newspaper. We have in mind political promises like shorter waiting times for medical treatment, or lower unemployment, for example. Such promises are easy to specify in terms of measures, and sometimes this is done. However, to go further and indicate the desired trade-offs on a more permanent basis may be considered problematic.

But in our opinion, to avoid testing the balanced-scorecard concept for this reason is to adopt the attitude of the ostrich. Responsible politicians and other officials have every reason to encourage discussion and debate on key issues by making use of this method of providing a better description of public service.

INFORMATION FOR WHOM?

In Chapter 10 we expressed some doubts about how openly a company might want to disclose its scorecard. For the public sector the situation is of course different, but here too, officials may vary in their enthusiasm about giving broad publicity to descriptions, for example, of service provided and of developments in a municipality or at a particular agency. For municipalities, present and presumptive inhabitants are an important interest group, and more than at the national level, there is an opportunity for different municipalities to cultivate different profiles by deliberately choosing how they allocate their resources for the future – there may also be differences by comparison with present priorities. On the home pages which are now showing up on the Internet, we can see that different municipalities emphasize different things. A municipality which describes its IT endeavours or its activities in the arts may reasonably be expected to give these efforts a conspicuous place in its scorecard, if it has one.

When RRV specifies how agencies should describe their operations, we should compare this reporting with both the managerial and the financial accounting of a company. The dialogue between agencies and the government,[5] particularly the functional ministries but in practice also the Ministry of Finance and sometimes RRV, is primarily conducted in the form of documents which are available to the public. However, at the same time it is a dialogue with a kind of "corporate management", so to speak. In more detailed requests for appropriations, and in the quality audits which will now be conducted at government agencies, it would be natural to use methods consistent with the balanced-scorecard concept.

SUMMARY

For non-profit operations, the multi-objective approach of the balanced-scorecard concept is both reasonable and attractive. However, measuring the performance of such operations has been attempted before and has often proved difficult. But that is no reason not to try. Using scorecards is related in an interesting way to experiments in performance measurement at both national and local levels of government. Perhaps the perspectives should be somewhat different; for example, the financial focus in unchanged form can hardly be viewed as the ultimate criterion in the same way as at a business run for profit, and the relationship of an agency to the public is hardly captured in a customer focus. Nevertheless, we see interesting possibilities for developing scorecards for the public sector, without undue complications. It remains to be seen, though, whether the rational ends–means approach of the balanced-scorecard concept has a place in political decision-making.

NOTES

1. Zero-base budgeting was originally a part of the program planning and budget systems developed at the US Department of Defense during the 1960s.
2. Compare the discussion on measures for IT in Chapter 7.
3. Unpublished material provided by Rolf Larsson.
4. Similarly, we could consider broadening the customer focus for certain companies to embrace a more general business-environment focus. In particular, so-called imaginary or virtual companies which are dependent on partners should have reason to monitor and measure the number and

attitudes not only of customers but also of other parties who are involved in the common enterprise.

5. Bergstrand & Olve (1996, pp. 150ff) relate objectives of government operations, requests for appropriations, etc. to how budgeting is used in companies.

Part V

Conclusion

12
Making the Scorecard Process a Success

The balanced scorecard gives us a language for introducing strategic thinking into discussions which we believe will involve an increasing number of people, both at companies and in society at large. A language may have different vocabularies and local dialects, depending on what is considered important to discuss. If we are to speak the same language, we must be familiar with the meaning of different words. The grammatical structure and the context are also important. When we start to use scorecards as our language, we must agree on the individual measures which are its words or terms. The scorecard is a format that is simple and easy to remember, but it has to be filled with purpose and content. Its purpose is no more remarkable than to remind us that no focus should be neglected, and to encourage us to think constantly about how the different areas of focus are related.

When we speak of the balanced scorecard, we are referring to several different kinds of balance: the balance between the short and long run, between different parts of the scorecard, between how others see us (perspective) and how we see ourselves (focus), and between measuring change and the situation at a particular time. Finding measures which achieve balance in these different respects is no trivial matter, even though the balanced scorecard may appear to be a simple tool. Nor is it as simple as it may appear to establish IT support systems and "keep the scorecard alive", to actively discuss linkages, and to use the scorecard for learning. Its apparent simplicity entails a risk that the balanced-scorecard concept, like so many other good ideas, may be misused. Merely putting a number of key ratios into four quadrants does not make a scorecard. If a scorecard is to work, it must command widespread support at a company. Employees must accept the scorecard as a relevant picture of the company, a picture that also includes long-term needs and ambitions. Managers must face up to difficult trade-offs, since everything cannot receive the same degree of attention – there is neither time nor money enough.

Although the history of the balanced scorecard is short, we have already witnessed some disappointments when scorecard projects have not lived up to expectations. In some cases they have been "saved" through a restart, but at a cost in terms of time, resources, and commitment. So in this final chapter, we will summarize our advice on how to make a scorecard project a success. The cases which we have described in previous chapters involve rather different approaches. Suggestions beyond the commonplace ones will probably be dependent on the situation and objectives of a particular company. For this reason, we also attempt to place our advice in the context of a company's development. We conclude by reiterating some of the essentials of why we believe scorecards to be important.

STRATEGIC VS OPERATIONAL CONTROL

Throughout this book, we have used a figure (Figures 3.1, 6.1, 8.1, 9.1) showing the different parts of the balanced scorecard process. Scorecards may be useful both for strategic as well as operational purposes. As the relevant figure illustrates, they enable a company to learn and to revise its strategy, and in turn to modify its system of management control and to gain new experience. Scorecards promote communication within the company, thus enhancing its capacity to adapt to its surroundings, but also to test new ideas.

It is widely believed that organizations move between different stages over time, and must therefore reassess their priorities – in response to impulses from outside, but also to internal changes.

In an article frequently cited, Greiner (1972) described a sequence of five phases of growth, separated by crises which compel a company to find a new set of organizational practices. Each new phase calls for new leadership, new systems of management control, and new ways of thinking. Hedberg speaks of myth cycles and sees a need for companies to reconsider their view of the world from time to time (see e.g. Hedberg & Jönsson, 1978). In our opinion, scorecards can make a significant contribution in this regard. Using a number of measures can increase the exchange of information. In addition, the process encourages a conscious effort to review cause-and-effect relationships. As we stated in Chapter 7, these can take two forms: experience – for example, how customers actually react; and as yet unconfirmed hypotheses about what will be profitable in the future. At the outset, the presumption is that management is correct in its view of the experience and hypotheses on which the business is to be based, particularly with regard to cultivation of competencies for the future.

However, the company must beware of trusting blindly in its knowledge of the world around it. Today's markets and technologies are changing so fast that management should continually test new hypotheses and opportunities. Both hypotheses and previous experience must be continually tested against reality; measurement and the use of scorecards must be focused on this purpose. New and relevant experience will then be gained; for example, the company will develop a better understanding of how customers react. We will have to change our thinking if our beliefs prove erroneous. As new experience is acquired, new patterns of reaction may emerge. Management control through scorecards thus interacts with knowledge management.

What we have seen leads us to believe that the scorecard process may be based initially on different views of what it will entail. For some, it is a question of changing the company's strategy, perhaps in response to the kind of crisis discussed by Greiner. For others, the process may be primarily one of further refining operational control. In Chapter 3 we noted that strategic or operational control may predominate to a varying degree at the outset of a company's scorecard process. In reviewing our cases, we find that different companies have chosen to emphasize and initiate their balanced-scorecard process in ways which may be linked to different phases of the circular figure which we have used in this book.

KappAhl clearly found itself in both a financial crisis and a crisis of confidence in its previous strategy. However, both the industry and the company were long established, so that there was good reason to trust experience. In this situation the balanced scorecard proved its value as a method for reaching consensus on a new hypothesis as to how KappAhl could exploit its strengths and be successful. Therefore, KappAhl had to emphasize the development of a new strategy in its balanced-scorecard process.

A new approach to the business was an even more dominant theme at BT. While neither the company nor the industry was new in a formal sense, deregulation and privatization had led to a situation where a new approach was essential. We find it significant that BT's scorecard project is completely integrated into its overall "strategic planning and management", as a means for group management to create a sense of meaning and to convey it to the organization. Here, too, we find a need for a tool which not only could make a large organization think along new lines, but could also translate strategy into specific goals and numerical measures. In other words, at BT the emphasis has been on developing strategy and a new management-control system and follow-up process.

The situation is different in a number of the other cases. Coca-Cola is building up a new operation in Sweden based on its many years of global experience and a comprehensive global strategy. The company operates in a competitive industry where it is important to ensure that the entire organization follows certain basic policies and the chosen strategy. Here the scorecard, which was formulated by a small group, later served as the foundation for developing the management-control and incentive systems, as well as personnel-recruitment handbooks; it is mainly an operational tool which continually tests the organization's learning capacity and strategy.

NWL is another recently established company. Here a small group made the decisions on both strategy and management control, ensured that various systems would provide the required information, and adapted the incentive system and recruitment procedures to the company's basic policies and strategy. The emphasis here is on operational control of an organization within a predetermined structure for management control. In other words, NWL can emphasize the later phases in our circle: ensuring that there is learning, an evolving organization which continually tests the company's strategy.

The above may be even more true of Xerox, where the company also appears to emphasize management information for operational control: building on previous experience, wider use of the best practice, etc. rather than "revolutionary" new thinking. Today's management control was developed during a period when Xerox found itself in a crisis. The company was losing market share in an increasingly competitive industry. There was a pressing need for a management-control model which could communicate strategy and show the way out of the crisis. While the focus was then on the development of strategy, in today's mature market it has shifted to more operational control.

Other cases may be classified as more intermediate. VCC was in a crisis in 1993. When the merger with Renault failed, two years of product development efforts were lost. A long-term strategy was developed in a short time. In view of the mature and highly competitive industry in which the company operated, there was a great need for a long-term approach in the core functions, combined with a short-term approach at the operating units. In other words, up to the present there have been substantial elements of both strategic and operational control.

Halifax is an example of operational control at the outset, with a successive reorientation towards strategic control. There the emphasis has been primarily on management control and the development of systems and IT. The operational tool which has been created makes it possible to follow what is happening in a large organization. Management has thus established a learning organization, and today – several years later – the time has come to adapt the strategic-planning process to the balanced-scorecard concept.

At British Airways' operations at Heathrow the operational use of the scorecard is even more obvious. The unit was going through a difficult time and it was essential to get control of the business and focus on what really mattered – as soon as possible. The great challenge was to find a pedagogic framework, a language, that not only described the business but also helped the managers to commit themselves to objectives in day-to-day operations. With this bottom-up approach, used at Heathrow, the managers have learnt an enormous amount about their own business and today they feel supported, instead of attacked, in their job of improving the business.

Skandia's endeavours in the area of intellectual capital combine features of a strategic and an operational focus. They originated to some extent in a division whose strategy and organizational model deviated from both company and industry tradition.[1] They are definitely an example of innovative strategic thinking, accompanied by a strong need for communication concerning the cause-and-effect hypotheses on which their international expansion is based. It should be noted that the scorecard process has also spread to other parts of the corporate group, where the approach has been from the bottom up, focusing primarily on operating efficiency.

Our conclusion may be summarized as follows. The quantity of experience which remains relevant is increasing with time. In mature industries and in companies with a long history, there is a greater pool of experience. Experience, however, needs to be tested for its continued relevance. Whether the experience is in a form which can be utilized is another matter – compare current discussions on knowledge management. The balanced scorecard could provide a valuable contribution in this respect.

For new companies, particularly in newer industries, hypotheses – as opposed to experience – will play a larger part in the scorecard process, which will also have a more strategic focus.

Perhaps most important, though, is the interrelationship between a more mature, stable phase and the revolutionary recasting, as illustrated by Greiner and Hedberg, each in a different way. When we speak of organizational learning as a purpose of the scorecard, we do not mean just elaborating on what our experience has told us about our company and its surroundings. It must also be possible to challenge this picture – conditions may have changed; if so, it is time to test new hypotheses.

Thus, the interplay between the strategic and operative functions of the scorecard is crucial. The circle must not look like Figure 12.1, where the connections have been broken! But this situation may easily arise:

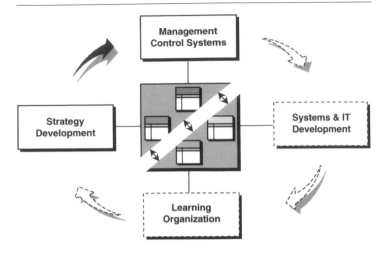

Figure 12.1 Breaking the circle, a danger to be avoided

- If we are content with the strategic discussion instead of continuing on and implementing the project operationally
- If we only consider the scorecard as an expanded form of operational reporting at the operational level, without testing management's basic hypotheses about the company and its business environment

WHAT CHARACTERIZES SUCCESSFUL IMPLEMENTATION OF BALANCED SCORECARDS?

From the discussion above it should be obvious that there are no standard solutions. We dare to make this statement after a number of years of working with the balanced scorecard. How a company's balanced scorecard will look and how management will proceed in implementing the concept will depend on a number of factors: the industry, size of the company, age of the company, culture, etc. In other words, it is very difficult to generalize. However, we can examine certain aspects of a balanced-scorecard project which we consider essential to its success.

Support and Participation

Without the firm support of top management, it is extremely
difficult to succeed in implementing a concept like the balanced
scorecard. Also, it often takes a long time before an entire
organization can be made to understand both the ideas involved
in the concept and its impact on the daily work of individual
employees. During this time it is of utmost importance for the
entire organization to feel that top management unreservedly
endorses the values, ideas, and management philosophy inherent
in the balanced scorecard. Top management must provide the
necessary resources in the form of sufficient time and training to
implement the scorecard. Companies which fail to gain the
requisite support for the concept have lacked a real enthusiast, or
at least one at a high enough level to keep the project moving
ahead in the face of adversity.

One of the primary purposes of a balanced scorecard is to
establish participation and communication concerning a company's vision and strategic aims. If the concept is improperly
applied, people in the organization may unfortunately view it as a
tool to control them rather than to ensure that the company is
making progress towards its established goals. It is therefore
important that a large part of the company participate in the
actual process of developing the scorecard, a process which begins
with the company's comprehensive vision. In this way the company can reach a consensus on how each individual can help to
achieve its strategic objectives. Another way to create a sense of
participation and of having a stake in the project is to let the
organization decide on a name for the company's own version of
the concept.

Priority

In recent years many companies have undergone major changes.
The rapid succession of change projects based on different theories
of organizational change has exasperated many employees. Seeing
the balanced scorecard as yet another three-letter acronym (BSC!),
they can easily perceive it as just one more "flavour of the

month", just another burdensome project. Its benefits may appear uncertain, as may the chances that the project will have any lasting impact. Proper timing is therefore essential. It is also critical that top management be able to explain the purpose of the scorecard project and its relationship to previous company projects. For example, if the company has already worked with multidimensional measures as part of TQM, management should build on this experience and show what scorecards can add.

Composition of the Project Group

The balanced-scorecard concept is intended to provide as complete a picture as possible of the company. Therefore, many different parts of the organization should be represented in the project group and contribute their views during the process of developing the scorecard. At some of the companies in our case studies, it was felt that too many members of the project group had their professional background in accounting. Not surprisingly, there was a tendency to favour the use of traditional financial measures at these companies.

The project groups have consisted of 4–15 people. It is impossible to generalize about an optimal number for success. While it is important not to let the group grow so large that efficiency and freedom of action are impaired, the group should not be so small that certain parts of the organization have no voice in the process.

Coverage of the Project

If a balanced-scorecard project is too broad in coverage and/or involves too many people, there is a danger that the work will balloon and overtax the company's resources. It may then take too much time to gain the necessary support for the concept, and the desired effects may not be obtained. Also, the project may consume too much of the time of key personnel, so that seeing it through to the finish is perceived as burdensome. Some companies seek to avoid this danger by starting with a pilot project at a subsidiary or department. The organization can then learn from its mistakes and have an easier time with further implementation of the concept. Another advantage of a pilot project is that it can help win the confidence of employees. What employees like and dislike about the concept may carry more weight than the pronouncements of top management or outsiders.

However, some companies believe in company-wide implementation of the concept from the very outset, reasoning that the balanced-scorecard concept raises issues with broader ramifications. This approach forces the entire company to change its philosophy of management control, and to look ahead to its goals for the future. The drawback is that the process – gaining support, spreading the message, and instilling appropriate attitudes – may take a very long time.

Basing the Scorecard on the Company's Strategy

It is fundamental that the balanced scorecard be based on the company's comprehensive vision and overall strategic aims. Before a balanced-scorecard process can go further, the company's strategy must be broken down into measures and goals consistent with it. If the scorecard is not based on strategy, there is a serious danger of suboptimization, with different parts of the organization working at cross-purposes. The principal challenge is to achieve a balance between maximum participation in the process of strategy formulation, and maintaining focus on operations. Experience has shown that many enjoy dreaming of a distant vision more than coming to grips with their day-to-day work. For that reason some companies have chosen to entrust the process of strategy formulation to a small group, while the rest of the organization formulates business plans, devises measures, and sets targets.

Clearly and Consistently Defined Measures

The measures used in a balanced scorecard should be defined precisely and in the same way throughout the organization. If a

corporation wishes to compare the progress of different subsidiaries and/or departments, it must be clear from the start in
formulating common definitions for the measures to be used. The
definitions should also be easily accessible in a data base or
manual, for example. If it is too difficult to find a measure, there is
a danger that this will be an excuse for not implementing any
measurement at all.

Balance and Cause-and-effect Relationships between Measures

Company objectives have traditionally been expressed in terms of
financial measures and goals. As a result, systems have been
developed to permit monitoring financial measures on virtually a
daily basis. Many companies lack the capability to monitor non-
financial measures, or have no tradition of doing so; here there is a
substantial risk that non-financial measures will be neglected. A
balanced scorecard is intended not only to give a company a
broader view of its business, but also to force it to determine how
the different measures affect each other.

Even if a company has no historical statistics on the latter point,
it is essential that it be discussed within the organization. When
cause-and-effect relationships cannot (yet) be verified, management must still have some idea about them. The reason for
emphasizing customer-sustaining activities, service, or development of competence is that they are presumed to benefit future
business and increase future profits. Here more or less formalized
simulations and scenario models may be of interest as management tools.

Setting Goals

Goals must be set for each measure. If a balanced scorecard is to be
credible, goals must first be consistent with the comprehensive
vision and overall strategy. Second, they must be realistic and
attainable. While goals must be ambitious enough to spur the

organization to develop, it is also important that employees throughout the organization find that most goals are generally met.

A company needs both short-term and long-term goals. Short-term goals should have a time frame of 3–18 months, and they may constitute subgoals in relation to a long-term goal. To maintain focus on measures related to short-term goals, measurements should be taken relatively often, perhaps even monthly. By contrast, long-term goals cover a period of two to five years, and they are commonly updated and modified during the process of strategy formulation. To function as instruments of control, measurements of progress towards long-term goals must be taken at least once a year, and preferably each quarter.

Relationship to Existing Control Systems

The balanced scorecard is a method for strategic control of a business or other operation. Naturally, it must be aligned with existing systems of control, particularly management control. Budgets, reports, and incentive systems must be adapted to the scorecard and in time co-ordinated, perhaps even integrated, with the measures used in it. Otherwise, traditional responsibility and rewards for monetary performance will probably continue to predominate, at the expense of responsibility for successfully meeting the commitments which have emerged from the scorecard dialogue. In addition, excessive resources must be devoted to administrative processes.

The situation may seem worrisome, even dangerous, to management, particularly at the executive level (board of directors and senior corporate management), with its customary view of the business in terms of financial measures. Moreover, this description may be the only possible one at the top level of a diversified corporation which operates in different industries and thus serves a variety of markets. Quite early on, a company must determine the desired combination of monetary and non-monetary responsibility for its managers, with appropriate adaptation to different parts of the business and different levels of the organizational hierarchy.

Ensuring the Feasibility of Measures and Measurements

If a scorecard is to be effective, it must be continually filled with current, relevant information so that it becomes a natural part of the company's strategic discussion and learning. The process of formulating the balanced scorecard often results in a number of measures which do not exist in the company's present systems. Here the project group must make sure that the necessary data will be provided. Otherwise the company may well find itself with a scorecard filled with a number of measures which cannot be followed. It will then be difficult to achieve a learning organization and to test strategy.

The company must therefore develop intuitive, flexible, and cost-effective systems and procedures for measurement, systems which will make it possible to use information from available data bases – both internal and external – and which also permit digitalization of measurement which has been performed manually in the normal course of operations.

IT-based Presentation and Support Systems

Many believe that a company cannot reap the full benefits of the balanced-scorecard concept unless the scorecard is linked to an IT-based presentation and support system. With computer-based diagrams and illustrations, an organization can quickly and easily obtain a comprehensive view of how the company is doing. In this way individuals can clearly see the impact of their work on overall company performance.

While an IT-based presentation and support system is required if data collection and reporting are to function in the long run, it is also important that the project not acquire an image as a "computer project" too early in the process. If it does, it may be considered too abstract by many people in the organization.

How much IT support should be used, and at what stage of the scorecard process, are questions to be decided from case to case. Clearly, a larger organization with more operating units will have different needs from a smaller company with more concentrated operations. Nevertheless, we believe that there will soon be

interesting opportunities for utilizing IT support in a more standardized way, and at acceptable cost, particularly for the strategic
discussions of top management on linking different factors and
measures.

Training and Information

In our experience, it is impossible to give an organization too
much information and training. It is essential that information on
the balanced-scorecard concept be readily available and easily
understood. Training and information can be provided with the
help of manuals, an intranet, or seminars. Experience has shown
that information is transmitted most easily to groups of 20 people
or less. In larger groups, people may be more reluctant to ask
questions and critically examine the ideas underlying the concept.

Development of a Learning Organization

In a balanced-scorecard process strategy is broken down into
measures and specific goals. This process develops participation,
awareness, a decentralized decision-making process, and responsibility for achieving the goals which have been formulated. As a
consequence, there must be a goal-achievement analysis, in which
the organization draws conclusions about what it is doing well,
what it is not doing so well, and what can be improved.

Following up the Concept

To remain competitive, a company must constantly review its
strategy. Most companies operate in an environment which com-
pels them to test their strategy continually. The link between a
company's strategic aims and the measures in its scorecard may be
regarded as a hypothesis of certain cause-and-effect relationships.
If there later turns out to be no correlation between measures
and strategic aims, that finding is an indication that the theories
underlying the choice of strategy should be re-examined.

Discussions of this kind should be held at least once a year, perhaps even on a quarterly or monthly basis. A balanced scorecard should not be regarded as a static product but as a living model of a company.

SUMMARY

In this chapter we have tried to illustrate some of the issues which must be addressed before a company decides on a balanced-scorecard project. Again we would emphasize that there are no standard solutions. A particular company must always consider a wide range of factors, which vary in the degree to which they can be influenced: e.g. the maturity of the industry, the age of the organization, organizational culture, existing systems of management control, age profile of company staff.

A balanced scorecard gives an organization a framework for communicating the company's vision and strategy by expressing them in the form of strategic objectives, measures and goals. A company will then find it easier to adopt new strategies, and gain greater flexibility in dealing with changing markets.

For large parts of the organization, a company's strategy is generally viewed as an abstraction, a document or a number of sentences which only top management understands. For successful implementation of a company's vision and strategy, operating plans must be developed and followed up. If properly used, a balanced scorecard is an excellent tool for expressing an abstract vision and strategy in tangible terms, so that these can be presented throughout the organization, and for providing follow-up so that the vision is achieved and the strategy is pursued as intended.

In our opinion, this kind of management control based on strategy is the principal reason why many companies began to experiment with different varieties of the scorecard in the 1990s. As a condition for success we would particularly emphasize the importance of the so-called virtuous circle of strategy, control, measurement, learning, and back to strategy. If the circle is broken, much of the potential of the balanced scorecard may be lost; on the other hand, if the circle is kept intact, the scorecard process will enable the company to benefit from a combination of some of the most significant elements of modern management control.

NOTE

1. We are referring to Skandia AFS – see Hedberg et al. (1997).

Appendix: Examples of Measures in the Different Perspectives

In this appendix we provide some examples of proposed measures for each perspective. They should not be seen as recommended metrics – as readers will understand from the main text, measures should always reflect the particular strategy and critical success factors of each company. They are collected from a variety of sources, including previous literature on scorecards.

As will be seen, both outcome measures and performance drivers can be found among the measures. But in the financial perspective it is of course natural to find outcome measures, whereas the renewal and development perspective contains almost exclusively performance drivers. However, a status measure like patents pending in the later focus could be seen as the outcome of development activities in previous periods. And when we look to the remaining perspectives, there is clearly a mixture of drivers and outcomes. For instance, under the customer perspective, time spent on customer relations is obviously a driver while customer loyalty could be seen as an outcome. But then, customer loyalty may in turn drive sales, illustrating what we said in Chapter 1 about the means–effect chain character of such measures.

FINANCIAL PERSPECTIVE

1. Total assets ($)
2. Total assets/employee ($)
3. Revenues/total assets (%)
4. Revenues from new products or business operations ($)
5. Revenues/employee ($)
6. Profits/total assets (%)
7. Profits from new products or business operations ($)
8. Profits/employee ($)
9. Market value ($)
10. Return on net assets (%)
11. Value added/employee ($)
12. Return on total assets (%)
13. Return on capital employed (%)
14. Profit margin (%)
15. Contribution/revenue, or contribution margin (%)
16. Contribution/employee ($)
17. Cash flow ($)
18. Shareholder equity/total assets, or solvency (%)
19. Return on investment (%)
20. Total costs ($)

Many other measures could be considered. A number of them are found in the financial analyst's arsenal of measures, and we would refer the interested reader to the specialized literature on accounting measures. However, it is apparent from the list above that some writers, for example Kaplan & Norton, would also include more market-related measures such as those showing the profitability of different customer segments. While these measures, too, present a picture of "yesterday" which – with a little effort – we could extract from the company's accounting, they could also be listed under the customer focus.

The measures are often quite appropriate for comparing different parts of companies and for relating the company to industry averages or its own historical data. For example, at Volvo (see Chapter 6), we have observed how the company makes active use of graphs and time series in its presentations. Measures both of status and of change – that is, related both to the balance sheet and to the income statement – should be included.

CUSTOMER PERSPECTIVE

1. Number of customers (No.)
2. Market share (%)
3. Annual sales/customer ($)
4. Customers lost (No. or %)
5. Average time spent on customer relations (No.)
6. Customers/employee (No. or %)
7. Sales closed/sales contacts (%)
8. Satisfied-customer index (%)
9. Customer-loyalty index (%)
10. Cost/customer ($)
11. Number of visits to customers (No.)
12. Number of complaints (No.)
13. Marketing expenses ($)
14. Brand-image index (%)
15. Average duration of customer relationship (No.)
16. Average customer size ($)
17. Customer rating (%)
18. Customer visits to the company (No.)
19. Average time from customer contact to sales response (No.)
20. Service expense/customer/year ($)

Some of the measures above are examples of "how customers see us": satisfied-customer index, various measures of attitudes, etc. These measures may in turn be broken down by customer category, marketing channel, and the like. They should reflect both our current standing with different target groups and how it has changed as a result of operations in the latest period – in other words, they should give us both a kind of balance sheet and a kind of income statement. For obtaining early indications on future sales, it has proven fruitful by experience to monitor measures which primarily are surrogates, such as customer awareness (brand recognition). There are still earlier indicators which are even more surrogate in nature; examples would be completed marketing efforts and visits to prospective customers. Sometimes these kinds of measures may be included in the renewal and development focus, as with resources spent to enter a market or to reposition the company there.

Depending on the situation (that is, on what has been identified as critical to success), we may also need measures showing the company's share of customers' purchases, the frequency of contacts, the number of employees with active customer contacts of their own, and other factors which we seldom find mentioned in the literature.

PROCESS PERSPECTIVE

1. Administrative expense/total revenues (%)
2. Processing time, outpayments (No.)
3. On-time delivery (%)
4. Average lead time (No.)
5. Lead time, product development (No.)
6. Lead time, from order to delivery (No.)
7. Lead time, suppliers (No.)
8. Lead time, production (No.)
9. Average time for decision-making (No.)
10. Inventory turnover (No.)
11. Improvement in productivity (%)
12. IT capacity [CPU and DASD] (No.)
13. IT capacity/employee (No.)
14. Change in IT inventory ($ or %)
15. IT expense/administrative expense (%)
16. Emissions from production into the environment (No.)
17. Environmental impact of product use (No.)
18. Cost of administrative error/management revenues (%)
19. Contracts filed without error (No.)
20. Administrative expense/employee ($)

Much of the reasoning in Chapter 7 is relevant here. For example, it may be important to measure not only the theoretical capacity and current performance of certain processes (actual quality, throughput times, etc.), but also reserve capacity and flexibility for handling larger quantities or a different product assortment. Here, too, both current status and the change during the period are of interest. If we do not want a special human-resources focus, many process measures will reflect the interaction of people and technology. In this case, what we noted in Chapter 7, under the heading "Measures for IT", becomes directly pertinent. The potential for improvement and the capacity for expansion often lies in teaching employees to make better use of existing technology. In this regard we may be interested in measures which relate employee competence to the capability of systems – for example, how many employees have mastered various applications of the company's computer system, how many employees actively use the Internet, or access the company's customer data base.

RENEWAL AND DEVELOPMENT PERSPECTIVE

1. R&D expense ($)
2. R&D expense/total expenses (%)
3. IT development expense/IT expense (%)
4. Hours, R&D (%)
5. R&D resources/total resources (%)
6. Investment in training/customers (No.)
7. Investment in research ($)
8. Investment in new product support and training ($)
9. Investment in development of new markets ($)
10. Direct communications to customers/year (No.)
11. Patents pending (No.)
12. Average age of company patents (No.)
13. Suggested improvements/employee (No.)
14. Competence development expense/employee ($)
15. Satisfied-employee index (No.)
16. Marketing expense/customer ($)
17. Employee's view (empowerment index) (No.)
18. Share of employees below age X (%)
19. Non-product-related expense/customer/year ($)
20. Ratio of new products (less than X years old) to full company catalogue (%)

As with the process focus, measures here often reflect the interaction of people and systems. We are often forced to use measures of what we do rather than of what we accomplish, or of effects, since we take our measurements at an early stage of a process over time. As we know, a high level of theoretical education at a development department is no guarantee that innovation will be forthcoming, just as building up a new business at great expense is no assurance that success will follow. Therefore, the measures chosen should enable readers to draw their own conclusions as to whether the reported combination of resources – human and otherwise – accomplishments, and results is convincing.

The measures appropriate for this purpose may vary substantially depending on the nature of the investment in the future. As with the other areas of focus, however, it is important to reflect both status and change. For an R&D or a systems-development department, it may be interesting to measure its size and accomplishments (patents, systems put in operation), and their impact (share of sales from new products; acceptance of new internal support systems). Such measures may also be related to previous periods and compared between different company units.

HUMAN-RESOURCES PERSPECTIVE

1. Leadership index (No.)
2. Motivation index (No.)
3. Number of employees (No.)
4. Employee turnover (%)
5. Average employee years of service with company (No.)
6. Average age of employees (No.)
7. Time in training (days/year) (No.)
8. Temporary employees/permanent employees (%)
9. Share of employees with university degrees (%)
10. Average absenteeism (No.)
11. Number of women managers (No.)
12. Number of applicants for employment at the company (No.)
13. Empowerment index (No.), number of managers (No.)
14. Share of employees less than 40 years old (%)
15. Per capita annual cost of training ($)
16. Full-time or permanent employees who spend less than 50% of work hours at a corporate facility (No.)
17. Percentage of full-time permanent employees (%)
18. Per capita annual cost of training, communication, and support programmes ($)
19. Number of full-time temporary employees (No.)
20. Number of part-time employees or non-full-time contractors (No.)

If a special human-resources perspective is desired, it should be related to those human-resource factors which are considered strategically important. While one factor would naturally be employee competence, others would be the distribution of employees with regard to age, sex, and perhaps other aspects of their backgrounds such as occupational experience and nationality. Employee turnover, attitudes, and opportunities for advancement or transfer within the company are additional factors. Furthermore, the measures chosen should reflect the relationship to other perspectives; examples would be employee contacts with customers and the ability to use computerized systems.

Interviews

The following persons were interviewed by the authors especially for this book.

ABB

Lennart Lundahl, Group Staff, ABB AB
Lennart Andersson, Manager, Business Consulting
Jan Frisk, Application Consultant

BRITISH AIRWAYS

Peter Read, Director of Heathrow

BRITISH TELECOM

Steve Walkin, Manager, Corporate Development (BT Quality and Business Management)
Gerwyn Williams, Manager, Corporate Development (BT UK Human Resources)

COCA-COLA BEVERAGES SWEDEN

Claes Tellman, External Affairs Manager
Per Widerström, Enterprise Project Manager

ELECTROLUX

Peder Zetterberg, Deputy Group Controller, Budget and Control

HALIFAX

David Fisher, Head of Retail Sales
Su R Kinney, Manager, Network Performance Information

KAPPAHL

Thommy Nilsson, President and CEO
Helene Duphorn, Project Leader for balanced scorecard project
Peter Karlsson, Business Controller

NATWEST LIFE

Theo van-Hensbergen, Head of Corporate Development, Life and Investment Services
David J Watts, Head of Corporate Development, NatWest Life

SKANDIA

Lars-Erik Petersson, President and CEO
Leif Edvinsson, Director of Intellectual Capital

SKF

Anders Forsberg, Group Controller

VOLVO CAR CORPORATION

Staffan Carlson, Vice-president and CFO
Hans Oscarsson, Financial Planning and Control

XEROX

Göran Möller, Director, Rank Xerox Quality Services
Lasse Säfwenberg, Quality and Customer Satisfaction

References

Adams, C. & Roberts, P. (1993). You Are What You Measure. *Manufacturing Europe 1993*, Sterling Publications Ltd, pp. 504–507

AICPA (American Institute of Certified Public Accountants) (1994). Improving Business Reporting – A Customer Focus, the comprehensive report of the AICPA Special Committee on Financial Reporting, chaired by Edmund Jenkins (a.k.a. The Jenkins Report). URL: www.aicpa.org

Andrews, K.R. (1980). *The Concept of Corporate Strategy* (3rd edn). Irwin, Homewood, Ill.

Anthony, R.N., Dearden, J. & Govindarajan, V. (1992). *Management Control Systems* (7th edn). Irwin, Homewood, Ill.

Barney, J. (1991). Firm Resources and Sustained Competitive Advantage. *Journal of Management*, **17**(1), 99–120

Bell, Timothy et al. (1997). *Auditing Organizations through a Strategic-Systems Lens. The KPMG Business Measurement Process.* KPMG Peat Marwick

Bergstrand, J. & Olve, N.-G. (1996). *Styr bättre med bättre budget* (Improved control through improved budgeting). Liber, Malmö

Brunsson, N. (1985). *The Irrational Organization. Irrationality as a Basis for Organizational Action and Change.* Wiley, Chichester

Collis, J.D. & Montgomery, C.A. (1995). Competing on Resources: Strategy in the 1990s. *Harvard Business Review*, July–August, 118–128

Dahlgren, L.E. et al. (1997). *Make IT Profitable!* Ekerlids, Stockholm

Davén, B. & Nilsson, H. (1996), *Kommunerna och decentraliseringen – tre fallstudier* (The communes and decentralization – three case studies). Finansdepartementet (Swedish Ministry of Finance) Ds 1996: 68

Davenport, T. (1997). *Information Ecology.* Oxford UP, New York

Davenport, T. & Prusak, L. (1998) *Working Knowledge.* Harvard Business School Press, Boston, Mass.

Davenport, T. et al. (1998). Successful Knowledge Management Projects. *Sloan Management Review*, **39**(2), 43–57

Eccles, R.G. & Pyburn, P.J. (1992) Creating a Comprehensive System to Measure Performance. *Management Accounting*, October, 41–58

Edvinsson, L. & Malone, M. (1997). *Intellectual Capital.* Harper Business, New York

EFQM (1998). *Self-assessment Guidelines.* European Foundation for Quality Management, Brussels

Falk, T. & Olve, N.-G. (1996). *IT som strategisk resurs* (IT as a strategic resource). Liber, Malmö

Garvin, D.A. (1993). Building a Learning Organization. *Harvard Business Review*, July–August, 78–91

Goldenberg, H. & Hoffecker, J. (1994). Using the Balanced Scorecard to Develop Companywide Performance Measures. *Journal of Cost Management*, Fall

Grant, R.M. (1993). *Contemporary Strategy Analysis*. Blackwell Business, Oxford

Grant, R. (1996). Prospering in Dynamically-competitive Environments: Organizational Capability as Knowledge Integration. *Organization Science*, 7

Greiner, L. (1972). Evolution and Revolution as Organizations Grow. *Harvard Business Review*, **50**, July–August. Reprinted (1998) with author's comments: **76**, May–June, 55–68

Hally, D.L. (1994). Cost Accounting for the 1990s. *Finance*, December, 129–182

Hamel, G. & Prahalad, C.K. (1994). *Competing for the Future*. Harvard Business School Press, Boston, Mass.

Hansson, J. (1997), *Skapande personalarbete. Kompetens och lärande som strategi.* RabénPrisma, Stockholm

Hedberg, B.L.T. & Jönsson, S.A. (1978). Designing Semi-confusing Information Systems for a Self-designing Organization. *Administrative Sciences Quarterly*, **21**, 41–65

Hedberg, B. et al. (1997), *Virtual Organizations and Beyond: Discover Imaginary Systems*. Wiley, Chichester

Helling, J. (1995). *Verksamhetsmätning* (Activity measurement). Studentlitteratur, Lund

Jansson, Å., Nilsson, F. & Rapp, B. (1997). Implementing Environmentally-Driven Business Development: A Management Control Perspective. Paper presented at the workshop "Environmental Management: Beyond Standardized Systems" arranged by School of Business, Stockholm University, 5–7 November, 1997

Johanson, U. et al. (1998). *Human Resource Costing and Accounting versus the Balanced Scorecard. A literature survey of experience with the concepts.* A report to OECD. School of Business, Stockholm University (draft version)

Johnson, T.H. & Kaplan, R.S. (1987). *Relevance Lost – the Rise and Fall of Management Accounting*, Harvard Business School Press, Boston, Mass.

Kald, M. & Nilsson, F. (2000). Performance Measurement at Nordic Companies. *European Management Journal*, **18**(1), 113–127

Kaplan, R.S. & Cooper, R. (1998). *Cost & Effect*. Harvard Business School Press, Boston, Mass.

Kaplan, R.S. & Norton D.P. (1992). The Balanced Scorecard – Measures that Drive Performance. *Harvard Business Review*, Jan–Feb, 71–79

Kaplan, R.S. & Norton D.P. (1993). Putting the Balanced Scorecard to Work. *Harvard Business Review*, Sept–Oct, 134–142

Kaplan R.S. & Norton D.P. (1996a). *The Balanced Scorecard*. Harvard Business School Press, Boston, Mass.

Kaplan, R.S. & Norton D.P. (1996b). Using the Balanced Scorecard as a Strategic Management System. *Harvard Business Review*, Jan–Feb, 75–85

Ljung, A. & Oftedal, O. (1976). *Social redovisning* (Social Accounting). SPF (Swedish Personnel Managers Organization), Stockholm

McNair, C.J., Lynch, R.L. & Cross, K.F. (1990). Do Financial and Nonfinancial Performance Measures Have to Agree? *Management Accounting*, November, 28–35

Maisel, L.S. (1992). Performance Measurement: The Balanced Scorecard Approach. *Journal of Cost Management*, Summer, 47–52

Manville, B. & Foote, N. (1996). Harvest Your Workers' Knowledge. *Datamation*, July. URL: www.datamation.com/PlugIn/issues/1996/july/07know1.html

Mintzberg, H. (1994). *The Rise and Fall of Strategic Planning*. Prentice-Hall, Englewood Cliffs, NJ

Mossberg, T. (1977) *Utveckling av nyckeltal* (Development of key numbers), EFI (Economic Research Institute at the Stockholm School of Economics)

Nilsson, F., Jansson, N.-H. & Jansson, Å. (1996). Systematisk implementering av miljöledning – en förutsättning för miljödriven affärsutveckling. *Balans*, No. 6, 22–27

Nilsson, F. & Rapp, B. (1998). Implementing Business Unit Strategies – The Role of Management Control Systems. *Scandinavian Journal of Management* (forthcoming)

Normann, R. & Ramirez, R. (1993). *Designing Interactive Strategy*. Wiley, Chichester

Olve, N.-G. & Westin, C.-J. (1996). *IT-mått. Hur kan IT-användning beskrivas?* (Measures of IT. How can IT use be described?) Report no. 96/2 from the Swedish government commission on IT

Peters, T. (1987). *Thriving on Chaos: Handbook for a Management Revolution*. Macmillan, London

Porter, M. (1980). *Competitive Strategy: Techniques for Analyzing Industries and Competitors*. Free Press, New York

Porter, M. (1985). *Competitive Advantage: Creating and Sustaining Superior Performance*. Free Press, New York

Quinn, J.B. (1992). *Intelligent Enterprise*. Free Press, New York

Quinn, J.B., Baruch, J. & Zien, K.A. (1998). *Innovation Explosion*. Free Press, New York

Roos, J. et al. (1997). *Intellectual Capital. Navigating in the New Business Landscape*. Macmillan, London

RRV (Riksrevisionsverket, The Swedish National Audit Office) (1996). *Balanced score card i myndigheterna – förbättrad resultatinformation för intern styrning* (Balanced Scorecard in the public authorities – improved result information for internal control). Stockholm

RRV (1994). *Resultat–verksamhet–ekonomi* (Result–activities–economy). Stockholm

Ruddle, K. & Feeny, D. (1998). *Transforming the Organisation: New Approaches to Management, Measurement and Leadership*. Oxford Executive Research Briefings

Rumelt, R. (1994). Foreword. In: Hamel, G. & Heene, A. (eds) (1994). *Competence-Based Competition*. Wiley, Chichester

Senge, P. (1990). *The Fifth Discipline*. Doubleday, New York

Shank, J.K. & Govindarajan, V. (1993). *Strategic Cost Management*. Free Press, New York

Smith T. (1992). *Accounting for Growth*. Century Business

Stewart, G.B. (1991). *The Quest for Value*. HarperBusiness, New York

Stewart, T.A. (1994). Your Company's Most Valuable Asset: Intellectual Capital. *Fortune*, Oct. 3

Stewart, T.A. (1997). *Intellectual Capital. The New Wealth of Organizations.* Currency Doubleday, New York

Sveiby, K.E. (1997). *The New Organizational Wealth.* Berrett Koehler, San Francisco

Van der Heijden, K. (1996). *The Art of Strategic Conversation.* Wiley, Chichester

Von Hippel, E. (1994). "Sticky Information" and the Locus of Problem Solving. *Management Science*, **4**, 429–439

Wallman, S. (1996). The Future of Accounting and Financial Reporting, Part II: The Colorized Approach. Remarks of commissioner Steven M.H. Wallman before AICPA, 23rd National Conference on Current SEC Developments. URL: www.sec.gov/news/speechess/spch079.txt

Wennberg, I. (1994). På väg bort från ekonomistyningen (Moving away from economic controls). *Ekonomi & Styrning*, No. 2, 6–10

Wennberg, I. (1996). Banken mäter med fler mått än pengar (The bank measures with more metrics than money). *Ekonomi & Styrning*, **6**, 8–10

Wernerfelt, B. (1984). A Resource-based View of the Firm. *Strategic Management Journal*, **5**, 171–180

Westin, C.-J. & Wetter, M. (1997). *Att hålla ett styrkort vid liv* (To keep a scorecard alive), CEPRO.

Index